W9-CND-673

Eyes
Without
Country

Souad R. Dajani

Eyes Without Country

*Searching for a
Palestinian Strategy
of Liberation*

Temple University Press
Philadelphia

Temple University Press, Philadelphia 19122
Copyright © 1995 by Temple University
All rights reserved
Published 1994

The title of this book is from a poem by Rashid Hussein, "Revolution in Transit," in *The World of Rashid Hussein: A Palestinian Poet in Exile,* edited by Kamal Boullatta and Mirène Ghossein (Detroit: Association of Arab-American University Graduates, 1979), 172–173. Reprinted with permission from The Association of Arab-American University Graduates, Normal, Illinois.

Portions of the material in this book are reprinted with permission from Souad Dajani, *The Intifada* (Amman, Jordan: University of Jordan, Center for Hebraic Studies, 1990).

The epigraph to the introduction is from a poem by Mahmoud Darwish, "Investigation," quoted in Fawaz Turki, *The Disinherited Journal of Palestinian Exile* (New York: Monthly Review Press, 1972), 27. Copyright © 1972 by Fawaz Turki. Reprinted by permission of Monthly Review Foundation.

♾ The paper used in this publication meets the minimum requirements of American National Standard for Information Sciences—Permanence of Paper for Printed Library Materials, ANSI Z39.48-1984

Printed in the United States of America

Library of Congress Cataloging-in-Publication Data

Dajani, Souad R.
  Eyes without country : searching for a Palestinian strategy of liberation / Souad R. Dajani.
    p.   cm.
  Includes bibliographical references and index.
  ISBN 1-56639-240-3(cloth)   ISBN 1-56639-241-1(paper)
  1. Jewish-Arab relations.   2. Palestinian Arabs—Politics and government.   3. Intifada, 1987—Influence.   4. Nonviolence.   5. West Bank—International status.   6. Gaza Strip—International status.   I. Title.
DS119.7.D2554   1995
956.95'3044—dc20   94-21706
                                                                   CIP

Nothing remains of my oldest dream, of revolution,
But scraps and stars stitched to the shoulders
   of those who justify defeat.
Nothing but battalions of essays
   pregnant with bank accounts
   and a green light for murder.
Nothing remains but a minstrel
She wails over Jaffa and Haifa
Banks in Jerusalem sweat.
(Revolution still searching for an alphabet).
A revolution, my friends, comes to life
   in eyes without country
   in peasants without land
   where the police is landlord.
A revolution comes to life
   when the writer and the blind
   See one truth.

   From "Revolution in Transit" by Rashid Hussein

Contents

Acknowledgments

Initial work on this book coincided with the outbreak of the *intifada* in the Occupied Territories. During 1987–1988, I was a postdoctoral fellow at the Program on Nonviolent Sanctions at Harvard University's Center for International Affairs. I was pursuing my research on Palestinian nonviolent civilian resistance to Israeli occupation. The *intifada,* the civilian uprising of Palestinians in the Occupied West Bank and Gaza Strip, seemed like a vindication of the direction my work was taking. I was studying a region where the language of force prevailed and where people reacted very skeptically to the notion that "nonviolence" could wield any kind of effective power. As the *intifada* escalated, so did my commitment to investigate this mode of civilian struggle. Lying at the heart of the issue, it seemed to me, was the question of the extent to which the *intifada* relied upon a coherent strategy to achieve its goals. It was soon apparent that my energies should focus on this question of strategy. More precisely, I would focus on the formulation of a strategy of nonviolent civilian resistance that could be undertaken by the Palestinians themselves to end Israeli rule.

This book would not have been possible without the support of two fellowships, one from the Program on Nonviolent Sanctions at Harvard University and one from the Albert Einstein Institution in Cambridge, Massachusetts. My thanks especially to Gene Sharp, who first invited me to Harvard, and to Chris Kruegler, who facilitated my return for a second year. Three people to whom I owe special gratitude are Chris Kruegler, Elaine Hagopian—a role model and former professor, and Zachary Lockman. They read the first draft of this manuscript and provided me with most incisive and critical comments. I hope they recognize their input here. I thank Jamal Nassar of the Association of Arab-American University Graduates for permission to use the phrase "eyes without country" from Rashid Hussein's poem "Revolution in Transit" as the title of my book, and for permission to reprint part of the poem here. I am grateful to Antioch College for awarding me a Knight Grant that enabled me to travel to the Occupied Territories in July 1993. I also thank Mustafa Hamarneh of the Center for Strategic Studies at the University of Jordan for securing permission to use portions of my monograph *Intifada* in this study. Special thanks go to Micah Kleit at Temple University Press, who first responded favorably to this manuscript and who remained unstintingly patient and helpful throughout. And thanks to editor Michael Ames at Temple University Press, for his insightful comments and his continued support throughout the process of publication.

Working on this topic has sometimes been like chasing a moving target. Throughout, it was the goal at the end, the hope for a just peace in the Middle East, that made it all worthwhile. Many dear friends—Palestinians, Americans, Arabs, Jews, and Israelis—share this vision with me. I would like to say to all of you—and to my parents, sister, brothers, and lovely niece and nephew—I was thinking of you all.

Introduction

Write down I am an Arab,
my card number is 50,000[1]

For decades, these opening lines of the famous poem by the Palestinian writer Mahmoud Darwish seemed to capture the essence of the Palestinian experience. These words captured the poignancy of Palestinian dispossession, resignation, and despair. They told of lives of longing and of the depths of pain and suffering from which were born the will and vigor to resist, to endure, and to prevail. When the Palestinian *intifada* erupted in December 1987, Palestinians had shifted from hope to disillusionment, and from waiting upon the world to acknowledge the righteousness of their cause to taking matters into their own hands to pressure Israel. For a while, inconceivable as it was, it appeared as though they might succeed.

By the summer of 1990, two and half years into the *intifada,* Palestinians believed that they had achieved no tangible gains. The same Palestinians who had defied the odds to finally take matters into their own hands and launch a largely nonviolent resistance against their occupiers had, by the time of the Iraqi invasion of Kuwait, almost succumbed to their own despair and frustration. Disillusionment and paralysis set in, and once again, as happened frequently throughout their history, Palestinians in the Occupied Territories assumed a stance of waiting. They waited for the Palestine Liberation Organization (PLO), for the United States, for Saddam Hussein, for any liberator who would end their plight. Then, just as most analysts had settled into a comfortable stance and were waiting for the peace talks in Washington, D.C., to produce some results, a dramatic event occurred that stunned the most seasoned and cynical of Middle East observers. In late

August 1993 newspaper headlines blazed with the news that "secret" talks had been going on between the PLO and Israeli officials in Norway for several months, and that these had culminated in an agreement between the two parties. What followed was an event that many thought they would never live to see: the chairman of the PLO, Yasser Arafat, and the prime minister of Israel, Itzhak Rabin, standing to either side of U.S. President Bill Clinton on the White House lawn, watching their joint "Declaration of Principles" being signed by their respective delegates. This momentous event had veteran Middle East analysts reeling. The document in question basically outlined the steps toward interim self-rule in the Gaza Strip and the West Bank town of Jericho. It also spelled out criteria for extending this rule to the rest of the Occupied Territories and for negotiating on the final status of these areas. No one had predicted such a "breakthrough," nor that it would be negotiated between the two sides with little intervention by third parties.

Beyond the drama of the moment, however, serious scholars were still left with the question of how to achieve a just and lasting peace in the Middle East. Mutual recognition between the PLO and Israel, announced shortly prior to the signing, may have been a start; and the agreement over "Gaza and Jericho first," the interim self-rule plan, may have been encouraging. But for those concerned with achieving Palestinian independence alongside Israel, critical outstanding issues remained. Foremost among these was how to get "from here to there." It is the Palestinian inhabitants of the Occupied West Bank and Gaza Strip who form the central focus of this study. Palestinians in other jurisdictions are not ignored. They are constantly there, as reminders that events that take place in the region as a whole inevitably impinge on the situation of Palestinians on the "inside."

This study contributes to the debate on strategic options available to Palestinians by evaluating these considerations in terms of the whole context of the Israeli occupation. In light of events that culminated in the 1993 accords, Palestinian strategy would need to take on two main, and somewhat related, foci. The first is the formulation of a strategy of nonviolent civilian resistance for the duration of Israel's direct rule over the Occupied Territories. This is the theme of the present study. It is predicated on the idea that Palestinians could launch concerted civilian action in the Occupied Territories to defeat Israel's political will to maintain its occupation. This topic will be elaborated shortly. A second, more long-term strategic imperative is to prepare Palestinians for a strategy of civilian-based defense (CBD) for the period beyond interim self-rule.

The interim period specified in the Declaration of Principles provides Palestinians with a window of two to five years in which to ensure that the final status of the Occupied Territories is negotiated to their satisfaction. Since the basic agreements over self-rule do not envision any major Israeli withdrawal except as its forces may be redeployed away from populated

Palestinian areas, occupation remains intact. During this stage, therefore, a civilian resistance strategy that targets this occupation remains feasible and highly relevant. Afterward, especially if negotiations do not achieve the outcomes Palestinians desire, the structures of the interim arrangements may become such that they are institutionalized into full autonomy, and thus irreversible. A strategy of civilian resistance that could work in the interim stages would likely be ineffective in a setting that would then resemble a kind of neocolonial relationship, in which the occupation is indirect and less tangible. A more appropriate Palestinian strategy at that point may be a kind of civilian-based defense. As elaborated later in the study, this strategy would require a two-pronged approach, based on deterrence and defense. Strategies for reengaging the occupying regime directly at that stage, to induce its full withdrawal, would become more complicated and would have to be assessed in light of existing realities and conditions.

The period ahead is fraught with dangers for Palestinians. The introduction of self-rule comes at a time when the Palestinian community under occupation is beset with fatigue and virtual paralysis and is in desperate need of economic development and a breathing space in which to revive. Arafat's deal with Israel may offer that space. However, Palestinians must also guard against becoming too complacent and abandoning strategic planning in favor of the benefits of the moment. They must realize, as many do, that political negotiations between a proposed elected Palestinian council in the Occupied Territories and Israeli officials do not necessarily guarantee their ultimate independence. The interim phase dangerously shifts the arena from Palestinian/Israeli to Palestinian/Palestinian—as, for example, in the outbreak of violence between supporters and opponents of the autonomy agreements. This is a potentially explosive situation that could even lead to civil war, especially if elected leaders do not handle the transition to independence as effectively as the population would expect. Palestinians would likely give Arafat the benefit of the doubt and await the fulfillment of his promises, both for immediate economic succor and for eventual liberation. Meantime, the Palestinians living under occupation would be sorting out their relations with the entity that rules them and keeping a close watch on the progress of their leaders. They would need to be alert to the pitfalls of pacification, lest they wake up, some five years down the line, and find themselves in a state of permanent autonomy in which the chance for total independence has been lost and the opportunity to regain it foreclosed.

Special emphasis is placed in this study on assessing the tactics and methods employed by Palestinians in the *intifada,* as well as analyzing this uprising as a turning point in the evolution of Palestinian strategy and resistance. A point that should be made at the outset is that there is no attempt in this work to be "neutral," though the analysis aspires to remain "objective." I take the position that the only acceptable solution to the

Palestinian/Israeli conflict at this point is a two-state solution. The decision to examine a nonviolent alternative has been taken on practical rather than ideological grounds—a position that coincides with perspectives of the "practical" and "strategic" school of nonviolent action.[2] Still, these conclusions cannot be easily dismissed as "one-sided," since I firmly believe in the right of both "sides," Israeli and Palestinian, to sovereignty in their respective states and to peaceful and secure coexistence in the region.

The strategy that is explored in this work operates at three levels: (a) the Palestinian community under occupation; (b) the Israeli body politic; and (c) international actors (principally the United States). By entering into the debates and dilemmas surrounding Palestinian resistance in the Occupied Territories, this study examines the roots of the Palestinian/Israeli conflict as seen essentially from the point of view of the occupied. Critical questions are raised surrounding the operation of nonviolent techniques at each of the three levels, followed by an assessment of strategic options available within each for resolving this longstanding conflict.

Based on an evaluation of Palestinian resistance throughout the years of occupation, two points immediately stand out. One is the dearth of long-term strategic planning for resistance in the Occupied Territories. Clearly, there are many valid reasons for this omission, some of which have to do with the conditions and social dynamics operating in these areas, as well as in the relationship between the Palestinians and the PLO. The second point is the impossibility of adopting an effective armed or guerrilla struggle to end the occupation. To acknowledge this may come as a psychological blow to some Palestinians who have internalized and emulated the examples of a whole repertoire of successful armed struggles of people worldwide against similar conditions of colonial domination—in Algeria, other parts of Africa, and Asia. One implication that resonates from these observations is that if indeed past "strategies" have not and could not work in the Palestinian context, then a viable alternative has to be found. The lesson of the *intifada* is that Palestinians must keep the initiative in their own hands, a lesson that has been underscored during the peace process. The *intifada* taught Palestinians that their greatest source of strength lies in the power of the people themselves, in their ability to organize and participate in resistance on a mass scale.

From a Jewish-Israeli perspective, a strategy that is universal and organized, particularly one that utilizes nonviolent means of struggle, may be especially threatening to Israel's control over the Palestinians. Indeed, evidence of Israeli vulnerability to massive Palestinian civilian resistance has been demonstrated throughout the *intifada*. Unlike earlier patterns of resistance, both from within and outside the Occupied Territories, the *intifada* underscored the asymmetrical nature of the conflict. Palestinians clearly have been unable to match Israel's military might and cannot, therefore, hope to defeat it on these terms. Yet Palestinians proved that they could still wield effective power by using the very asymmetry of the conflict to their own advantage. The *intifada* demonstrated that Palestinians could rely on a most unexpected weapon. This "weapon" was precisely the power of their opponent, which the resistance could wield to cause Israeli power to rebound against itself. Used effectively, this element of strategy would enable the Palestinians, and not Israel, to define the terms of the struggle. It would keep the initiative largely in Palestinian hands, empower them and their community, and thus advance their political cause.

The *intifada* incorporated another strategic element that would set the opponent off balance—Palestinian noncooperation. By refusing to obey the occupier, Palestinians established that it would be costly for Israel to continue to govern the Occupied Territories. I will examine closely how these and other elements of the *intifada* could be incorporated into future strategies of resistance.

Chapter One examines the context of the occupation and its impact on the West Bank and Gaza Strip since 1967. Beginning with early Palestine under the British Mandate, the disintegration of the Palestinian community in the face of Zionist Jewish immigration, and the creation of the State of Israel, it sets the stage for tracing the transformation of indigenous social and economic structures in the Israeli Occupied Territories. This history of colonization establishes the social context in which Palestinians have organized their resistance. Israeli laws and measures, land expropriation and settlement, and other issues are examined here.

Chapter Two traces the emergence and development of resistance in the Occupied Territories and the debates surrounding these initiatives. It starts by examining the relationship of the Palestinians under occupation to the PLO outside. It outlines the means and objectives of the Palestine national movement during the early years, and analyzes the shift in the strategic focus to give more weight to the participation of the population inside the Occupied Territories in their national struggle. Palestinian resistance to occupation before the *intifada* illustrates both the potential of Palestinian strategy and the limitations imposed by conditions under occupation.

Chapter Three examines the *intifada*. This uprising is, as implied in the term itself, "a shaking up" of both the Palestinian society under Israeli rule and of the Israeli occupation regime against which it was launched. Its character as a civilian and largely nonviolent struggle that spread quickly across the Occupied Territories is analyzed. But the *intifada,* as I will argue, turned into a double-edged sword, one that caused a backlash within the Palestinian community itself. Strategic debates and dilemmas, along with the ways in which the Palestinian community has been both strengthened and divided by the *intifada,* are outlined. This chapter considers some of the lessons that can be drawn from the *intifada* and points to various strengths and weaknesses of Palestinian strategy in the Occupied Territories.

Chapter Four synthesizes the material presented in earlier sections to provide a theoretical basis for a comprehensive evaluation of strategy. Theoretical perspectives are reviewed, and comparisons are made with other relevant conflict situations. A significant part of this chapter is devoted to an examination of the concept of nonviolent action. Various perspectives are outlined to review their central understandings, their techniques and mechanisms, and the dynamics of their operation. Reference is also made to the technique of armed struggle and the problematics of adopting this technique in the Occupied Territories. Also included is a discussion of the issue of power and how different perspectives on power relations can be worked into a viable strategy of nonviolent resistance. Nonviolent civilian resistance and civilian-based defense are examined here as they may contribute to different facets of strategic formulation during different phases of the Palestinian struggle.

Chapter Five constitutes the core of this study. This chapter examines the specific application of a strategy of nonviolent civilian resistance to the Palestinian case and analyzes the conditions that would determine its success or failure. A central theme is the internal coherence of the strategy, whereby its components, including objectives, techniques, and tactics, are selected and organized in view of how they promote the overall goal. At one level, Palestinians need to maintain internal cohesiveness and unity of purpose. They need to build adequate support systems that would strengthen their communities and secure the weaker sectors of Palestinian society that could otherwise be exploited by Israel. Mobilizing the Palestinian people to overcome leadership and factional problems is another strategic focus. At the second level, Palestinian strategy should target the opponent, Israel, and in so doing, establish the unsustainability of its continued occupation of the West Bank and Gaza Strip. The strategy should exploit weaknesses within the Israeli army, government, and public in order to defeat Israel's political will. The third strategic focus comprises Israel's international allies, foremost among them the United States. By adopting a total strategy of resistance, Palestinians would try to ensure that their struggle is interpreted correctly in Israel and abroad as one of resistance against occupation and for the legitimate rights of Palestinians to self-determination. Different levels of Palestinian action that could target the international community are evaluated in Chapter Five.

The complexity of emerging realities in the Middle East has given my work an added incentive. It is my view that as long as the occupation persists and as long as Israel does not publicly commit itself to a full withdrawal from the West Bank and Gaza Strip, a strategy of resistance remains vital. Diplomatic and political initiatives would constitute a single component of a broader strategy: Negotiations would neither replace strategy, nor would they preclude alternative forms of resistance being undertaken where necessary. The essence of this resistance strategy must be civilian based and largely nonviolent. In the summer of 1993, Arafat repeated his pledge (first voiced in 1988) that the PLO had renounced violence. There is, therefore, no better time than the present to seriously investigate and perfect the methods of nonviolent civilian resistance and to formulate a coherent strategy based on such resistance. It may well be the only means available to Palestinians to take them beyond autonomy toward complete independence. The *intifada* provides precisely the kind of powerful precedent that could be built upon in future resistance.

Although this study focuses mainly on the situation in the Occupied Territories, it is clear that the Palestinian *intifada* will have ramifications that go far beyond the boundaries of the West Bank and Gaza Strip. Palestinians themselves may have been influenced by comparable struggles in South Africa, the Philippines, and other countries. It is not difficult, therefore, to envision scenarios where the Palestinian *intifada* and the tactics of civilian resistance and civil disobedience provide examples that are emulated by civilian populations elsewhere in the world—wherever dispossessed and disaffected peoples struggle to gain their civil and political rights and freedoms.

One

The Context and Background of the Intifada

Historical Overview

The total Palestinian population worldwide is estimated at more than five million people. Since their dispersal following the establishment of the State of Israel in 1948, Palestinians have come to fall largely under three distinct jurisdictions—inside the Occupied Territories, in the diaspora, and as citizens of Israel. By far the largest single concentration of Palestinians comprises those living under Israeli rule in the West Bank and Gaza Strip.

Estimations vary on the size of the Arab population in these areas. Meron Benvenisti, former deputy mayor of Jerusalem and head of the West Bank Data Base Project, maintains that official figures quoted by Israel's Central Bureau of Statistics (CBS) are as much as 22 percent lower than actual numbers. He estimates that in 1988 the total population of both these areas was 1.74 million, of which 1.09 million resided in the West Bank and 650,000 in the Gaza Strip. By the early 1990s, the estimated figure was closer to two million.[1] The population is skewed in favor of youth. More than 45 percent are under 14 years of age, which means that over half the Palestinian population of the Occupied Territories has known no life other than occupation. This fact may explain in part the Palestinian determination to struggle against the hardships they have been forced to endure for over two decades.

Though close to 70 percent of West Bank Palestinians are village residents, over 40 percent consist of refugees, dispersed in the refugee camps, towns, and villages of the area. In the Gaza Strip, the proportion of refugees rises to almost 70 percent of the population, although, unlike the West Bank, the majority of the Gaza Strip population is urban based.[2]

Palestinians who live outside the Occupied Territories are the second-largest grouping. They include the hundreds of thousands of Palestinian refugees living in the surrounding Arab states who were forced to leave Palestine in 1948 and the West Bank and Gaza Strip in 1967. Significant numbers of other Palestinians live in the diaspora, scattered throughout the Arab world and around the world.

The third group, the Israeli-Arabs or Israeli-Palestinians, includes the Palestinians who remained in Israel after 1948 and became Israeli citizens. They constitute close to 750,000 people, or about 17 percent of the total Israeli population.

The Palestinian claim to the West Bank and Gaza Strip—even as these areas continue to be occupied by Israel—is rooted in a history that is as controversial as it is long and complex. Analysts of every persuasion have written extensively on the emergence of the "Palestine Problem" in its various dimensions. A number of historical conditions are cited in common by both Jewish and Arab analysts. The problem emerges with interpretation, what is made of these "facts," and how they are articulated—including the very terminology used to articulate them.

Most observers agree, for example, that well before the emergence of political Zionism in the late 1800s, and while the region was still under Ottoman rule, the area called Palestine had long been inhabited by an indigenous population. This population consisted mainly of Arabs, both Muslim and Christian, and a small community of Jews.[3]

To claim that Jews immigrated to a largely barren and uninhabited land is simply inaccurate. In 1920, 80 percent of the Arab rural population were *fellahin* (peasants), who earned their livelihood from agriculture.[4] On the other hand, to acknowledge the existence of an indigenous people but to dismiss this as a marginal or irrelevant detail in the Zionist movement's settlement plans is another matter altogether.

Political Zionism and its manifestations in the nationalist movement that sought to "reconstitute" Palestine as the Jewish homeland emerged in the late 1800s within the same atmosphere that characterized the emergence of other colonial movements. Its origins are usually traced to Theodore Herzl, who in 1896 published *The Jewish State,* in which he advocated the establishment of a Jewish state in Palestine. Although the roots of political Zionism lay in the discrimination and persecution suffered by Jews in feudal Europe, the solution to the "Jewish problem" was soon interpreted by the wealthy Jewish capitalist classes of Europe in territorial and political terms. This interpretation coincided with the interests and ambitions of Britain, their main patron at the time. Political Zionism shared with European colonialism a view of indigenous peoples as somehow inferior, backward, and less than human. It was in this way that many of the French and British colonial conquests in Africa and in the Middle East (among others) could be justified. These colonial powers could ignore the "natives' " existence altogether, except insofar as they served the economic and political interests of the colonial power. A more charitable view regarded the natives as "benefiting" from colonial rule, by being afforded an opportunity to become "civilized" through exposure to Western values and beliefs. It was in this way that the Zionist movement largely disregarded the prior presence of Arabs on the land they wished to settle. Some liberal Zionists occasionally referred to the benefits that would soon accrue to Arabs from their close encounters with Jews. For the most part, however, their existence was ignored. What distinguished the Zionist movement from other colonial ventures was an ideological focus that regarded Palestine as the eternal land of the Jewish people. In this view, indigenous Arabs were not so much a people to be exploited as they were obstacles that had to be ultimately removed. Thus Herzl would insist on the all-Jewishness of the proposed state. Concerning the indigenous population, he wrote,

> When we occupy the land, we shall bring immediate benefits to the state that receives us. We must expropriate gently the private property on the estates assigned to us.
>
> We shall try to spirit the penniless population across the border by procuring employment for it in the transit countries while denying it any employment in our own country.[5]

Understanding the present situation and the structural conditions of Israel's colonial occupation of the West Bank and Gaza Strip would not be possible without examining the ideological underpinnings of the Zionist movement. This statement is intended to suggest neither a monolithic nor a homogeneous definition of Zionism. However, this ideology has defined the national liberation of the Jewish people in Palestine. Insofar as it has facilitated and legitimated the actions that uprooted Palestinians, it is this Zionism that defines the political ideology underlying the Jewish colonial venture in Palestine.[6] Tracing Zionism's course in Palestine reveals the continuity between Jewish colonization of Palestine in the early part of the twentieth century, the subsequent establishment of the State of Israel in 1948, and the occupation of the West Bank and Gaza Strip since 1967.

International observers, including Jewish and Palestinian critics alike, have identified in Zionist political ideology a basic dismissal of the Palestinians and a denial of their rights. There are, for example, prominent Jewish writers who warned about the implementation of Zionism.[7] The Russian Jewish writer Ahad Ha'am (Asher Ginzberg) was one of the first to urge caution. As early as 1891, Ha'am tried to alert Jews to the fact that Palestine was already inhabited and that they should make the effort to understand Arabs and try to coexist with them. Other prominent Jews expressed similar concerns. Judah Magnes, an American rabbi, advocated a binational state in Palestine; Martin Buber, a German philosopher, wrote about the need for cooperation with Arabs. Other respected personalities, such as Rabbi Elmer Berger, would claim, "The source of the conflict was always Zionism."[8] Berger added, "Paradoxically, this ethno-centered, exclusivist, aggressive ideology has been virtually accepted as a benevolent, liberating, progressive phenomenon." He insisted that only by understanding this "total confrontation" with "the Arabs," can there be a way to a clearer vision for a just peace. Despite the efforts of Berger and others, many, especially in the United States, who have tried to expose political Zionism for what it has done to Palestinians, have faced intimidation and efforts to silence and suppress alternative points of view.[9]

The official launching of the Zionist enterprise in Palestine can be traced to 1897, the date of the First Zionist Congress. Taking place a full 20 years before the Balfour Declaration, the Basle Program, as it is known, established the Zionist Organization, which would henceforth be assigned the task of establishing "a publicly and legally secured home in Palestine for the Jewish people."[10]

The Zionist Organization is the key to understanding the Zionist underpinnings of the State of Israel. This organization was formally recognized by the British as officially representing the interests of the Jewish people and ensuring the fulfillment of the terms of the Balfour Declaration.[11] It was the Zionist Organization that undertook to negotiate with the British over the wording of the Balfour Declaration; the indigenous Arab inhabitants of Palestine were not invited to participate in determining the fate of their homeland.[12]

As for the coincidence of Zionist and British imperial interests in Palestine, this passage from Herbert Sidebotham, who worked with the British government (dated 1934), is revealing:

> So complete, indeed, is the ideality of British and Zionist interests in Palestine, that if there were no Zionism, our policy would have been driven to make it.[13]

The Jewish National Fund (JNF), which was to be entrusted with the task of acquiring lands in Palestine, was established at the Fifth Zionist Congress in 1901. The Jewish Agency was formed in 1929, to take over some of the responsibilities of the Zionist Organization for realizing their "national home" in "cooperation" with the British government. It drew up a constitution concerning land acquisitions and holdings. Article 3(d) of this constitution specifies that "title to the lands acquired is to be taken in the name of the JNF, to the end that the same shall be held as the inalienable property of the Jewish people."[14] The consequence of transferring land to the JNF was to render these lands, to use Sir John Hope Simpson's words, forever "extraterritorialized."[15] This process first started before 1948, continued in Israel itself after the establishment of the state, and was later extended to the Occupied West Bank and Gaza Strip after 1967. The significance of this practice should not be underestimated. What it entails is that Arabs are forever barred from buying, leasing, cultivating or in any way working on these lands.

Registering land with the JNF establishes "extraterritorialization" in another way. Land so registered does not belong to individual Israeli citizens (even Jews among them, to whom the lands can only be leased), nor even to the Israeli government itself. That land belongs to "the Jewish people," whoever they are, whatever different citizenships they may hold, and wherever in the world they may reside.[16] This is a point that is little known or appreciated, since in most countries the property and resources of a particular state can be owned privately by its citizens or by their representative government for its own use. Indigenous resources are not usually held for some amorphous group of people who may not even reside in that state, to whom lands are guaranteed in perpetuity. This peculiar situation came about in Israel after the establishment of the state, when the World Zionist Organization/Jewish Agency (WZO/JA) entered into a formal "covenant" with the state to continue to serve the interests of the "Jewish people." By virtue of this agreement, which was later enshrined into law in Israel, each subsequent Israeli government was entrusted with fulfilling the tasks required by the state. Meantime, the WZO/JA would be responsible for securing Israel and its lands and resources for the whole Jewish people. As I will show, there is a division of labor, but the tasks overlap. In essence, the State of Israel exists for the benefit of its Jewish citizens (and all Jews everywhere), not for its Arab citizens, and certainly not for the Arabs under occupation, who are not citizens. This discrimination is codified in a Basic Law that distinguishes between "nationality" (afforded only to Jews) and "citizenship" (which Israeli Palestinians may hold). This differentiation culminates in a process that makes discrimination against the Arab citizens of the state legal and official.

In practice, extraterritorialization means that the WZO/JA together are the legal and official international wings of the Israeli government. Their function is one step removed from that of the State of Israel, beyond the immediate citizens, to the service of a Jewish homeland for Jews everywhere in the world.[17] In this context, David Ben-Gurion, the first prime minister of Israel, is reported to have stated, "The Zionist Organization is able to achieve what is beyond the power and competence of the state, and that is the advantage of the Zionist Organization over the state."[18] In order for this expectation to be fulfilled and assume the status of law, the Israeli Knesset (parliament) in 1952 enacted the Basic Law "The World Zionist Organization/Jewish Agency for Israel (Status) Law."[19] Henceforth defined as "national institutions," the WZO/JA would be responsible for immigration, settlement, and dissemination of information about the state, as well as cooperation with other organizations and countries. The final piece of legislation that defined the WZO/JA "Status Law" is officially termed a "covenant" between Israel and these organizations.[20] Whether they are considered an integral part of the government or agents of the State of Israel, there is no mistaking the extraterritorial functions and responsibilities provided for in this law.

Many Israelis and Jews continue to point to the PLO Charter as one indication that the PLO has not abandoned its goal of dismantling the Zionist State of Israel.[21] However, it is significant that Israel maintains its own "covenant" that includes a set of laws serving distinct functions. These are (a) to define "Eretz" Israel within borders that remain unspecified but ones within which the WZO has clearly included the West Bank and Gaza Strip; (b) to define Israel as a permanent expression and realization of the Zionist movement; and (c) to define the overarching interest of the state as the "Jewish people" rather than its citizens. This is a "covenant," in other words, by virtue of which the permanent occupation of the West Bank and Gaza Strip has basically been legalized.[22] Within this scenario, Arab Palestinians—citizens of Israel and residents of the West Bank and Gaza Strip alike—are defined by law as second class or worse: Arab Israelis can be citizens but never nationals, and Palestinians under occupation remain an oppressed minority who have watched their lands being usurped for the permanent benefit of the "Jewish people" and the Zionist movement.

These issues cannot be understood apart from some of Israel's other Basic Laws: the Law of Return and the Law of Nationality. The 1950 Law of Return grants a Jew anywhere in the world the right to immigrate to Israel. The 1952 Nationality Law confers the automatic right of citizenship upon any Jew who wishes to settle in Israel.[23] As Berger explains, by virtue of these laws, "the Jewish people" are elevated to form the "nationality constituency" of the State of Israel. The implications of this "supranationality" are unmistakable. First, Jews, even those who are already citizens of other states, are part of the "Jewish people" that have automatic rights in this state. Second, "nationality" is determined in Israel by religion and not by citizenship, thus disqualifying native Arab residents and citizens of the rights and privileges afforded Jews. Third, Israel as the declared state of the Jewish people, whose primary goal and raison d'être are dedicated to the task of "ingathering of the exiles,"[24] cannot but practice racism and discrimination against its Arab citizens. This discrimination is therefore institutionalized in law and constitutes the essence of how Zionism operates against Palestinians.[25] Because they are not Jewish, the original Arab inhabitants of Palestine are forever barred from returning to their homeland or assuming citizenship there. The same applies to their descendants. Meanwhile, Jews, from the Soviet Union, from Ethiopia, or from any other place in the world, can immediately acquire citizenship in Israel. They can do so even if they have no physical connection to the land, have never set foot on it before, and have not descended from anyone currently residing there. The inescapable conclusion, then, is that Zionism and democracy (as far as non-Jews and particularly Palestinians are concerned) are simply incompatible. One person who dared express this reality, albeit to support his own agenda, was the late Rabbi Meir Kahane, leader of the right-wing Kach movement. Kahane, who was frequently dismissed as a fanatic, even by Jews and Israelis, was assassinated in New York in the fall of 1990.[26]

During the Mandate period, the Jewish Agency had also established a "Population Transfer Committee." Joseph Weitz, the director of the JNF who served on this committee, outlined its policy. This was not limited to the "transfer" of Arabs from Jewish areas, but also included the evacuation of lands that Arabs themselves held and cultivated, in order for these lands to be acquired by Jews.[27] Mentioning the "transfer" policy in this context is to point out that although it has not been recognized as official policy in Israel, it continues to operate in practice, albeit indirectly, in the form of deportations, land expropriations, and the like, in the Occupied Territories. Moreover, "transfer" was formalized as an official position within the Israeli government in 1988, when three political parties advocating this measure were first elected to join the government.

An official "transfer" policy, combined with the existence of Israel as the state of the "Jewish people," and one that has increasingly encroached on Palestinian lands in the West Bank and Gaza Strip, poses a real danger for Palestinians. Since the 1967 occupation, these lands have been gradually appropriated by the JNF and the government. As Matiyahu Drobles, author of the Five Year Plan (later known as the "Master Plan" of the WZO), insists, "There is to be not a shadow of a doubt regarding our intention to remain in Judea and Samaria."[28] For the Palestinians of the Occupied Territories, therefore, and despite agreements concerning self-rule, the question of their final status remains in doubt.

All these practices raise critical questions concerning Palestinian resistance, where a central issue is whether there can be any compromise with Zionism. Given the history just outlined, compromise would almost seem impossible. Zionist legitimacy has necessarily precluded a Palestinian legitimacy, especially where the Zionist movement has defined itself as a "nation" whose boundaries are fluid and expansionist, and not a state whose boundaries are fixed.[29] Rabbi Berger was among those who apparently believed that had Israel left the Zionist Organization behind at the time of the creation of the state, there would have been room for both legitimacies and for the creation of a Palestinian state. In his view, an Israel that is "normal" and separate from a "Zionist" Israel may be able to envision and achieve peace.[30] Maxime Rodinson seemed to agree that this eventuality would have been possible, had the "colonial situation" "been left behind" at the time of the 1947 UN Partition Plan.[31] Can Zionism be contained within the 1948 borders, so to speak, with Israeli law changed or amended accordingly? The implications for Palestinian resistance are very intricate, since, as is shown, theirs is not simply a struggle against foreign domination of their lands, but against a dominant ideology that claims those lands exclusively and by right for Jews and sees no place for Palestinians in the definition of its "nation." Various anticolonial movements and national liberation movements around the world have engaged in struggles that were somewhat less complicated. Those "occupied" usually had to contend with a colonial occupation without the complications of a settler colony whose underpinning is an exclusivist ideology.[32] Palestinians have, over the years, made a painful and conscious choice to change their objectives: from dismantling the Zionist basis of the State of Israel and establishing a secular democratic state for both Jews and Arabs, to ending Israel's occupation of the West Bank and Gaza Strip and coexisting within two separate sovereign states. Palestinian critics wonder whether they can separate the "reality" of colonial occupation from the ideology motivating it, and whether one could end without destroying the other. Yet most Palestinians (including their leaders) are willing and committed to do just that—separate their struggle against occupation from their overriding concerns and misgivings about Zionist ideology. They wonder whether Jews and Israelis can reciprocate by, in a sense, splitting "legitimacy"—secularizing the conflict in order to allow for the creation of a Palestinian state alongside their own.[33]

To attempt to condense close to one hundred years of history into only a few paragraphs is impossible. One can make claims and counterclaims, and there is no end to the debates or the recriminations and accusations by both sides. Does Palestine belong to the Jews? Many Jews would argue this claim on biblical or historical grounds, or on the rights won through conquest and war and the imperatives of security concerns. Arab Palestinians would lay their claim on the basis of thousands of years of continuous living on the land. They were, in fact and in deed, a continuous presence on that land throughout the centuries, through which they were able to trace their ancestry and identity. And so the impasse continues to plague the two parties.

The Impact of the Israeli Occupation

Following the establishment of the State of Israel in 1948, in which it claimed 80 percent of the land of Palestine, what remained came under different Arab jurisdictions: The West Bank fell under Jordanian rule, while the Gaza Strip came under Egyptian administration.[34] During the June 1967 War, Israel captured both these territories, and they have been under Israeli occupation ever since. Zionist colonial domination of early Palestine was soon extended into these areas to enable Israel to seize control over available land and resources at the expense of the indigenous Arab population.[35]

Prior to the 1967 occupation, traditional social structures in the West Bank had remained largely intact. West Bank society was characterized mainly as peasant based, with large family farms or sharecropping arrangements and expanding intellectual, merchant, and business classes in the cities.[36] Since 1948, under Jordanian rule, indigenous agricultural and industrial sectors reached essentially the limit of their absorptive capacity, and the number of agricultural workers seeking supplementary incomes as wage laborers in the cities began to rise. Palestinian refugees forced out or fleeing the creation of the Israeli state, combined with economic difficulties facing Jordan during the period of its rule, created some hardships for the residents.

In contrast, the Gaza Strip underwent fundamental changes as a result of the 1948 war, when its population was more than tripled by the influx of refugees from Palestine. The prime farming areas and fishing sites of the Gaza Strip were lost to Israel. Also lost were vital trade routes to the rest of the region. Difficult conditions prevailed and even intensified under Egyptian rule, as the material resources and economic structures available in the Strip remained insufficient to meet the needs of the largely dispossessed population. Between 1948 and 1967, the social structure of the Gaza Strip was dominated by a contrasting picture of an indigenous class of merchants and landowners, who managed to salvage part of their livelihood by exporting citrus fruits abroad, and a large dispossessed group of refugees who desperately sought a livelihood within this area.[37]

The initial debate within Israel after the June 1967 War revolved around whether or not to annex these territories.[38] Israeli officials decided to pursue a policy of economic integration without formal annexation. This would maximize the advantages of occupation while minimizing economic and political costs.[39] However, Israeli officials were quite frank about the eventual outcome. General Moshe Dayan, regarded as a "minimalist" because he favored the gradual integration of the Occupied Territories into Israel without outright annexation, stated, "Judea and Samaria is Israel and we are not here as foreign conquerors but as returners to Zion."[40]

Following the June 1967 War, Israel embarked upon a course of mass expulsions. Three entire West Bank villages were destroyed in 1967: Emmwas, Yalu, and Beit Nuba, which are now the site of Canada Park. The destruction of these villages alone displaced between 4,000 and 10,000 people.[41] A conservative estimate of the total number of Palestinians forced out during the few months immediately following the war is about 300,000.[42]

The Israeli authorities demolished a large number of Palestinian houses. One report claims that 7,555 houses were demolished in the West Bank between June 11, 1967, and November 15, 1969.[43] Although such demolitions and mass expulsions gradually ceased by the early 1970s, Israel continued to try to "depopulate" the area. According to Ann Lesch, between 1968 and 1978, 1,156 people were deported from the West Bank (in some cases as whole families).[44] Fewer than one-tenth of all those who left or were forced out since 1967 were allowed to return. These figures lend credence to the view that Israeli policy has been geared toward reducing, to the extent possible, the Arab population of these areas.[45]

Economic integration of the Occupied Territories proceeded, accompanied by the growing dependence of these areas on Israel. Before they could embark on land expropriations and settlements, however, the Israeli authorities realized they did not have automatic jurisdiction over these areas, especially in matters that would "alter the status" of the Occupied Territories, to use a phrase from the Fourth Geneva Convention of 1949 (Convention Relative to the Protection of Civilian Persons in Time of War). Since the West Bank had been under formal Jordanian rule, legally Jordanian law would continue to apply. In order to circumvent any restrictions imposed by Jordanian law, but without suggesting outright annexation, the decision was taken to issue "amendments" to this law in the guise of military and security requirements.[46]

These and other measures gave an official stamp to Israeli policies in the Occupied Territories. They were soon accompanied by a process of Israeli settlement that some analysts suggested amounted to a deliberate policy to create a "fait accompli" that would justify political annexation later on.[47]

Of the most significant measures taken to dispossess Palestinians and transform the Occupied Territories into a type of internal colony under Israeli control, were laws concerning land expropriation and settlement. Some are reviewed in the following section.[48]

Land Expropriation and Settlement

U.N. Special Committee Report—1971: Report of the Special Committee to Investigate Israeli Practices Affecting the Human Rights of the Population of the Occupied Territories—5 October 1971.

Findings: On the basis of the testimony placed before it or obtained by it in the course of its investigations, the Special Committee has been led to conclude that the Government of Israel is deliberately carrying out policies aimed at preventing the population of the Occupied Territories from returning to their homes and forcing those who are in their homes in the Occupied Territories to leave, either by direct means such as deportation, or indirectly by attempts at undermining their morale or through the offer of special inducements, all with the ultimate object of annexing or settling the Occupied Territories.[49]

The total land area of the West Bank is approximately 5,500 square kilometers or 2,126 square miles. Various policies to expropriate land and build Jewish settlements had by 1988 resulted in over 52 percent of West Bank land being confiscated. On the eve of the *intifada,* in 1987, more than 65,000 settlers (compared to only 1,182 in 1972) inhabited the 120 or so settlements in the West Bank. In comparison, the 850,000 to 1,090,000 Arab residents of the West Bank, scattered in 400 villages and towns, were left with less than 48 percent of the land. The area of the Gaza Strip is about 352 square kilometers (140 square miles). By 1987, over one-third of the land had been expropriated by Israel. Eighteen Jewish settlements were built in the area, with a population of more than 2,700 settlers.[50] Land expropriation and settlement accelerated significantly in the aftermath of the Gulf crisis. By late 1991 the number of Jewish settlers was estimated at 250,000, residing in some 157 settlements, with over 70 percent of the West Bank alone estimated to be in Israeli hands.[51] Upon coming into power in 1992, the Rabin government announced new policies on settlement building that were to greatly restrict government-funded construction. Emphasis was placed on building "security" settlements, completing housing units already under way, providing for the "natural growth" required, and settling throughout the area of "Greater Jerusalem." There have been indications, however, that this policy has not been strictly adhered to and that widespread settlement and road building have proceeded unhindered.

Over the first ten years of occupation, successive Labor governments generally adhered to the policy of justifying settlements on military and security grounds. In view of the hopes pinned on the more "moderate" Labor Party to withdraw from the Occupied Territories and achieve a permanent peace, what deserves mention is that it was the very same Labor Party that first launched settlement activities in the these areas.

Various analysts, including many Israelis, denied that there is a strategy expressly designed to drive out the Arabs and facilitate the eventual annexation of these areas.[52] However, settlement activities through successive Labor, Likud, and then combined "National Unity" governments, seemed to bear out this hypothesis. The first settlements established under Labor rule took the form of military and agricultural outposts along the Jordan valley, areas that were expected to remain in Israeli hands in the event of any future settlement. By 1977, when the first Israeli government headed by the Likud Party assumed power in Israel, some 25–30 settlements had already been established in the West Bank, a significant number of which departed from the original intention of underlying security considerations.

The Likud government pursued an aggressive and intensified settlement policy. In the view of Likud supporters and other right-wing groups in Israel, the Occupied Territories constituted inalienable Jewish lands that Israel had "liberated" in the June 1967 War, and on which Jews could settle by "right."[53] If the annexation of the Occupied Territories could not be accomplished de jure, then the process of "creating facts" would continue on the ground.[54] The 1978 Camp David Accords, calling for "autonomy" for Palestinians, gave added urgency to the drive to establish settlements with a view to preempting independence or even genuine autonomy for the Palestinians in these areas.[55]

Several legal measures were enacted to enable Israel to confiscate Arab land in the West Bank and Gaza Strip. Many of these were adopted by the first Labor governments that ruled over the Occupied Territories between 1967 and 1977.

Military Order 59, "Order Concerning Government Properties—1967," and Military Order 364 (Amendment No. 4) of December 1969, give the military administration powers to "possess and dispose of all government property" of the previous Jordanian government in the West Bank and administer state lands in the Gaza Strip.[56] Only land that is "duly registered" and ownership settled by Israeli standards is legally considered as private property. The amount of this land is estimated at 30 percent of the West Bank.[57] Journalist Danny Rubinstein explains that since these military orders were "rediscovered" by the Likud Party after 1977, "there is hardly any problem in seizing lands in the West Bank for settlements."[58]

There are a number of military orders that authorize the administration to seize privately owned land for "vital and immediate military requirements." These lands would later be handed over to prospective Jewish settlers.

The military commander possesses full authority to declare certain areas "closed areas," usually on "security" grounds. The declaration of closed areas means that the Arab owners cannot enter to cultivate the land. After three consecutive years, the area can then be declared "state land" and confiscated. Many Israeli settlements have been built on lands expropriated in this manner.

Various military orders permit confiscation of land for the establishment of parks, roads, and the like. Such orders have frequently been used to expand the lands in and around Jewish settlements. The Israeli authorities have also "amended" laws to include the provision that "force be used to evacuate the owner of the land if he refuses to vacate it within the period decided upon by the Area Commander."[59] This military order has basically defined the "taking of land for Jewish settlements" as a "public purpose." In theory, any privately owned Palestinian land may be expropriated for the purpose of establishing Jewish settlements.[60]

It is interesting to note the similarity between laws enacted to expropriate land in the Occupied Territories with those in force in Israel. One example is the Absentee Property Law. Military Order 58, "Order Concerning Abandoned Property—(Private Property)—1967," which is based on the Absentee Property Law of 1950, defines an "absentee" as anyone who left the West Bank and Gaza Strip before, during, or after June 7, 1967.[61] The "Custodian of Absentee Properties" is authorized to "possess and control fully as an owner" all properties of those declared absentees. In some cases, where the land in question was being coveted for a settlement and the owner was not "absent," the custodian simply "leased" the land to the Jews, and the desired settlement would be established.[62]

Palestinians have no control over the lands that remain in their hands. Contrast this with the Jewish settlers in the Occupied Territories, who through their local councils, participate in decision-making and planning concerning land use in their areas. For example, road plans are designed to benefit Israeli settlers rather than the Arab residents. Major road networks have cut through Palestinian land, connecting Israeli settlements to Israel and to each other and bypassing existing Arab towns and villages.[63]

Palestinians also have little control over planning within their legally designated municipal boundaries. Once a civilian administration replaced the military administration in 1981, the Israeli civilian administrators took advantage of their authority to transfer some of the Arab municipal lands to surrounding Israeli settlements.[64]

Palestinian lands were thus expropriated for "military" purposes, for "public" purposes, by being declared "abandoned," and by being designated as "state" land. Other laws pertained to the declaration of "closed areas" and to the category of "absentee property." Land expropriation in an occupied territory, illegal under international law, constitutes just one dimension of the total process of expropriation that has been pursued in these areas. The economic integration of the West Bank and Gaza Strip was accompanied by the exploitation and control of vital resources, such as water, electricity, and labor. Moreover, Palestinian productive sectors, in industry and agriculture, have been marginalized in an unequal competition with the Israeli economy.[65]

The Integration of the Economy of the Occupied Territories into Israel

It is beyond the scope of this study to analyze in depth the transformation of the West Bank and Gaza Strip into virtual "peripheries" that serve the Israeli "core" economies.[66] However, land expropriation and settlement have essentially provided Israel with the best farmlands.[67] These same processes

resulted in the separation of Palestinians from productive work and facilitated their transformation into a proletariat in the Israeli economy. In all,
the Occupied Territories became markets for Israeli products. As indigenous
productive activities stagnated and atrophied, further barriers were placed
in the way of indigenous development. Unequal taxation, stiff tariffs, and
strict regulations governing exports and imports all served to reinforce this
trend.

The processes of integration and dependence proceeded in other spheres.
The Israeli government assumed complete control over water and electricity
resources in the Occupied Territories, rendering their use and allocation by
Palestinians limited and strictly regulated. In another vein, the Israeli
occupation regime has, since 1967, imposed severe restrictions on the
functioning and authority of local and municipal officers and councils. Such
restrictions inhibited indigenous development by such means as limiting
funding to municipalities and using funds as rewards or punishments,
among others.

Agriculture

Various analysts have documented the growing dependence of West Bank
agriculture on Israel.[68] In the Gaza Strip, the situation has been even more
critical; an extensive process of deterioration and marginalization of this
sector has taken place under Israeli occupation.

Instead of developing an indigenous subsistence economy, agricultural
production in these areas has been forcibly channeled into an unequal
relationship with Israel. Agricultural goods are produced to suit Israel's own
industries or for export abroad, as long as the exports do not compete with
Israeli produce. Credit facilities are lacking, cooperatives are restricted,
importing agricultural machinery is often prohibited or else highly taxed,
and market conditions remain insecure. As a consequence of these policies,
Palestinian direct producers have been forced into a position of a casual
labor force for the Israeli economy.[69] The policy of integration was
acknowledged by Israel. A report issued by the Ministry of Defense in
1981[70] claims that closer economic links between the West Bank and Israel
have integrated the agricultural sector within the Israeli economy, rather
than with other sectors of the occupied regions themselves.

Prior to 1967 agriculture, especially citriculture, constituted the major
economic activity in the Gaza Strip, accounting for over 33 percent of all
employment and 90 percent of all exports.[71] By 1984, only 18 percent of the
Gaza Strip labor force worked in agriculture.[72]

Analysis of the agricultural sector in the Occupied Territories would not
be complete without discussing water. Israel's exploitation of this essential

resource provides a further indication of its economic strangulation of these regions. As an Israeli Ministry of Defense report points out,

> Subterranean aquifers in Israel as elsewhere in the Middle East, do not correspond to political demarcation lines, and so far as water resources are concerned—Judea-Samaria is inseparable from the territory of Israel within the Green Line.[73]

The problem of water is especially crucial given the scarcity of water resources in the region as a whole and the dependence of land irrigation on water from underground wells.

In the West Bank, the Jordanian regime had anticipated difficulties in obtaining water and had accordingly drawn up a series of laws to regulate the drilling of new wells so as to ensure equal distribution and adequate supplies. After 1967, Israel "amended" these laws to the following effect: "It shall not be permissible for any person to set up or assemble or to possess or to operate a water installation unless he has obtained a license from the Area Commander."[74] This and other regulations have resulted in an almost total ban on the drilling of new wells by Arabs. Jewish settlers are exempt from the ban.[75]

Industry

Industry in the West Bank and Gaza Strip have remained underdeveloped relative to agriculture.[76] One effect of the 1967 War was to cut the Occupied Territories off from their traditional trading partners. For the West Bank, this separation resulted in an abrupt decline in industrial activity, though by 1969 it had recovered somewhat and resumed small-scale industrial production. West Bank industries have been unable to compete with Israeli ventures, and along with the restrictions on markets, credits, facilities, and machinery, limitations have been placed on the potential for further development. The expansion that has occurred has generally reflected Israeli investments in subcontracting ventures in the Occupied Territories, for example, in clothing and furniture. The Israeli government facilitated this process by offering large subsidies and loans to Israeli investors. As noted by Meron Benvenisti, this "business cycle closely follows the fluctuations of the Israeli economy, pointing to the absolute dependence of West Bank industry on Israel."[77]

Israeli subcontracting became an important activity for the Gaza Strip, and this area has remained heavily dependent on Israel for raw materials and exports. An almost identical situation to that in the West Bank has existed with regard to the integration of the Strip's industry into the Israeli sector.[78]

Until the *intifada,* these areas continued to constitute Israel's second-largest market after the United States. For each year until the *intifada,* an estimated US $800 million worth of Israeli goods were dumped into these markets.[79]

Proletarianization

Various analysts agree that proletarianization is one of the most serious consequences of the occupation, as well as a most revealing indicator of the degree to which the West Bank and Gaza Strip have been integrated into Israel.[80]

In 1984 the West Bank labor force comprised some 154,000 workers (36.7 percent of the total working age population in the West Bank). In the Gaza Strip, the figure for 1984 was 87,200. Yusuf Sayigh estimates that by 1983 close to 40 percent of all Palestinian workers in the Occupied Territories were working in Israel.[81] By the early 1990s, and especially after the Gulf War, the number of Palestinian workers in Israel had been drastically reduced, to a total of about 120,000. Israeli measures taken in March 1993 that cut off Jerusalem from the rest of the Occupied Territories, and the north and south of the West Bank from each other, reduced further the number of Palestinian laborers in Israel.[82]

Palestinians have generally been concentrated in menial and low-paid jobs that Jews would not perform. Sheila Ryan writes, "Workers are channeled into those menial jobs by a systematic Israeli policy."[83] In the mid-1980s, about 51 percent of West Bank laborers in Israel worked in the area of construction. Industry constituted 17.9 percent, agriculture 9.8 percent, and other sectors (including services) 2.8 percent.[84] Figures for the Gaza Strip in 1984 showed 45.1 percent in construction, 19.6 percent in agriculture, 18.1 percent in industry, and 17.2 percent in services.[85]

Palestinian laborers in Israel face exploitive and insecure working conditions. For example, although 30–40 percent of a worker's salary is deducted for basic benefits and compensation, in practice Palestinians (compared to Jewish laborers) have not benefited from any of the services for which they paid. Palestinian laborers have received some 40–50 percent of wages paid to Jews.[86] As migrant laborers, they received daily wages and worked without contracts. This practice made Palestinian workers easily expendable in times of economic slowdowns, and as such exceedingly vulnerable to fluctuations in the Israeli economy. Before the *intifada,* the unemployment rate had already become one indication of the severity of Palestinian dispossession. Between 1970 and 1983 some 99,000 Palestinians from the West Bank were said to be unemployed. Partial amelioration of this condition occurred through emigration to the Gulf, Jordan, and other states in the region. However, by the 1980s, opportunities in the Gulf had declined, and thousands of Palestinians, laborers and professionals alike, were forced to return to face renewed unemployment within the Occupied Territories. This situation was further exacerbated in the summer of 1990, when tens of thousands of Palestinians were forced to flee Kuwait as a result of the Iraqi occupation. Not only were hundreds of thousands of Palestinian families left without a means of livelihood, but remittances from workers in the Gulf to their families at home also came to an end. By the early 1990s the staggering rate of unemployment was one of the most critical issues facing Palestinians. At the same time there was increased pressure to employ "Jewish labor only." This is reminiscent of the measures adopted by the early Zionist community in Palestine to employ only Jews.

Apart from serving economic and political ends, the revival of this practice revealed the racist stereotypes that have historically operated against Arabs. These beliefs have in turn reinforced the particular class and ethnic distinctions between Jews and Arabs and contributed to the perpetuation of the occupation.[87] There are a number of derogatory and discriminatory racial stereotypes used against Palestinians—for example, the Hebrew term concerning Arab labor *avoda aravit,* which denotes "Arab work" and refers to a job poorly done, and *aravi melukhlah,* or, "dirty Arab." Several racial stereotypes depict Palestinians in general. For example, former Prime Minister Menachem Begin was reported to have spoken about Arabs as "almost as subhumans."[88] In 1988, Prime Minister Itzhak Shamir was said to have referred to Palestinians as "grasshoppers." At other times, Palestinians have alternatively been referred to by leading policy makers as "two-legged animals" and "drugged cockroaches in a bottle."[89]

The manipulation of racist stereotypes against an oppressed group is a familiar tactic in situations of colonial domination. In the case of Israel and the Occupied Territories, these racist assumptions lend credence and justify (in some Israeli eyes), the continued domination of these territories and their Arab inhabitants. Later sections examine elements of the Israeli social structure that have bearing on this issue.

Purely economic benefits of cheap Palestinian labor to the Israeli economy are supplemented by various political advantages that accrue from the process of proletarianization. Israel over the years has been able to exploit Palestinian labor to finance its continued occupation of the territories. Huge sums of money have been collected from the Palestinians in the form of wage deductions, taxes, and fines.[90] Instead of being reinvested into their respective economies, these sums have, in effect, been channeled to finance both the occupation and the establishment of Jewish settlements in these areas.[91]

Unlike other facets of Israeli rule, proletarianization, especially as it approaches its more complete form, may be both unintended and unwelcome to Israel. Palestinian labor from the Occupied Territories could be characterized as a largely migrant labor force, whose subsistence needs are met in the occupied areas themselves (especially in the West Bank). Israel on the other hand, remains responsible for meeting its productive needs. As the process of expropriation and dispossession continues, one would expect that Israel will increasingly be forced to pick up the costs of maintaining a growing dispossessed population, thus risking additional economic and political costs to its continued control of these areas. As a result, Israel may be caught in a set of contradictory policy responses. The first favors the dislocation and dispossession of Palestinians: to benefit from the exploitation of cheap labor in the short term, and to eventually remove Palestinians from these areas in the long term. The second regards increased dispossession and disaffection within Palestinian ranks as risky, since they may intensify the Palestinians' sense of frustration and despair and threaten Israel with unwanted political repercussions.[92] These developments may explain, in part, Israel's reasoning behind the interim autonomy plan for the Occupied Territories. By 1993 the policy of "integration" and "dependence" can be said to have come full circle. Pressures to "accommodate," by ridding itself of its responsibility for the Palestinian population of these areas, coincided with Israel's need to maintain some control over lands and resources. Hence, the autonomy plan was founded on the principle that the Occupied Territories will remain dependent economically on Israel for the foreseeable future.[93]

Marginalization of Palestinian Institutions

The ever-expanding Israeli monopoly over the lands and resources of the Occupied Territories is consistent with a pattern of colonial domination, and the Palestinian inhabitants find themselves increasingly dispossessed and marginalized in their own land. The processes whereby Israel has been consolidating its control over Palestinian resources and raw materials have been accompanied by deliberate measures to deprive the indigenous Palestinian population of the means for reproducing its independent existence on the land. These developments lie at the heart of the Palestinian struggle. Throughout the years of occupation Palestinians have regarded their first and foremost responsibility as staying on the land, remaining steadfast, and trying to reduce their dependence on Israel.

Measures taken to marginalize indigenous sectors and integrate the Occupied Territories into Israel have been reproduced in nonproductive spheres as well. Israel has interfered extensively in the functioning of Palestinian municipalities, the only local and official governing bodies of the Arab inhabitants.[94]

The Proclamation on Law and Administration, No. 2 of June 7, 1967, transferred to the commander of the Israeli Defense Forces (IDF) in the West Bank, "any power of government, legislation, appointive or administrative."[95] The Israeli military government proceeded to change laws in force in the West Bank by issuing a series of military orders and regulations that radically and systematically "amended" Jordanian law. In the Gaza Strip, amendments applied to all previously existing laws, from the Ottoman regime to the British Mandate regulations. As Benvenisti explains, "The military governor is the executive, legislative, and judicial authority."[96] From June 1967 until the imposition of a civilian administration in November 1981, the West Bank and Gaza Strip continued to be ruled directly by a military government. After that date, a civilian administration was in force in these areas. However, the ultimate authority remained in the hands of the military administration, in a chain of command responsible directly to the Israeli minister of defense.[97]

As the Israeli occupation got under way, the municipalities constituted the only official Palestinian national bodies that were recognized by Israel. Yet municipal authorities were prohibited from carrying out even the most basic of their functions without receiving prior permission from the military governor. For example, Israel at first banned municipal elections. Immediately following 1967, the terms of office of the mayors were extended by Military Order 80. This action was taken because the Israelis feared that holding elections would "endanger public order."[98] Municipal elections took place for the first time under occupation in 1972 and resulted in the victory of the traditional leadership.[99] The next municipal elections were permitted in 1976, when a majority of West Bank cities elected officials with a distinct pro-PLO stand. Israel then moved again to outlaw elections, freezing them in 1980 and beyond.[100] Candidates deemed "unacceptable" were expelled, and others were removed from their posts.[101]

The situation in the Gaza Strip differs slightly in that local municipal laws continued to be based on British Mandatory law, specifically, the Municipal Law of 1934. No elections had been held in the Gaza Strip since 1946. Following the 1967 occupation, Israel "amended" British laws to "legalize" its appointment or dismissal of municipal councils and further restrict municipal activities.

In addition to restrictions on the local functions of each municipality, the Israeli military government placed numerous obstacles in the way of their regional functions. Specific regulations were issued at different times to forbid West Bank mayors from coming into direct contact with each other, even at social gatherings. They were also forbidden to establish "any cooperative regional programs."[102] Several observers document the role of the military government in preventing the implementation of development projects. Benvenisti refers to Israel's economic policy of "prevention of independent economic development that would enable Palestinian political forces to establish power bases, and eventually a Palestinian state."[103] Until 1982, West Bank mayors were occasionally allowed to travel to the Arab states to collect funding for their municipalities. After that date, the direct receipt of *sumud* (steadfastness) funds was banned by military order.[104] All funds from abroad destined for the municipalities had to be channeled through a special Regional Development Fund controlled by Israel. This fund would decide for which projects, if any, money could be released.[105]

The Israeli government's apparent intention of holding onto the lands of the West Bank and Gaza Strip was clearly illustrated in its policies toward indigenous municipal planning. In 1971 the Israeli authorities issued Military Order 418, "Order Concerning Town and Village Construction Law." Under the relevant Jordanian law, planning committees had comprised various levels of municipal, regional, and national elements. With the new order, these functions were usurped by the Israeli authorities.[106] The marginalization of Palestinians from control over their own lands and livelihood became especially pronounced after 1977, when the Likud Party came into power in Israel. To quote Benvenisti, "The physical planning process reflects Israeli interests exclusively, while all the needs and interests of the Palestinian population are treated as constraints to be overcome."[107]

Far from being random historical incidents, measures and policies taken during the early period of the occupation provided the groundwork for future Israeli government policies vis-à-vis the Occupied Territories. During the peace process that began in 1991, for example, even the most flexible Israeli "concessions" envisioned no more than offering the Palestinians "autonomy." The geographic sites of this proposed "autonomy" were strictly defined, to comprise a mere 4–6 percent of the total land area of the Occupied Territories.[108] What was apparent was Israel's total opposition to any form of Palestinian indigenous development that would ensure the continuity of a Palestinian entity in the Occupied Territories. There was, moreover, opposition to any Palestinian national expression, despite Israeli claims to be searching for a representative Palestinian leadership in these areas and despite the Israeli government's pledges of "autonomy" for the Palestinians.[109] This contradiction is evident when we examine the Camp David Accords and the imposition of a civilian administration in these areas.

The Camp David Accords, signed in 1978 by President Anwar Sadat of Egypt, President Jimmy Carter of the United States, and Prime Minister Menachem Begin of Israel, provided a framework for the settlement of the Palestinian problem that was referred to and reactivated in limited form during the peace process of the early 1990s. What these agreements called for was "self-rule" for the inhabitants of the Occupied Territories, which, as it was interpreted by the Israeli government, applied to the people and not the land. Benvenisti explains Israel's view of the "autonomy" contained in these plans, whereby land and water would remain under Israeli control. He states that this "was used as a program of action guiding the government of Israel and the military government in steps taken toward annexation."[110] These agreements required that the final status of the Occupied Territories be left open for a period of five years, after which the "inhabitants" of the area would participate in "negotiating" their future status. That these inhabitants will necessarily be Arabs was not specified in the text. Theoretically Israel could, and in reality Israel has, taken advantage of the ambiguity in order to step up settlement activities in the area, further dispossessing Palestinians and affording Israel greater control over vital land resources.[111] Neither Palestinians nor their representatives in the PLO were invited to participate in these talks that were to determine their fate. Consequently, most Palestinians rejected these accords and until 1993 remained largely skeptical of all autonomy plans.

Settlement activity was immediately escalated (in violation of the agreements at Camp David), but there was no "autonomy" forthcoming to the Palestinians. Meantime, by 1981, the Israeli authorities realized that more active measures had to be taken to deter the emergence of an independent Palestinian national existence. The National Guidance Committee (NGC), which was formed in the wake of the Camp David Accords to resist the implementation of self-rule, was banned, and many of its leaders were imprisoned or deported. When the Palestinian municipalities also refused to cooperate with the new civilian administration, these were dissolved and replaced by Israeli military officials acting in the capacity of mayors.[112]

The civilian administration was established in the Occupied Territories by virtue of Military Order 947 of November 8, 1981. It is important to note that the transition to the civilian administration did not mark the end of military rule. What the order did achieve was to create two distinctive sectors of authority. The military sector remained in control of all matters pertaining to politics and security, while the new civilian sector assumed "administrative" powers only.[113]

The shift to a civilian administration did little to enhance Palestinian involvement in decision-making within their own communities. On the contrary, the establishment of the civilian administration arguably enabled Israel to legalize the military occupation itself. As various lawyers and other analysts have pointed out, all preceding military orders have virtually been elevated to the status of permanent—as opposed to temporary—laws.[114] In other words, the occupation itself would be legalized—as a civilian government and no longer as military government. With military rule thus "withdrawn," Israel retained power and has since claimed the authority to determine the future of the areas. How far the institutionalization of the occupation proceeded was evident in the Israeli government's continued insistence on referring to the West Bank and Gaza Strip as "administered" or "disputed" areas during the peace negotiations. Even the autonomy plans did not specify that these areas would ultimately revert to full Palestinian sovereignty.

Laws and Regulations

Economic and political measures taken by Israel against indigenous institutions are only one facet of the repression of Palestinians under occupation. A whole series of laws and measures were enacted to regulate the activities of Palestinians, both individually and collectively. The cumulative effect of these regulations was to control practically every aspect of Palestinian existence. These measures are illustrated in the latitude of freedom enjoyed by the military government in defining what are considered "security offenses." Almost any expression of Palestinian nationalism or identity, any protest, and any attempt to develop one's society in the Occupied Territories may be defined as "security violations." Once a Palestinian is charged with a security offense and sentence passed, the person has no right to appeal the decision. The result has often been severe punishment: imprisonment, administrative detention, or deportation.

The family or community from which the "offender" originates has also not been immune. The Israeli authorities have frequently imposed "collective punishment," such as sealing or blowing up houses of families of the offenders. These measures have often been taken merely on the suspicion of having committed an offense, that is, without having been formally charged or tried, let alone sentenced. Another means of collective punishment is the imposition of curfews on whole camps and villages.

More than 1,400 military orders have been issued since the beginning of the occupation; together with the British Emergency Regulations, these constitute the basis for the preservation of "law and order" in the occupied West Bank and Gaza Strip.[115] As for relevant international law, Israel maintains that the Fourth Geneva Convention is not applicable to the West Bank (and Gaza Strip) because Jordan's annexation of the West Bank was not legal. In the Israeli view, therefore, these areas are "administered" rather than "occupied."

Between the 1960s and the late 1970s, close to 20,000 houses were demolished or sealed in whole or in part.[116] Demolition is frequently carried out before a person is charged for an offense, and it is used as a form of collective punishment against the family as well, even if the individual in question no longer resides there. In some cases the suspect is later acquitted—too late to save his house. Israeli officials have openly admitted that the purpose of these measures is not simply to punish offenders and suspected offenders, but also to deter others.[117] By the third year of the *intifada,* soldiers were demolishing or sealing homes of Palestinians who belonged to popular committees, or those whose members had been involved in stone-throwing activities and other demonstrations, or simply those from whose vicinity stones were thrown.[118] An estimated 2,000 houses were demolished or sealed during the first five years of the *intifada,* including some 182 homes (mainly in the Gaza Strip) that were destroyed by antitank missiles.[119]

Israeli military authorities may declare an area closed and under curfew without prior notification. This is a means of collective punishment that has often been imposed on refugee camps and other communities as punishment for strikes and demonstrations. The use of this measure increased during the *intifada.*[120] Declaring a curfew means declaring a closed area; journalists are not allowed in, and the residents are generally not allowed outside their homes. Curfews may extend for days or weeks, causing severe hardships for people who need food or medical care. During curfews, Jewish settlers may continue to travel unrestricted in these areas. This measure was used extensively during the Gulf War. All the Palestinian inhabitants of the Occupied Territories were placed under a blanket curfew lasting from January 15 to February 25, 1991, with virtually no interruption.

The Israeli authorities may at any time place a restriction order against any individual, forbidding the person from meeting with others in groups of more than ten people. Restrictions may be issued on travel permits, and sometimes residents of whole villages or areas are barred from travel. Teenagers and young adults face a particularly difficult situation. If they wish to travel outside the Occupied Territories, they are generally not allowed to return for at least nine months.[121]

Police and soldiers in the Occupied Territories are authorized to make arrests "upon suspicion" and without a warrant. Military Order 378 empowers soldiers and police to arbitrarily stop a Palestinian at any time or to enter and search his house.[122] Before the *intifada,* when restrictions were intensified, a person could be held for up to 18 days without being officially charged or brought before a military judge. Throughout this time, a detainee would not be permitted to consult with his lawyer. Often, International Red Cross officials would also be barred from meeting the prisoner, and although Israel is bound to report detentions to the International Red Cross within 12 days, it would not always comply. A Palestinian could be held up to six months without trial. The detention period could then be renewed or canceled after six months.[123] Many persons placed under administrative detention had their detention periods renewed several times, sometimes extending into several years. This type of detention was frequently used against leading national and institutional figures. They included mayors, municipal officials, heads of research organizations, university professors, teachers, leaders and activists in charitable and other organizations, labor unionists, students, lawyers, journalists, physicians, and other professionals.

Some administrative detainees have sometimes been punished without charge, or for such offenses as writing articles in newspapers.[124] Raja Shehadeh refers to a 1984 Amnesty International report that states, "Many people were restricted for nonviolent expressions of their political opinions."[125]

Reports of mistreatment of prisoners abound and have come to the attention of international and humanitarian organizations. In late 1987 there was an outcry in Israel over the disclosure that over the years the General Security Service (GSS or Shin Bet), which first interrogates Palestinians upon their arrest, had systematically mistreated and tortured Palestinian detainees for the purpose of extracting "confessions." Benvenisti says that among the methods used by the GSS are solitary confinement, cold showers in winter, arrests of relatives, threats, verbal abuse, and forcing the prisoner to stand for long periods.[126] The *Jerusalem Post International Edition* of November 17, 1987, disclosed the results of the Landau Commission, which was set up to examine the Shin Bet's interrogation methods. The report confirmed what Palestinians and their lawyers, Amnesty International, and others had been claiming for years concerning Israeli torture.[127] Reports since 1971 have revealed that the Shin Bet "on numerous occasions lied to the courts in connection with the methods with which confessions were extracted from suspects." Rather than being "irregular" occurrences, "physical pressure," indeed, torture, has been systematically employed to extract confessions.[128]

Articles that appeared in Israel in essence defended its practices, noting that, when working against "terrorist activities," the state must use all the means at its disposal to protect itself. As a result, the use of force against Palestinians became legalized and routine, and was practiced freely, especially during the *intifada*.[129] However, the tragic part of the whole affair, as Palestinians were quick to point out, was that this type of violent interrogation has been systematically practiced against innocent Palestinians, frequently youth, whose "terrorist" activities consisted of nothing more than throwing stones, participating in demonstrations, or raising the Palestinian flag.[130]

In June 1993 new revelations concerning torture in Israel came to light during a conference on torture, sponsored by the Association of Israeli-Palestinian Physicians and Public Committee Against Torture, when an official document called the "Medical Fitness Form" was circulated. It was established that participating physicians had been asked to complete this form for prospective prisoners, in order to ascertain their overall health and their ability to cope with different degrees of "physical pressure."[131] A prisoner is frequently tortured to "persuade" him to inform on others or to obtain a confession that would convict him, regardless of whether he had indeed committed a security offense. A number of cases were reported during the *intifada* where imprisoned Palestinians died in "suspicious circumstances." There are strong indications that these Palestinians were beaten or otherwise tortured to death.[132]

Palestinians regard deportation, the permanent exile from one's homeland, as the most severe measure that can be taken against them. Prohibited in international law, even the 1945 British Emergency Regulations specify that deportations are only to be carried out when they are necessary to preserve law and order, or to put down revolts and riots.[133] Israel has resorted to deportations in order to deprive the Occupied Territories of its nationalist leadership, or simply as a warning to other resisters. More than 2,000 people have been deported since 1967. Hundreds of them have never committed any violent act; their activities have been totally nonviolent, and they have been undertaken in the effort to develop their communities. These include municipal leaders, professionals, university professors, trade unionists, women active in various organizations, and many others. Abdul Jawad Saleh, former mayor of El-Bireh, who was permitted to return to the West Bank in 1993 after 20 years of exile, describes the anguish experienced by those forced out of their homeland.[134] He was deported without trial on December 10, 1973, the International Day of Human Rights. He writes, "If serving one's people with the most possible devotion is a crime . . . then I am glad to write down my confessions that I am the most dangerous terrorist and a devoted criminal."[135]

Between December 1987 and early 1991 close to 70 people were officially deported from the Occupied Territories. Most were expelled during the first year of the *intifada,* between 1987 and 1988.[136] In December 1992, 413 Palestinians were expelled en masse from the Occupied Territories to Southern Lebanon, allegedly for being *Hamas* activists. This was the largest single mass expulsion since the 1967 War, and their fate was for a long time a major point of contention between the Israeli authorities and the residents of the Occupied Territories. About half were permitted to return in late summer 1993 and the rest were allowed back at the end of the year.

Other regulated activities that stand out are censorship of the press and censorship of books. Newspapers in the West Bank are required to submit all their articles to the Israeli censor on a daily basis. Failure to comply could result in the paper being confiscated temporarily or being banned or closed down altogether. Shehadeh and Kuttab note that words such as "the sail," "the stalk of wheat," and other symbolic terms were regularly censored.[137] Sometimes, to evade these restrictions, Palestinian journalists attempted to print articles that had already appeared in the Hebrew press. These were also subject to censorship. All references to disturbances, demonstrations, land confiscation, and other similar occurrences would be routinely banned. During the *intifada* violations of press freedom became even more acute. A number of press offices, newspapers, and other publications were closed down, and several journalists were detained or expelled.[138]

Similar prohibitions exist with regard to books. For example, a book taken from East Jerusalem into the West Bank or Gaza Strip for personal use was expressly forbidden unless a permit had been issued. Punishment for violating this regulation could result in five years imprisonment or a huge fine.[139] At any given time, book lists ranging from tens to hundreds could be banned. These have been changed periodically, and have even reached the 1,000 mark. The topics cover literature, politics, poetry, and history, including school texts and other works, particularly those dealing with Palestinian nationalism.

Given that almost any expression of Palestinian rights to self-determination or resistance against the occupation could constitute a security violation, it is not surprising that tens of thousands of "incidents" have occurred over the years and that hundreds of thousands of Palestinians have been arrested and detained. Military Order 101, "Concerning the Prohibition of Incitement and Adverse Propaganda," of August 27, 1967, defines several areas of security violations in the Occupied Territories. Article 9 of this order reads in part, "Every soldier shall have the power to use the necessary force to execute any order issued by virtue of this order or to prevent the commission of any offense which is contrary to this order."[140] One survey, taken before the *intifada* in 1986, found that 90 percent of the population 15 years and over had experienced one or more forms of Israeli repression: beatings, physical abuse and threats, harassments, insults at checkpoints, fines, bans on travel, property or land confiscation, sealing or demolition of houses, arrests, detentions, and so on.[141] Such punishments were often imposed even where the acts were clearly nonviolent.[142]

* * *

By 1993, 26 years into the occupation, Israel's strategic interests remain as the central factor in determining the fate of the Occupied Territories.[143] Uppermost in these conceptions is the issue of land. Even its most liberal interpretations of a political settlement have not shown Israel inclined to withdraw completely from these territories. For many in Israel, the issue of land is nonnegotiable. The Camp David Accords that envisioned some "autonomy" for the Palestinian people and the introduction of a civilian administration in the Occupied Territories—both of which were heralded as "positive developments" at the time—did not offer Palestinians anything more than limited self-rule. This was in keeping with the overarching Zionist ideology of the State of Israel, one that defines the Jewish nation as belonging to the "Jewish people." Similarly, the PLO/Israel accords signed in September 1993 leave the issue of full withdrawal from lands in the Occupied Territories deliberately vague.

The structural changes in Palestinian society engendered by the occupation left an indelible mark on existing social relationships within the Palestinian community. New social relationships emerged to reflect the transformed social conditions. These in turn have been the driving force in the emergence of the types of resistance in these areas. The following chapter reflects extensively on these issues. As we will see, Palestinian concern over the destruction and marginalization of their society has been significant in shaping their assessments of the appropriate targets for their struggle. In the final analysis, it is the occupation as a whole, and not the individual manifestations of Israeli rule, that remain the focus of Palestinian resistance.

Two

Twenty Years of Occupation: Palestinian Resistance Before the Intifada

The Emergence of a Palestinian National Liberation Movement

Tracing the course of resistance in the Occupied Territories is difficult without first taking into account the Palestinian national liberation movement as a whole, embodied in the Palestine Liberation Organization (PLO).

Palestinian resistance emerged initially in response to British rule and Jewish settlement in Mandate Palestine in the early part of the twentieth century—a resistance that has persisted in one form or another to the present day.[1] There is a distinct historical continuity in the context that defined the genesis of Palestinian resistance, even though goals have not remained the same and the modalities of resistance have changed. Both have evolved and have been restructured in light of specific historical events in the region. Nevertheless, the Palestinians' response to the colonization of their lands is neither unique nor unprecedented in history. Their experience is shared with numerous national liberation movements around the world, as a reaction of an oppressed people to the conditions of their oppression and dispossession.

There are interesting parallels between the perceptions of the Zionist movement vis-à-vis the indigenous inhabitants of Palestine and those of the Palestinians in the PLO vis-à-vis the Zionist movement. The Zionist conquest of all of Palestine ultimately succeeded by force if one keeps in mind that the whole venture was initially conceived in total disregard of the indigenous inhabitants. Thus, if Zionism emerged within the distinct atmosphere of European colonization in general, the antithesis, the response of the Palestine national movement, emerged within a comparable context of prevailing anticolonial movements and incorporated their specific understandings about the nature and goals of the struggle. Without implying symmetry or making any value judgments concerning either of the two movements, what this comparison suggests is that if such movements—whether colonial or anticolonial—emerge in specific historical contexts, then there may be room for modifying the content and objectives of each movement once a particular historical period has passed. The "historical necessity," if one can put it that way, that gave the impetus to the Zionist movement at a particular time culminated in the establishment of the State of Israel. It was a similar "historical necessity" that gave birth to its antithesis, in the form of the Palestinian national liberation movement. This movement sought to reverse that specific expression of colonialism that took the form of the State of Israel. However, in the past few decades, this goal has been superseded by new events and forces in the Middle East. The fulfillment of part of the Zionist goal—the Jewish state established in 1948—has already been achieved. Yet the continued occupation of additional Palestinian lands since 1967 has signaled to Palestinians that the Zionist movement may still be unfinished.

The establishment of a Palestinian national liberation movement began in the 1950s.[2] As the founding members of the PLO saw it, the occupation of Palestinian land comprised both a specific ideology—Zionism—and an actual colonial presence. The two could not be separated. The Palestinian movement sought to terminate the one by eradicating the other. They sought to restore an Arab Palestine, one where Jews, Muslims, and Christians could coexist. In their eyes, Palestinians had been unjustly and violently removed from their lands, and replaced by another people who were regarded as foreign and who did not permit them, the original inhabitants, to return to claim their homes, their belongings, or their lands.

Many analysts have addressed issues pertaining to the dynamics of resistance under colonial rule. Among these are the writers Frantz Fanon and Albert Memmi, who argue forcefully that colonialism contains the seeds of its own destruction.[3] The Palestinian national movement grew up into precisely the atmosphere of resistance to colonialism that was so eloquently portrayed by these writers. The injunction of the total cleansing of the colonized through violence and the imperative to totally destroy the colonial entity voiced by Fanon and Memmi were familiar to the PLO and greatly influenced its outlook. The arguments posed by Fanon were particularly compelling because he wrote about Algeria under the French, a settler colony that Palestinians would compare to Palestine.

For Fanon and Memmi, the antithesis of colonialism is inherent in its inception. They acknowledge the violence and total oppression that the colonizer can bring to bear, with its readiness to exploit, discriminate against, and even massacre the colonized. But there are countervailing forces: Because the existence of the colonial system is predicated on the very presence of the colonized, the decimation of the subjugated population can never be total; the colonized cannot be physically annihilated. Eventually, the opposed forces collide, tearing the colonial system apart. What contributes to this process is the dehumanization of the colonized by the colonizer. This operates through racism and other ideological underpinnings that serve to separate the two peoples and legitimize the oppression of one by the other. Neither can this process be total, and soon the dehumanization of the oppressed backfires against the oppressors, causing their own sense of estrangement from self and their own dehumanization.[4]

Meanwhile, the colonized are also being transformed. The dehumanization and violence practiced against them awakens hatred, anger, and self-awareness of being "other." The colonized become determined to shrug off this yoke they carry and meet violence with violence. Decolonization has begun. Fanon suggests that no half measures are possible. He believes that the only way a complete "cleansing" and removal of the oppressor can be achieved is through violence.[5] Fanon sees this violence as "creative," in that it gives birth to a people who are empowered, who have shrugged off both their oppressors and the internalized image of themselves acquired through their oppressors. They are a people reborn through violence.

We can take issue with Fanon by comparing his analysis with the circumstances surrounding the Palestinian national liberation movement. For Fanon—with due consideration to the historical period in which he wrote (the Algerian Revolution of the 1950s)—there appears to be little distinction between a strategy that would effectively end "oppression" and one that would create the new free person. Violence is posited as the only effective means because it is "cleansing" and empowering, and not necessarily because it ends the situation of colonization.[6]

What if there exists an alternative strategy to "violence," one that could have an identical effect, not only in ending a system of colonial rule, but also in exorcising the mentality of the colonizer from the colonized? If violence is adopted mainly for the sake of "cleansing," what if another strategy can also accomplish that purpose, and perhaps end the physical presence of an occupier/colonizer as well? What if this strategy is a nonviolent civilian resistance strategy? One can challenge the PLO and other national liberation movements that have been quick to adopt, at face value, the notion that violence can only be met with violence, and that only armed struggle can be effective against a colonizer.

No national liberation movement necessarily extols "violence" for violence's sake. It is adopted out of what is perceived as sheer necessity in the face of the magnitude of oppression endured by the colonized, and as an outpouring of reaction from the bottomless well of their suffering. Fanon recognizes these other dimensions of violence, as well as the purification and empowerment they afford. The PLO adopted armed struggle in much the same way, seeing it as the heroic, purging, dynamic, exciting, and in many cases—with the exception of their own—successful form of struggle.

The challenge to the PLO is to reevaluate the tenets they have taken for granted all these years. If armed struggle has occasionally succeeded in other places, why did it not or could it not succeed in liberating Palestine? Is armed struggle supposed to liberate the land or the people? Or both? What about the fact that with clear exceptions, Palestinians living under direct colonial rule in the Occupied Territories overwhelmingly rejected armed struggle as a technique to liberate themselves and their lands? Instead, and in spite of individual acts of violence against Israeli soldiers or settlers, Palestinians under occupation have chosen the *intifada*. What if these Palestinians have concluded that another strategy, one that uses the power of nonviolent civilian resistance, may accelerate decolonization? What if they can establish that this strategy operates not by overthrowing the oppressor but by forcing it to become aware of its oppression and by causing the dehumanization to backfire against this oppressor? Such thought-provoking questions could be considered in the Palestinian-Israeli conflict. One then realizes that historical possibilities are there to be seized and not left waiting to happen.

One issue confronting the Palestinian movement and the PLO has not been choosing between armed struggle and another strategy, but defining the real objectives of the movement itself. The question that could be asked is whether Palestinians have been struggling against colonization in the West Bank and Gaza Strip, or whether their ultimate goal has been to defeat Zionism and colonialism combined. Responding to this question may require a Palestinian acknowledgement that their acceptance of a two-state solution may always remain only partial decolonization. If so, they should be clear that partial decolonization is not necessarily synonymous with partial "cleansing" of the oppressed. The latter could be total while the former remains partial. That being the case, then there has to be a letting go, an abandonment of Palestine, the "homeland," regardless of whether it is Zionist or colonial in their eyes, in favor of Palestine, the state. There needs to be a conscious selection of means in light of these ends. Even if armed struggle were somehow suited to total decolonization, it may well backfire both as a technique and a strategy in the Occupied Territories. These are issues with which Palestinians have been grappling since the inception of their movement. Palestinians have incorporated their responses into specific ideological leanings and perspectives—perspectives that have constantly been challenged and revised over the years.

The Palestine Liberation Organization—the PLO

The emergence of the PLO is a classic example of the embodiment of the axioms and precepts of anticolonial movements. These movements came to incorporate what has almost become a principle of such resistance: the notion that what has been taken by force can only be returned by force. As Fanon would say, "Decolonization is always a violent phenomenon."[7] Most national liberation movements have concluded that armed struggle would be used during at least some phases of the struggle against foreign domination. Amilcar Cabral, a prominent leader and activist during the struggle of the people of Guinea-Bissau against Portuguese domination, expressed it thus: "The normal path of national liberation, imposed on the peoples by imperialist repression is armed struggle."[8]

The PLO apparently concurred. Armed struggle was to become the overarching tenet guiding the movement, at least in the early years.[9] Since 1967, the focus of PLO/Palestinian national resistance activities shifted gradually from the goal of liberating all of Palestine to concentrating on the Occupied Territories as the location of a future Palestinian state. Even this transformation, however, could not be understood without examining what the anticolonial movement actually comprised and how the PLO sought to incorporate this understanding in its own struggle.[10]

A redefinition, on the Palestinian side, of what the struggle is about (whether it is Zionism, colonial occupation, or both) inevitably necessitated a reevaluation of means. If it is no longer a struggle for the negation of Zionism/colonialism, then is "armed struggle" still required? Is it justified or feasible? Moreover, if their struggle is limited to the liberation of the Occupied Territories, how are Palestinians to address Zionism within the state that occupied these lands in the first place? How is Zionism to define itself, within the State of Israel, or beyond? Are Palestinians responsible in any way for such a redefinition on the part of Israel?

Far from being rhetorical questions, these are fundamental issues that Palestinians have confronted throughout their recent history. These are also issues that have fashioned their responses and resistance to Israeli colonization of their lands, first in Palestine, then in the Occupied Territories. It is their continued grappling with these questions that has in part contributed to the emergence of various factions within the PLO, as well as to the factional and fractional problems between the PLO and the inhabitants of the Occupied Territories. It is also in this context that the emergence of radical Islamic groups, as alternatives to the "secular" PLO, can be more readily understood.

In 1964 the Arab states established the PLO as part of an attempt to coopt a rising tide of Palestinian uneasiness and to contain demands for action that were being voiced across the Arab world.[11] The move for an independent

PLO began after 1967, when the defeat of Egypt, Syria, and Jordan by Israel, along with the Israeli conquest of additional lands, discredited the Arab states in the eyes of the Arab peoples (especially among Palestinians). Between 1968 and 1969, the emerging leadership in exile, including Yasser Arafat, Khalil Al-Wazir (Abu Jihad), and the rest of the *Fatah* core, took control of the PLO. From then on, the PLO became a uniquely Palestinian organization and assumed growing popularity among the Arab peoples. People flocked to join *Fatah*, the largest PLO faction, as well as other factions that were established in later years, especially the Popular Front for the Liberation of Palestine (PFLP) and the Democratic Front for the Liberation of Palestine (DFLP). Despite major ideological differences, these factions coalesced into a single PLO, the overarching organization of the Palestinian national movement.

The history of these early years was often quite stormy as the PLO tried to define itself in relation to the Arab world. In asserting its right to independent action and decision-making, it had to acknowledge its dependence on, and hence susceptibility to, the control of the surrounding Arab states in which the Palestinian organizations were located. Constraints on independent action were complicated by shifting loyalties and interests. These in turn reflected changing conditions both in the area and internationally. Mostly, these centered on a division between "right" and "left" in the Arab world (though not in the classic Marxian sense) and on the distinct ideological affiliations of the participant PLO factions and their supporters in the Occupied Territories. For example, early in the occupation, Jordan was regarded, especially by some in the West Bank, as the champion of the Palestinian cause. Syria then commanded a relatively minor role. Later, it was Syria that became known as the defender of the Palestinian left, while Jordan, Egypt, and Saudi Arabia were condemned as the benefactors of the right. However, there were strong incentives to maintain ties with the Jordanian regime. It was there that the Jordanian-Palestinian Joint Committee, established in 1978 to fund Palestinian "steadfastness" in the Occupied Territories, was located. These ties persisted despite an earlier falling out between the PLO and Jordan, when the PLO was expelled from the kingdom after the 1970–1971 civil war.[12] As a consequence of the Camp David Accords of 1978, Egypt was marginalized somewhat and condemned for signing a separate peace with Israel. Placing complete trust in Syria, however, was precluded by its stand against the PLO during the Lebanese civil war in the mid-1970s. Syria was also suspect for its encouragement of dissident PLO factions in 1983, which resulted in a virtual breakup of the PLO. This situation lingered until the 1987 meeting of the Palestine National Council on the eve of the *intifada.*

Added to the confusion of conflicting and fluctuating alliances and dependencies was a problem facing the PLO since its inception that inevitably compromised its ability to achieve an overriding strategic consensus. The question was whether the struggle for Palestinian independence should take place before or after "unification" of the Arabs. "Unity to struggle" or "struggle to unity" became the code words of this debate. There were those who perceived that the Palestinian struggle was dependent on and inseparable from the "Arab nation," and those who emphasized that the priority of the Palestinian movement was to achieve Palestinian independence and statehood before tackling the larger issue of Arab unity and nationhood.[13] Predictably, the increased politicization of Palestinians inside the Occupied Territories, who were experiencing the direct impact of Israeli occupation and subjugation, influenced Palestinian thinking on the matter and accelerated demands for immediate and independent Palestinian action. Complicating the scene in the 1980s was the emergence of militant Islamic movements, both in the Arab world in general and in Palestinian society in particular. Labeled "fundamentalist," some strands of this resurgent and radical Islam revived calls for "unity" under Islam throughout the whole Arab world, while others posited the first responsibility of Muslims as the liberation of all of Palestine. Palestinian Islamic groups generally rejected a two-state solution and thus came into direct conflict over objectives and means with the main groupings of the PLO in the Occupied Territories.

The controversial issue of armed struggle, as it has been equated with "terrorism" in the Palestinian case, and consequently delegitimized in the eyes of the West (and Israel), has tended to overshadow and preclude any objective evaluation of the role of the PLO in the Palestinian community. As a national liberation movement, the PLO has functions and a role that are not limited to actions against an opponent but revolve essentially around what it does for its own people, especially in the absence of a state. Without either condemning or praising the PLO, our intention is to assess its ability to prosecute a strategy that would succeed in achieving its stated objectives. Evaluating PLO strategy in this regard is contingent upon assessing its ability to target distinct loci of power in three areas:

1.   *The resistance movement:* The success of the PLO in mobilizing supporters and providing social services, defense, and other services to the Palestinian community both inside and outside the Occupied Territories.

2.   *The opponent:* The achievements of the PLO and the resistance movement in trying to cause Israel to withdraw from the Occupied Territories and advancing national independence.

3.   *The opponent's international allies:* The ability of the PLO to affect international opinion, especially in the United States, Israel's main ally, and to recognize Palestinian rights.[14]

The principles that define the coherence of any given strategy should remain valid regardless of value judgments concerning the technique of struggle. However, the technique itself—in this case, armed struggle—needs to be evaluated in the light of its ability to achieve strategic objectives. Not only the feasibility of armed struggle is called into question, but also the usefulness of any of the violent and terror tactics adopted by the PLO over the years, where the victims were often innocent civilians and bystanders. A statement by Hani al-Hassan, a senior *Fatah* official in 1980, to the effect that "the armed struggle sows and the political struggle reaps," is of questionable value in the Palestinian case.[15]

What the PLO did provide the Palestinian community was to restore a sense of hope and dignity, and most importantly, to revive the national cause and bring it to the forefront of international attention. The establishment of the PLO guaranteed that the Palestinians were no longer a mass of helpless and voiceless refugees, victims of the whims of various governments in the region. Therefore, Palestinians, regardless of whether they agreed or disagreed with specific ideologies or practices of the PLO, continued to rally strongly behind this national symbol. In the language of strategy, the PLO performed an invaluable function: It gave a sense of purpose and a common cause, and to a large extent (in theory if not in practice) it united resistance against Israel.[16] However, this unity was never complete in a strategic sense. There appeared to be no conception of how symbolic unity would be translated into practical means to involve the "constituents" in the actual national liberation movement. Part of the reason for this failure rested in the emphasis on armed struggle. This technique necessarily precluded the participation of a large majority of the Palestinian population, both on the inside and outside. Guerrilla warfare did not and could not take root in the Occupied Territories.[17] As a result, for many years, the population inside these areas was relegated to a rather passive role in the national movement.

The strategic considerations surrounding the technique of armed struggle go beyond whether or not we approve of it as a legitimate means of resistance. The right to armed struggle by national liberation movements has remained enshrined in international law. Jews themselves claimed the right to use arms, against both the British and the Arabs, in their struggle to establish their state. Without weighing the legitimacy of various national claims, the point for Palestinians to consider is that the evaluation of the correct technique has as much to do with what is strategically possible as with blind reliance on what is theoretically legitimate. In the Palestinian view, an important strategic function of armed struggle was not simply to force Israeli concessions and liberate the Occupied Territories single-handedly, but rather to direct efforts at two fronts: (1) to mobilize and unify Palestinians, and (2) more significantly, to draw Arab states into a military conflict with Israel so as to liberate Palestine.[18]

The "debate" over armed struggle between the interior (Palestinians under occupation whose situation urgently needed redress) and the exterior (the PLO outside) was never fully resolved. The PLO outside preferred to keep a rather tight rein on resistance in the Occupied Territories. Meantime, the Palestinians under occupation were trying to make known to the PLO their immediate concerns and priorities, and to incorporate policies and decisions that reflected these concerns into the official position of the PLO.[19] Some of these debates were preempted by the eruption of the *intifada,* during which widespread support, both inside and outside the Occupied Territories, emerged for the mode of civilian action. Other developments, such as the rise of Islamic movements and deliberate attacks on Israeli soldiers and settlers by their followers, revived the debate over armed action in the Palestinian community.

Since the launching of the peace process in 1991, many of the questions surrounding the technique of action—indeed all questions pertaining to "alternative" modes of struggle, whether violent or nonviolent—were for all intents and purposes put on hold. The Palestinian population under occupation became restive and frustrated with the lack of political success. For its part, the PLO (in Tunis) appeared largely unwilling to entertain proposals that would give people "on the ground" in the Occupied Territories the chance to break the stalemate and reinvigorate the *intifada.*

Other elements of PLO strategy had bearing on issues of unity within the movement and the allegiance of the "masses" to the organization. The PLO represents several major factions, each with its own ideological perspective on the goals of the struggle. *Fatah,* the first to be formed and the largest, is characterized as "nonideological," in the sense that it derives its appeal from a shared nationalism. For many years this faction tried to steer a neutral course between Arab governments and the different pressures and demands that were placed upon it. This course was followed precisely in order to preserve a degree of independence of action, and in order to mobilize Palestinians generally and obtain support and funding from various Arab regimes. This tactic earned it (and its leader, Yasser Arafat) the label "reactionary." On the left in the PLO, the two main factions are the DFLP and the PFLP.[20] Characteristic of these factions is their focus on the need for social reform within the Arab world, including the overthrow of "reactionary" regimes. This is important, in their view, so as to mobilize the Arab masses in a common class and political struggle.[21] Since the mid-1970s, political factions have competed actively for the support of the Palestinian population in the Occupied Territories, and factionalism has become particularly acute there.

With each passing year the PLO has exhibited signs of increasing political maturity, flexibility, and awareness of strategy. However, there have been several drawbacks. One was the lack of clarity concerning short- and long-term objectives. In failing to define precisely the objective of the national movement, the PLO would also fail in deciding exactly how to relate to Israel, to its society, and to its allies, particularly the United States. There existed no clear definition of the mechanisms for causing the opponent to accommodate to its point of view, especially since the PLO sometimes sent out contradictory signals on what it regarded as its ultimate goal. Meanwhile, Palestinians under occupation were becoming reconciled to the reality of Israel's existence, and they began to direct their energies toward urging both the PLO and Israel to work to end the occupation and establish Palestinian (or joint Jordanian/ Palestinian) sovereignty over these areas. After a spate of violent and terror acts in the early 1970s, the PLO also started coming around to this view. This change was coupled with a realization that the effort to end the occupation had to involve Israelis as well.[22] Starting around 1972, the PLO began to consider the role of diplomacy and political struggle, and to invite the direct participation of the people in the Occupied Territories in such efforts.[23] Gradually the PLO defined a clearer strategic view, that of establishing an independent Palestinian state in the West Bank and Gaza Strip to coexist side by side with Israel. However, it did not appear to resolve the contradictions between different techniques, nor did it adopt a clear strategy for ending the occupation.

Whether by design or default, after the PLO's ouster from Lebanon in 1982 the locus of power shifted to the Occupied Territories.[24] This shift was accompanied by a reevaluation of techniques that permitted political efforts to operate in conjunction with a civilian struggle.

Palestinian Resistance Before the *Intifada:* Social Formations and Changing Social Relationships Under Occupation

Within the Occupied Territories, Palestinian resistance against Israeli occupation in the West Bank and Gaza Strip was acquiring a specificity of its own. Although there were some social and structural continuities between the Palestinian territories of the West Bank and Gaza Strip, significant differences remained. These came to define the particular forms of resistance that evolved in each of these areas.

Throughout much of the period of Jordan's rule in the West Bank, political organizations and parties were largely suppressed. One exception was the Islamic movement. The overarching organization of this movement, the Muslim Brotherhood, had existed in the region since the 1930s, and Jordan allowed this organization to operate rather openly, though it was banned in the Gaza Strip under Egypt. Apart from political restrictions, however, worsening economic conditions in both the East and West Banks during the 1960s prompted a large portion of the Palestinian population to emigrate rather than seriously challenge Jordanian political control.[25]

In the case of the Gaza Strip, the period spent under Egyptian rule was notable for the high level of political mobilization and the strong tradition of protest and resistance. These occurred in spite of the often harsh and repressive Egyptian rule. As in the West Bank, local political parties and organizations were suppressed, especially those at odds with the interests of the Egyptian government.

The persistence of traditional forms and relations of production in the West Bank enabled the traditional leadership, particularly landowners and prominent families, to continue to represent the population. In contrast, in the Gaza Strip, the dislocation caused by the establishment of the Israeli state created a kind of vacuum that was marked by the absence of any organized leadership or authority capable of representing the people. This vacuum was later filled by the Palestinian national liberation movement.[26] This erosion of the basic feudal organization of Palestinian society, gradually in the West Bank and more abruptly in the Gaza Strip, signaled a decline in the system of patronage that had earlier characterized Palestinian social formations.[27] A number of factors contributed to this demise. These included the loss of land, increased proletarianization, more educational opportunities, the emigration of young professionals and workers abroad, the shrinking of clan based agricultural production, and the erosion of the power of the established merchant classes. New social forces, organized around different class and social concerns, came to dominate the social scene and to compete for the allegiance of Palestinians. In the West Bank, these were dominated by the educated professionals and businessmen in the major cities who later came to comprise the backbone of the "nationalist" movement. These figures took the lead in organizing resistance to the occupation within such organizations as the Palestine National Front and the National Guidance Committee, and their prominence on the scene coincided with growing support for the PLO within the Occupied Territories.[28]

The relationship between the emergent social forces in the Occupied Territories and the PLO alternated between cooperation and competition, with both sides vying for the control and allegiance of the population. This point is central to our understanding of patterns of resistance in the West Bank and Gaza Strip.

As we saw in Chapter One, the impact of proletarianization and, increasingly, pauperization of the Palestinian community was to create a largely disgruntled and increasingly radicalized sector of the society. Despite heavy dependence on Israel for its livelihood, this sector was swiftly reaching a point where indigenous support networks had been eroded and where it had nothing left to lose.

The family was another area where the Israeli occupation transformed social relations. Considered the most basic social unit in Arab society from which all other social relations flowed, the Palestinian family under occupation gradually became marginalized. It found itself unable to perform its expected functions as a self-sufficient unit responsible for securing the livelihood of its members. The Israeli occupation has perhaps unwittingly unleashed the very social forces that would later turn against it with special vigor during the *intifada.* The occupation "liberated" the two sectors that would prove the most active in organizing resistance: students (and young people in general) and women. As we shall see, during the uprising especially, other community organizations—most recently Islamic groups— assumed some of the functions of the traditional family. Responsibility for meeting the subsistence and support needs of the family passed to some extent to "public" organizations; at the same time, other factors, such as education and activism among youth, emigration, and the independence of sons and their families, as well as female wage labor, all combined to produce a solid challenge to the traditional notions of patriarchal authority and family honor.

The contradictory social dynamics operating in the Occupied Territories throughout the period of Israeli rule can be illustrated in another area, that of rising religious extremism, especially among Muslims. It should be stated that the Palestinian people cannot be regarded separately from their religious cultural heritage, whether as Muslims or Christians. These affiliations are firmly rooted in the very identity of the land and its people. Religious manifestations are frequently found in national liberation movements, where elements of tradition—particularly religion—take on new forms and meanings as symbols of an indigenous and authentic culture juxtaposed against the alien presence of an oppressor. Religion comes to define and reinforce the separate identity of the subjugated population.

The phenomenon of religious extremism, particularly Islamic fundamentalism, as it has taken root mainly in the Gaza Strip, has sometimes appeared to work at cross purposes with the task of national liberation. It has set back the Palestinian community in some respects. Ironically, the religious factions that became a special source of concern in the Occupied Territories in the early 1990s were initially courted and encouraged by Israel itself as alternatives to the PLO. The Islamic groups were meant to offset and discredit the secular national movement and curb its following. For the first few years of occupation, the impact of these Islamic forces was negligible as the secular PLO established its appeal among the Palestinian people. The resurgence of the Muslim Brotherhood did not occur until after the 1973 October War, when both Jordan and Israel began to view it as an alternative to the PLO.[29] Islamic *Jihad,* an offshoot of the Brotherhood, was established in the early 1980s.

Though both the Muslim Brotherhood and Islamic *Jihad* adhered to the notion of an Islamic state in all of Palestine (Israel) they differed over the tactics and steps necessary to achieve this.[30] The Muslim Brotherhood gave priority to the reeducation and Islamization of societies throughout the Arab world prior to liberation. The Islamic *Jihad,* on the other hand, advocated armed struggle against Israel and the primacy of the nationalist cause. Neither the Muslim Brotherhood nor the Islamic *Jihad,* however, could be described as totally homogeneous. They have both drawn their support from various sectors in Palestinian society that include secular and religious Palestinians, professionals, and working-class people. They have also based their strength on their organizational skills and their ability to provide necessary support services to the population at large.[31]

Most of the Islamic efforts during the *intifada* were channeled into the immediate task of resistance against the occupation regime. Islamic *Jihad* tended to subsume itself under the overall consensus of the Unified Nationalist Leadership of the Uprising (UNLU). Meanwhile, the Muslim Brotherhood established its radical offshoot, *Hamas* (acronym for the Islamic Resistance Movement), to conduct the struggle and to compete with the UNLU for the allegiance of the Palestinian people. Over subsequent years of the *intifada, Hamas* and its fighting wing, the *Ezzeddin Al-Qassam* units, emerged as a powerful political force to be reckoned with, particularly in the Gaza Strip. Support for *Hamas* has been fueled by the daily hardships of life under occupation and by increased disillusionment over the inability of the PLO to achieve real political gains. *Hamas* responded by organizing popular committees and structures to support the weakened population, and so has gained many adherents.

The Islamic message, a return to culture, religion, and tradition, has resonated among Palestinians who perceived the failure of the secular nationalist ideologies and who rejected all ideologies emanating from the "imperialist" West and the Zionist enemy. How far *Hamas* and the Islamic movement could succeed in winning the allegiance of Palestinians would depend in part on the ability of the secular factions and the PLO to achieve real political gains in the *intifada* and in the peace process.[32] The immediate impact of the PLO-Israeli agreements of 1993 was to rein in the influence of *Hamas.* Future prospects for this group and for the Islamic movement as a whole would likely depend on several factors, including the success of autonomy plans and programs to alleviate poverty and suffering in the Occupied Territories, the power of Islamic groups in surrounding Arab countries, and most crucially, progress toward Palestinian independence.

Palestinian Resistance to Occupation: Shaping the Debate and Launching the Resistance

Palestinian resistance to Israeli occupation was circumscribed by existing social formations and social relations in both the West Bank and Gaza Strip. The forms of struggle were also conditioned by the special integral relationship of the Occupied Territories to the Palestine national movement as a whole, and to the PLO in particular, as well as by shifting expectations and strategies.

For the most part, Palestinians in these areas remained adamant in their insistence that the PLO was their "sole legitimate representative" and that, no matter how distinct or independent, their role would never be totally separate from this movement. There are immediate and valid reasons for this stand. One is that the PLO represented the interests, demands, and aspirations of all the Palestinian people, including those in the diaspora. Palestinians originating from or residing in the Occupied Territories may represent themselves on certain crucial matters. However, they were not expected to represent the Palestinian people as a whole in deciding such issues as the right to return, compensation, and the like that would need to be dealt with to settle the Palestinian issue in its entirety. Another reason for the widespread support for the PLO among Palestinians under occupation was their perception of this organization as a symbol and representative of a legitimate national cause. The Palestinian "problem" did not emerge in 1967, nor can it be reduced to the question of some minority group (Palestinians) in a disputed territory. The existence of the PLO remains an affirmation and a reminder that the Palestinian issue goes well beyond narrow "political rights" into the fundamental and inalienable rights of a people to liberation and national self-determination in their own homeland. This is not to deny that over the years of occupation serious disagreements arose between the PLO and the population and organizations of the Occupied Territories over objectives and tactics. But for the most part, and until the first few rounds of the peace talks in the early 1990s, the representational authority of the PLO was never in serious dispute.

One of the questions that Palestinians addressed during the early years of occupation was whether permitting the normal functioning of indigenous institutions would be construed as a betrayal of their cause and a legitimation of the occupation. Palestinians debated whether or not to "cooperate" with the Israeli regime. They were fearful that the population would suffer should they discontinue the normal operation of their institutions. They also sensed that a more appropriate response to the unwanted occupation would be to boycott the Israeli military authorities altogether. Palestinians struggled with the idea of refusing to obey the occupier. In education, on the issue of elections, on the role of lawyers—these were all areas where Palestinians seriously weighed the consequences of given courses of action.[33]

Complicating the picture, and generally frustrating any Palestinian efforts to achieve strategic consensus, were a number of internal and regional factors in which a rapid succession of events defied predictability and control. The predominant response to Israeli rule in the early years of the occupation, especially in the West Bank, was to look toward Jordan for leadership and guidance. A significant sector of West Bank elite engaged in political activities to pave the way to an accommodation with Israel based on a territorial compromise with Jordan.

This period lasted essentially until the October 1973 War. Meantime, other forces emerged. In the Gaza Strip, for example, the population was responding to the occupation with a spate of guerrilla attacks against the occupying forces. Israel clamped down hard on this activity. A forceful suppression of resistance was accompanied by the demolition of large numbers of Palestinian residences, killing and arrests of people, and the massive "relocation" of refugees to other localities. In the West Bank as well, the situation was not static. As the political leadership inside failed to achieve any political results and as the PLO outside gained in popularity, the demise of the traditional leadership accelerated in the West Bank.[34]

The creation of the Palestine National Front (PNF) in the Occupied Territories in 1973 was perhaps the first instance of organized resistance in these areas since 1967.[35] Analysts, however, disagree over the precise position and relationship of the PNF to the PLO, Jordan, and Israel. Lisa Taraki states simply that the Front was "endorsed" by the PNC in 1973 and maintains that the PNF closely defined itself in the framework of the whole Palestine national movement and the PLO.[36] In contrast, Shaul Mishal depicts the politicking and vying for influence between the PLO, Jordan, and political forces in the Occupied Territories characterizing this period as the driving force behind the creation of the PNF.[37] Whatever the case may be, it is clear that the influence of the PLO continued to grow in the Occupied Territories. Its status was given an additional boost in 1974, after the Arab League declared the PLO the "sole legitimate representative of the Palestinian people."

Ironically, a factor that helped to cement a closer relationship between the PLO and the Occupied Territories was Israel's policy of expulsions. Over the ensuing years, several of the deportees assumed prominent positions within the PLO and its institutions, through which they conveyed the interests and concerns of the population in the Occupied Areas and helped influence the PLO's stand. The influence was mutual. People from the Occupied Territories who had emigrated to the Gulf and other Arab states returned periodically, carrying with them a broader understanding and appreciation of the PLO and its objectives.[38] This is not to say that tensions did not exist. Competing factional interests had always been one of the salient features of political activism in the Occupied Territories.[39] The issue of control was not limited to the relative strength of various factions, but pertained to the very idea of political action in the Occupied Territories. While the PFLP and DFLP generally favored independent decision-making and activity, *Fatah* preferred to retain centralized control and oversight. The rise of the Islamic movement during the years of the *intifada* posed an additional challenge to the dominance of the main PLO groups, especially *Fatah*.

The victory of the nationalist forces in the 1976 municipal elections ushered in a new strategic focus concerning organized resistance against the Israeli occupation. Members of the Palestine National Front and others could now work through the elected official institutions, principally the municipalities, to promote nationalist goals.[40] The PNF continued to play a significant role until it was superseded by the formation of the National Guidance Committee (NGC) after the signing of the 1978 Camp David Accords. The driving force behind the NGC was the threat to Palestinians under occupation emanating from the "autonomy" plans defined in these agreements. The NGC was composed of various official representatives of the Palestinians, such as mayors, professional figures, and businessmen, as well as the emerging "unofficial" or grassroots and popular leadership of voluntary organizations and committees, trade unions, and student groups.[41]

From all indications, it appears that the NGC was so successful in mobilizing the population behind its resistance to the occupation, as well as in initiating concerted efforts to develop real and viable indigenous Palestinian alternatives, that it posed a special threat to certain Israeli and even PLO interests. Abdul Jawad Saleh states categorically that "the PLO official leadership never recognized the National Guidance Committee."[42] Perhaps it would be more accurate to qualify this statement by mentioning *Fatah*'s concern that an independent leadership would emerge in the Occupied Territories that would challenge its authority. From the point of view of the NGC and other nationalist forces in the West Bank, support of the PLO as the ultimate representative of the Palestinian people was never seriously questioned. More likely, Palestinian activists in the Occupied Territories sought more freedom in formulating resistance tactics and in running the day-to-day affairs under occupation. Both were in full agreement that the main target was the autonomy plan, together with the unilateral peace agreement between Israel and Egypt. This was especially the case following the Likud victory in 1977 and the subsequent escalation in land expropriation and settlement activities. Mishal notes that these developments provoked "a series of civil disturbances, public strikes, riots and demonstrations initiated by the National Guidance Committee" in the Occupied Territories.[43]

Throughout the occupation the Israeli authorities targeted "peaceful resistance" just as fiercely as violent struggle.[44] Geoffrey Aronson explains as a possible reason for this policy the enormous difficulties Israel would face should it be perceived as responding violently to Palestinians engaged in confronting the occupation nonviolently and constructively. He maintains that Israel's goal was "to keep civilian resistance—strikes, boycotts, protest, demonstrations and anti-Israel propaganda—to a minimum."[45]

The effectiveness of the role of official Palestinian institutions in organizing resistance against the occupation was apparent in 1981, when one of the first uprisings in these areas broke out. This followed the announcement of the imposition of civilian rule in these areas. Not only were Palestinians then involved in protest activity—of which they already had experience—but they were also becoming involved in direct intervention and in the creation of alternative structures—activities which later underscored the *intifada*. In the early 1980s, Palestinians were still in the process of learning and perfecting their struggle. They were learning to withhold obedience, refusing to cooperate, and boycotting the occupation and its institutions. They did not then, nor indeed later, have sufficient viable alternatives to separate themselves from Israel. But Palestinians were prepared to resist, and that resistance assumed more than mere symbolic expressions of protest.[46] Underlying the success of the NGC was the emphasis on organizational diffusion and decentralization. Perhaps for the first time, an effort was made to establish local guidance committees at the community level, in villages, towns, and cities of the West Bank. This precedent of moving away from the traditional concentration on urban areas set an example that was not forgotten by the gradually expanding grassroots committees.

In 1981 the Israeli authorities banned the NGC, and many of its members and sympathizers were jailed, put under house arrest, or deported. When Israel moved to establish the civilian administration in the Occupied Territories in 1981, and later in 1982 when it dissolved the majority of the Palestinian municipalities in the West Bank, most official and overt organized resistance against the occupation came to an abrupt and final end. The task for Palestinians became one of continuing resistance in different forms, and the stage was then set for the transformation in the mode and organization of resistance. This transformation, from overt and official to underground and unofficial, could be largely attributed to the role of the grassroots and popular organizations that expanded in the Occupied Territories between the mid-1970s and late 1980s.

The Emergence of the Grassroots Organizations

The popular appeal and success of grassroots committees rested in their ability to mobilize ordinary Palestinians around issues of daily concern, while at the same time maintaining a strong national stand. This dual focus helped to institutionalize these organizations into something approaching an alternative Palestinian social and economic structure in the Occupied Territories. Their successes were most pronounced during the Palestinian *intifada,* when the grassroots committees rapidly organized and proliferated into local committees and other supportive groups to form virtual "parallel institutions" in the West Bank and Gaza Strip.

Given the absence of a national government and the vacuum left by incomplete and inadequate government services, it was up to the emerging grassroots groups, together with the remaining official institutions of Palestinian society, to assume responsibility for the well-being of Palestinians under occupation. However, existing official Palestinian institutions, in health care, education, and the like, were not subsumed under the direction of the grassroots committees. To do so would have been neither realistic nor desirable. What had changed was the focus of the resistance. Instead of protests, noncooperation, and steadfastness characteristic of earlier periods, resistance efforts shifted toward long-term local indigenous development. This new focus was expressed in the Palestinian determination to establish viable alternatives to the occupation regime. Such perspectives did not emerge immediately or spontaneously. Rather, they evolved gradually since the early 1980s, in response to new realities on the ground and based on the Palestinian experience of the ever-increasingly harsh conditions of occupation.

In an era of renewed attention to the problems facing "civil society" and the relationship between the structures of civil society and democracy in various parts of the world, the Palestinian situation presents a challenging case study. One could certainly argue that the grassroots committees, in their various sectors and spheres of influence in the West Bank and Gaza Strip, constituted a prime example of the very structures of civil society that are crucial for the protection and operation of democracy. The absence of a national government in this case precludes the idea that Palestinian social structures emerged to counter the power and hegemony of an indigenous "state," but it does suggest that civil society has discernible roots in the Palestinian community. Such precedents, if sustained, could be reinforced to ensure democracy and counterbalance centralized power in a future Palestinian state.[47] Another consideration in this instance is that militant Islamic groups in the Occupied Territories, whose popular appeal is based on grounds comparable to those of other grassroots groups, have posed a special challenge to prevailing notions of what constitutes "civil society." The existence and popularity of such groups raise questions as to whether democratic participation is possible in an atmosphere of growing religious militancy in the Palestinian community.[48] The concept of "loci" of power, as articulated by Gene Sharp, and by Anders Boserup and Andrew Mack, among others, explores similar ideas and has relevance to our understanding of civilian resistance in the Occupied Territories.[49]

During the *intifada* it was quite evident that grassroots committees had gradually evolved (through the popular local committees that were established) into relatively effective alternative loci of power. These pitted themselves in turn against the seemingly absolute power of the occupation regime. For the grassroots committees and their subgroups, it was not an issue of competing authority or legitimate social power, since the occupation and its agents had been completely discredited. Rather, the task for Palestinians was to consolidate political power by providing viable alternatives for the residents and by establishing their ability to act independently of Israeli control and interference. While the formative period of these grassroots committees, especially in the early 1980s, concentrated on the first concern—consolidation of power—the immediate period of the *intifada* established the latter. The quick proliferation of local committees, together with the almost complete reorganization of these associations to administer the uprising and implement calls for the escalation of civil disobedience, quickly established these popular groups as independent actors on the scene. Subsequent stages of the *intifada* simply confirmed this view. The grassroots and other local institutions quickly guided the Palestinian population from noncooperation and defiance of the occupation, to constructive strategies for survival, and to the building of indigenous Palestinian sectors independent of the occupation regime.

The expansion and flourishing of the popular grassroots committees reflected the emphasis of the PLO on direct action within the Occupied Territories. These changes also ushered in a period of increased factionalism and competition, as the very committees that were established to assume responsibility for mobilizing the population against the occupation were themselves rent by opposed ideological and political stands. Thus four different women's committees were created, each belonging to a different PLO faction. Within the trade union movement, the student movement, and other sectors, it was the same story. Meantime, individual committees succeeded in recruiting thousands of Palestinian women, workers, and students in the cities, villages, and camps of the West Bank and Gaza Strip. In other grassroots activities, voluntary, medical, and agricultural committees multiplied in the Occupied Territories. One message was increasingly clear: Social and community concerns would constitute an integral part of the national cause. By working on the former, Palestinians would also be struggling for the latter.[50]

Women's Committees

The women's movement in the Occupied Territories is a culmination of a long history, stretching back to the early part of the twentieth century, when organized political and social protest began to take root in Palestine. During the Mandate period, women were very active in their own right in expressing their opposition to Jewish settlement and in protesting British policies in the region. The first Arab Women's Congress was held in Jerusalem in 1929. Throughout the ensuing years, women were active in sending delegations to meet with British officials, leading demonstrations, and otherwise organizing protest activities.[51]

The General Union of Palestinian Women was formed within the PLO in 1965. It was not until the mid-1970s, with the formation of the popular Women's Committees, that the process of direct mobilization and politicization of women took root in the Occupied Territories. The Women's Committees aimed at creating a unified mass women's movement to reach all sectors and classes of Palestinian society. Their goal was to mobilize Palestinian women together in a joint struggle for defending their rights as women and for improving their socioeconomic position within the context of a total national struggle. Such goals derived from the basic premise of Palestinian Women's Committees, that strengthening the role of women in the national struggle would change women's roles. During the 1990s, Women's Committees began to unify their activities and redirect their energies toward the articulation of a distinct women's agenda. No longer were specific women's concerns to be subsumed under the national cause. For the first time, some Palestinian women were publicly using the term "feminism" to describe their agenda. Research centers devoted to women's issues were set up, and many Palestinian women geared themselves toward the task of addressing problems long neglected in their communities. These included early marriage, wife abuse, unemployment, and particularly the implications for Palestinian women of the rise of militant Islam. An early focus of their efforts was to examine the possibilities of creating a civil code to regulate "personal" affairs (marriage, divorce, inheritance, and the like), which, as elsewhere in the Arab world, are regulated by Personal Status Laws that are rooted in religion—particularly Islam.[52]

In contrast to the formal character of the traditional charitable societies, Women's Committees could be described as nontraditional, unofficial, and popular groups. Their members derived extensively from the villages and camps in the West Bank and Gaza Strip. These areas were traditionally neglected by the earlier established societies, although the daily problems of life under occupation were particularly acute there.

In the West Bank where they first emerged, four Women's Committees were created to sponsor women's activities.[53] Goals and activities of these committees overlapped. All stressed the need for productive work, education, and vocational training for women. They also emphasized involving housewives in productive activities. Some of the committees focused specifically on the concerns of working women, and all stressed the importance of cultural activities that would contribute toward the preservation of the Palestinian identity.[54] Several of the Women's Committees made it a point to work with other grassroots movements, such as Medical Relief Committees, Agricultural Relief Committees, and Voluntary Work Committees, as well as development-oriented institutions and trade unions. Funding has been a constant problem. Much of the work of Women's Committees has been hampered by the prevalence of traditional attitudes toward women, although these changed somewhat during the *intifada*. Women's Committees have also been targets of Israeli restrictions and harassment; female activists have frequently been subjected to detention or imprisonment. During the peace process, some Palestinian women and their committees turned their attention to the implications of these talks for women. They set up a technical support team to place women's issues on the national agenda, and began positioning themselves to play a role in the anticipated Palestinian entity. Theoretical considerations, such as articulating national and social agendas, the role of women under Islamic law, and other questions that had preoccupied women, seemed to have receded in the face of these new developments.[55]

Trade Unions

Trade unions cannot be defined as "unofficial" grassroots groups because they enjoyed official status in Palestinian society well before 1967.[56] However, their role has grown in importance, especially since the 1970s, in view of the specific hardships faced by Palestinian workers. The rise of trade union activities under occupation (the West Bank is estimated to have over 100 such unions), can be attributed to the increase in the number of dispossessed Palestinians forced to join the labor market. These included the 150,000 or so laborers from the Occupied West Bank and Gaza Strip who, until the *intifada,* worked in Israel. These workers were particularly vulnerable, since Palestinian unions for workers within the Occupied Territories had no control over conditions in the Israeli workplace. Apart from the officially registered workers, there were thousands of "illegal" workers— Palestinians who, before the *intifada* and before the closure of the Occupied Territories, commuted daily to work to Israel.[57]

Trade unions provide their members with such services as health insurance, rights to better wages and improved work conditions, and arbitration with Palestinian employers. During the *intifada,* some unions established workers' committees at the job site to provide additional protection for workers.[58] Some attempts were made to extend these committees into the Israeli workplace, but these were resisted by the Israeli Histadrut. Palestinian committee organizers involved in such activities were reportedly fired from their jobs.[59]

One problem facing the operation of trade unions has been divisive factional conflict. This has led to the formation of branches of trade unions split along factional lines. Palestinian unions have also been the target of severe Israeli repression and restrictions. The Israeli authorities have issued various orders and regulations restricting the licensing of unions, limiting their activities, exercising control over their membership, and otherwise suppressing union activities. These measures included occasional raids on union offices, confiscation of materials, and closure of unions.[60] Trade union activists have been subject to harassment, interrogation, detention, arrests, and even deportation from the Occupied Areas. In a number of such cases, as Joost Hiltermann asserts, "They have not been charged with any specific offense."[61] The greatest threat to Israel, as Hiltermann points out, is that "the peoples of the Occupied Territories are finally witnessing a sense of their collective strength."[62] Trade unions, along with other popular and national organizations in the Occupied Territories, were involved in organizing the Palestinian community precisely along these lines.[63]

Voluntary Work Committees

Voluntary work as a collective movement was launched during the early 1970s under the guidance of several popular municipal leaders in the West Bank. It fed on the impetus generated by the rapidly growing student movement in the Occupied Territories. This type of work was envisioned as a productive and exciting alternative for young people to participate in projects that would benefit their communities. These activities included cleaning streets, building schools, paving roads, picking olives, and others. Affording young people a sense of their worth as active members of the community and putting them in direct contact with ordinary people living on their lands would discourage young Palestinians from engaging in undesirable social habits and activities, such as drug use and delinquency, and encourage them to become responsible adults and leaders.[64] This movement grew to encompass many towns and villages in the West Bank and Gaza Strip, as well as the town of Nazareth in the Galilee in Israel. Voluntary work camps became a regular feature of the summer holidays in the Occupied Territories. Throughout the rest of the year, certain days would be designated as "voluntary work days," when such activities would extend across the Occupied Territories. This movement quickly expanded into an institutionalized feature to promote development and self-sufficiency in the Occupied Territories.[65]

A Higher Council was established in 1980 to coordinate the activities of the Voluntary Work Committees and draw up a constitution to guide their activities. Birzeit University in the West Bank began to require voluntary work as part of its regular credit hours.[66] Land reclamation was central to the activities of these committees; voluntary work provided a venue for actively confronting the Israeli authorities and for challenging their plans to further dispossess Palestinians of their lands. From voluntary work came the guard units, groups of local residents and others who assumed responsibility for guarding a plot of land against the uprooting of crops and trees by

Israelis.[67] This experience gave the Voluntary Work Committees valuable training in community work on a mass scale. It also provided the basis for their forthcoming role in organizing and administering the Palestinian *intifada* in the Occupied Territories.[68]

Participants in voluntary work activities were frequently subjected to harsh Israeli repression, and at least one popular mayor, Abdul Jawad Saleh of El-Bireh, attributes his eventual deportation from the West Bank to his active participation in such work.[69]

Medical Relief Committees

Reliance on voluntary work for the establishment of alternative Palestinian institutions was also adopted by the professional sector in the Occupied Territories. One example was the effort to create alternative health services for Palestinians under occupation.

The first Medical Relief Committee was established in the West Bank in the late 1970s. It emerged as a response, in part, to the poor health conditions and deteriorating services then prevailing in these areas.[70] Several mobile clinics soon operated under the mantle of the Union of Medical Relief Committees. These clinics traveled to camps and outlying village areas. Their emphasis was on the provision of preventive care and on addressing the health problems of Palestinians within their own communities. Participating pharmacists, lab technicians, doctors, nurses, and other health personnel increased in numbers over the years, as did the number of mobile clinics and other services.[71]

By the start of the *intifada,* more than 265 mobile clinics had served 47,000 patients in 180 locations in the West Bank and Gaza Strip. The number of health professionals participating also rose dramatically, from only 150 in 1983 to 730 by 1988.[72] Some health care personnel elected to work full-time for these committees, for a small salary. The establishment of permanent health centers was considered a major achievement of these committees. Medical Relief Committees also cooperate with local hospitals for the provision of both curative and specialized care.

As they grew in strength and numbers, the Medical Relief Committees began providing basic health education as well as training in health care to local women in the communities they served. As with the other popular grassroots committees, the reasons for the expansion of the Medical Relief Committees rested in their ability to address basic concerns of the population and to mobilize people for appropriate activities. Mustafa Barghouti, a doctor and founder of the Medical Relief Committees, insists that Medical Relief Committees remained motivated by a spirit of professionalism, and consequently may have been less prone to in-fighting and factional divisions within their ranks. Such factionalism, however, was not altogether absent.[73]

The successes of the Union of Palestinian Medical Relief Committees in producing some tangible medical gains for the needy Palestinian population has earned their members severe Israeli reprisals. In 1986, for example, the Israeli authorities raided and closed a clinic operated by the Medical Relief Committees in Gaza's Jabaliya camp and arrested four doctors. Following an international outcry, the clinic was reopened and the doctors were released.[74] It was during the *intifada* that the success of the Medical Relief Committees in developing alternative services became apparent. As Barghouti points out, the *intifada* "showed us the importance of this view and its priority."[75] Existing health institutions were unable to provide adequate services. Nor were they flexible enough to respond to this emergency situation. Barghouti notes that within two weeks of the start of the *intifada,* the Medical Relief Committees had reached almost all camps and villages and had served more than 6,000 patients. As the *intifada* progressed, the Medical Relief Committees were able to establish a system of health care somewhat independent of the Israeli authorities.[76]

The closure of the Occupied Territories in 1993 gave the work of these committees added urgency. Palestinian residents of the Occupied Territories were generally barred from reaching medical facilities in East Jerusalem, which in many cases were their only source of specialized services and facilities. To complicate matters, many Palestinians had also lost their health insurance or were otherwise ineligible for medical care coverage in Israel and the Occupied Territories. Services provided by the Medical Relief Committees were probably the last resort for those Palestinians who were in need.[77]

Agricultural Relief Committees

The agricultural sector was hit especially hard by Israeli occupation policies, particularly by unrelenting land expropriations. The absence of a national authority to undertake development projects in the interests of the local Palestinian residents made it especially imperative to prevent the total disintegration of this sector.

Through volunteer work, efforts to help Palestinians remain steadfast on the land and resist dispossession were combined with efforts to create viable long-term alternatives for Palestinian peasants and farmers.

Agricultural Relief Committees began forming in 1983, and they have grown to comprise a variety of specialties in agricultural engineering, botany, and other related areas. These committees concentrated on working with Palestinian farmers to improve the quality of the soil and their produce, and to protect their trees and crops from disease.[78] Committee members helped farmers extend water pipes made of nylon ("plastic tunnels") for irrigating the land, or helped build pools for conserving water.

Marketing agricultural produce from the Occupied Territories has always been a problem. Palestinians were generally barred from exporting their produce to Israeli markets, while Israeli produce, heavily subsidized by the government, was allowed unrestricted entry into the Occupied Territories. Export of Occupied Territories' produce to the Arab world faces high tariffs and taxes, and has also been restricted because of competition from the local products of these countries. The result has been severe economic losses for Palestinian farmers and producers. Palestinians have come to realize that the situation is not likely to stabilize until a Palestinian national authority is established that would protect their economic interests. Meantime, they have organized marketing cooperatives to regulate trade, both internally and with the European Economic Community (EEC).[79]

Creating facts on the ground in the form of independent and self-sufficient Palestinian agriculture was one way of resisting the occupation. This became a central feature of the *intifada*. As one article points out, "Self-sufficiency is now the catchword of the protest."[80] Even if, practically speaking, Palestinians did not end their dependence on Israel, they realized their ability to create their own individual areas of self-sufficiency. Many of these efforts slackened in the wake of the Gulf War and the intensified restrictions imposed by the Israeli authorities. Funding for all Palestinian institutions and activities in the Occupied Territories was a major problem. The PLO outside lost its major sources of income from Arab states, while Palestinians in the Occupied Territories lost their sources of remittances from relatives in the Gulf. Because of the closure of the Occupied Territories and the high rates of unemployment that resulted from being barred from jobs in Israel, Palestinians found themselves in a position where eking out a daily living became their main concern, and other long-term plans were largely put on hold.

The Youth Movement

The genesis of an organized student movement on which the youth movement was based can be traced as far back as the mid-1950s. It was then that the General Federation of Palestinian Students was first established in Cairo. At the same time, students in the Gaza Strip mobilized in youth cells. Both became the forerunners of the General Union of Palestinian Students of the PLO.[81] Student activism in the West Bank prior to the occupation was concentrated in the Jordanian Students Union, then dominated by the Communist Party.[82]

The youth and student movements came to form the "vanguard," so to speak, of resistance in the Occupied Territories.[83] Palestinian students were commonly described as the "most highly politicized constituency," and universities were widely regarded as centers of resistance and activism.[84] During a few years preceding the *intifada,* as well as during the uprising itself, students and youth became highly politicized. They expanded their movement to comprise social and community activities, clubs, sports, games, and the like, all of which incorporated an explicit political message. By the mid-1980s students had taken the initiative in organizing their own spontaneous demonstrations and protests against the occupation.[85] Political mobilization among youth was fed by the frequent jailing and subsequent release of young activists, who contributed in turn to the radicalization of the larger student body. Young Palestinian boys would often be imprisoned for the first time for a minor "security offense," such as throwing stones or demonstrating. They would emerge from prison transformed by their experiences. In the eyes of their peers, these youth become heroes, graduates whose time in prison "has won them respect and admiration."[86]

Factionalism and competing ideologies posed a problem right from the start, one that was exacerbated throughout the years of occupation by competition between groups vying for allegiance of their members. Political developments in the area, along with continued Israeli repression, served to radicalize students even further. By the early 1980s, several student "blocs" had formed. Several were affiliated to the major PLO factions, mainly *Fatah,* while others were based on affiliation to the newer Islamic groups.[87] Initially the pro-PLO factions were more or less united in opposing the Islamic groups. Subsequent events in the area, especially changing relations between the PLO, Jordan, and Egypt and the aftermath of the Gulf War, caused these pro-PLO groups to split internally and pit themselves in competition with each other. The factionalism and divisiveness were so serious at times that student council elections at the main universities erupted into violent confrontations between opposed blocs. The peace process generated its own concerns. Beginning with the Madrid Conference in 1991 and for the next several years, the major factions of the PLO displayed distinctly different reactions to the talks. While *Fatah* and the People's Party (the latter with some reservations) basically continued to support the bilateral talks in Washington, the DFLP (which had split into two groups) and the PFLP were largely critical of these talks. These rifts in the PLO were inevitably reflected on the ground in the Occupied Territories, including in the ranks of the *shebab* and the student movements.

The Islamic Movements

Discussion of the emergence of grassroots committees in the Occupied Territories would not be complete without reflecting on the Islamic movement. Islamic groups in the region predated both the occupation and the *intifada.* However, it was in the years immediately preceding the uprising that newer strands of militant Islam organized and proliferated in the Occupied Territories, particularly in the Gaza Strip. There, these movements found a fertile ground, fed by years of harsh repression under Israeli rule and by the particularly acute conditions of daily life during the *intifada.* Developments in the region at large—foremost among which was the Iranian revolution—also helped these strands of resurgent Islam gain strength and popularity. The fall of the shah of Iran and the subsequent establishment of the Islamic regime of Ayatollah Khomeini in 1979 were powerful examples to radical Muslims throughout the Middle East. The appeal of Islam was especially potent in light of the perceived failure of secular politics, and in view of hardships and worsening economic conditions, in such countries as Algeria, Egypt, and Jordan.

Although we do not suggest the existence in the Occupied Territories of any monolithic Islam, or "Islam International"[88] as some have been wont to call it, Islamic groups began to enjoy widespread appeal among certain sectors of Palestinians. Islamists rejected secular politics and perceived its failure at two levels. The first was the absence of concrete political gains. The second was the inadequacy of support services for the increasingly destitute Palestinians. Newer groups such as *Hamas* and its fighting wing in the *Al-Qassam* units, as well as more established groups such as the Islamic *Jihad* and the Muslim Brotherhood (the latter revitalized during this period), formed a distinctive "popular" movement that should not be underestimated in any evaluation of popular and grassroots efforts.[89]

Analysts agree that Palestinian Islamists resemble their Arab counterparts in many important respects; most significantly in their ultimate goal of establishing an "Islamic state" and in their assessments of the general failure of secular politics of both East and West. Islamic ideologies in the Arab world, particularly in the Palestinian case, were encouraged by the continuation of the Israeli occupation (the status of Jerusalem was a special sticking point). The dominance of Zionist and imperial interests in the area was, in the view of these Islamists and their supporters, a signal to devise more authentic Arab ideologies and mobilize more effective resistance. The emerging Islamic movements were thus able to feed off the discontent of the population and suggest alternatives that were more readily accepted by virtue of being rooted in custom and tradition.

Without going into great detail on these developments, two issues relevant to the Islamic movements in the Occupied Territories stand out. One concerns their broad appeal as "opposition" movements. Both Iyad Barghouti and Ziad Abu-Amr emphasize that the real test would come if these groups actually gained power. Both question whether they would be successful not only in criticizing existing structures, but also in constructing viable alternatives. Indeed, Barghouti questions whether these Islamic groups have any concrete proposals or strategies to that effect, and what they would do to maintain support for their goals.[90] Another point is that despite the apparent appeal of Islamic ideologies in some sectors, Palestinian society has remained secular in outlook and very protective of its aspirations to achieve democracy and respect for human rights. *Hamas* and the other Islamic groups have had to adjust to this reality; and *Hamas* in particular has toned down its rhetoric and amended its strategy so as not to alienate potential supporters. It began to refer to the immediate goal of ending occupation rather than focusing exclusively on the ultimate goal of an Islamic state in Palestine. It addressed issues of democracy and civil rights, and became less strident in its attacks against women's activism. Thus it won more adherents, especially among those Palestinians opposed to the peace process and to PLO "concessions" to Israel.[91]

In the immediate aftermath of the peace agreements signed between Israel and the PLO in September 1993, it was not yet clear whether the Islamic groups would be able to retain the stature they had achieved, or whether, indeed, they had a strategy for pursuing their objectives. *Hamas,* for example, was always categorically opposed to any kind of interim solution of "self-rule." Yet its ideological appeal among the Palestinian people in the Occupied Territories did not rest so much on political grounds as on its ability to provide needed services and support to the local population. It was largely able to accomplish this purpose because it continued to receive funding and support in the aftermath of the Gulf War, at a time when the secular PLO factions had their sources of funding cut off. The Declaration of Principles of September 1993, however, may have reversed this trend. This agreement stipulated quite clearly that major development projects were to be undertaken in the Occupied Territories. These would be accomplished with the support of international donors and investors, so as to raise living standards in these areas.[92] Channeling development funds into major Palestinian and PLO institutions would serve to counter the monopoly enjoyed by the Islamic groups as providers of needed services. Perhaps it would eventually diminish their appeal, especially if the PLO succeeded in its negotiations with Israel, both to advance autonomy in the short-term and to establish a sovereign state in the long term. The PLO would have to tread a thin line: While it would prefer to crush opposition to its deal with Israel emanating from its main challenger, the Islamic groups, it would need to do so without appearing antidemocratic, dictatorial, and overly harsh.

The Islamic movement in the Occupied Territories has established itself as a significant player in civil society in these areas, and it has to be acknowledged as such. It remains a movement that could yet be mobilized and reinvigorated, should the peace talks collapse or should they lead to what Palestinians perceive as too many concessions.[93] From all indications, however, Palestinians in the Occupied Territories were gearing up through their respective grassroots movements, both religious and secular, to "monitor" the implementation of the Israeli-PLO agreements. They were preparing to protect human rights and democracy, and to counter or check, as needed, any abuse of power by the "interim authority" of the PLO in these areas.[94]

*   *   *

The decolonization process has not progressed smoothly for Palestinians, partly because of Israel's stranglehold over the West Bank and Gaza Strip and their inhabitants, and partly because of the nature of Palestinian society itself under occupation. The variety of official and unofficial organizations to which Palestinians belong, as well as the factionalism and rivalry between groups and organizations claiming to represent them, remained a constant problem. These conditions have compromised the ability of Palestinians to arrive at a strategic consensus on how to proceed with their resistance.

These points underscore the basic issues that have confounded Palestinian strategic thinking. Often, Palestinians seemed to find comfort in Fanon's and Memmi's suggestion that colonialism carries the seeds of its own destruction. For many Palestinians, this was a vindication of their belief, articulated occasionally in their resistance, that "historical forces" were on their side. Yet, even in light of the September 1993 agreements, many Palestinians felt vulnerable. They continued to fear that Israeli leaders would seek to outwit history, so to speak, and create historical conditions that would fulfill the Zionist vision and at the same time permanently preclude opposing forces from destroying it. Some Palestinians perceived the agreements reached between the PLO and Israel in 1993 in precisely such a light. In their view, the possibility of the emergence of some kind of Palestinian self-rule, even limited "statehood," has been at the expense of Palestinian nationhood. An editorial in *Middle East International* notes,

> In other decolonization agreements of recent decades, the occupied have more often than not forced the imperial power to withdraw and so have been able to secure favorable terms for decolonization. Not so here.[95]

So the Palestinian struggle continues. Reaping the rewards of mobilization efforts of the mid-1970s, the Palestinians launched their *intifada*.

The following chapter examines the *intifada* and its predominantly nonviolent civilian resistance character. The conclusions drawn from this experience are then incorporated into the theme of Chapters Four and Five, which is to examine the feasibility of a nonviolent civilian resistance strategy for ending the Israeli occupation.

Three

The Intifada *as Palestinian Civilian Resistance*

The exact date of the following incident is not known. It may have occurred just prior to the *intifada* or during its early phases. It is recounted here because it captures so vividly the spirit of this uprising in the Occupied Territories.

Dheisheh camp, near the West Bank city of Bethlehem, has long been a site of confrontations between Palestinian refugees and Israeli soldiers and settlers. Because of its location overlooking one of the main roads traversed by settlers, Dheisheh has frequently been the source of stones thrown at passing cars. Some years ago, a group of Jewish settlers led by Rabbi Moshe Levinger, a vocal leader of the ultraright Gush Emunim movement, staged a deliberate, prolonged, and aggressive "sit-in" outside the camp. Levinger and his followers were determined to remain in place until the Israeli authorities solved the "problem" of stone-throwing Palestinian youth. They finally erected a huge fence all along the outskirts of the camp, bordering the main road. As one West Bank Palestinian told me, from then on the Palestinian camp dwellers were like "monkeys in a circus," trapped behind their wire fences.

At the time of the incident in question, Israeli army personnel had cleared a piece of land just across the road from one of the main entrances to the camp. They had installed utility poles, had erected tents, and were preparing to set up an army unit on the site. The camp dwellers of Dheisheh were evidently disturbed by these moves. They did not want an army presence at such close proximity, so they decided to protest. For three nights in a row, Palestinian women stood just inside the fence and spent the long hours of the night shouting and ululating across the road at the soldiers. After three nights of such continuous commotion, the Israeli soldiers packed up and left the site. The army later set up its camp a few miles down the road, away from Dheisheh. At some point during recent years, however, the army returned.[1]

The moral of this story is not that the army was afraid of the Palestinians or seriously disturbed by the noises of the women. According to the West Bank Palestinian who recounted the tale, what concerned the Israelis most was that through such action, Palestinians would learn something about their own power. They feared that Palestinians would organize and employ direct action against their opponent, action that does not rely on the force of arms to be effective.

Much has been written about the events immediately preceding the *intifada*—both in the Occupied Territories themselves and the region at large.[2] It is not really necessary to go far beyond the boundaries of the Occupied Territories themselves to locate the origins of the *intifada*. Palestinians viewed Israel as intransigent and unwilling to reach a political settlement. Frustration with the political process had been accumulating for years. Palestinians never accepted their situation passively, and they soon said "enough is enough" and took matters into their own hands to change the situation.

Before a full-fledged civilian struggle could be launched, a firm commitment from the PLO was required for the mass movement in the Occupied Territories—whereby the civilian population would struggle against the occupation with largely nonviolent means—to be legitimate in its own right. Perhaps the PLO was caught by surprise by the specific timing, but there can be little doubt that the PLO not only approved of such a struggle, but had been actively involved in laying the groundwork for it. Helena Cobban quotes the Palestinian leader Faisal Husseini to the effect that Abu Jihad, the military commander of the PLO, had been planning for "offensive nonviolence" in the Occupied Territories at least as early as 1985. By Cobban's own account, the PLO consciously adopted this strategic focus after its ouster from Lebanon in 1982. It was then that the PLO realized the limitations of armed struggle and decided to shift the locus of power to the civilian population under Israeli rule.[3]

This shifting emphasis signaled a division of labor in the national movement. The PLO would retain responsibility for the formulation of general policy (grand strategy), while the population in the Occupied Territories would be responsible for formulating and coordinating the tactical steps of the *intifada*. They would be the ones to employ direct and generally nonviolent resistance against the occupation regime (the nonuse of lethal weapons was specified by the PLO from the start). Ideally, there would remain a close dialogue and exchange of ideas between the activists on the inside and outside.

However unprecedented the *intifada* may have appeared in the eyes of the outside world, the methods of resistance employed in these areas were not really new. What was new was the convergence of a number of key factors and the emphasis on concerted—and, for the first year or two, largely nonviolent—civilian action.

The Impact of the *Intifada* on Palestinian Society

The official starting date of the *intifada* was December 9, 1987. As the weeks, months, and then the first few years unfolded, this uprising came to fulfill the role implied in its name, as a "shake-up" of Palestinian society and of the relationship between occupier and occupied. The initial selection of mainly nonviolent methods was directed at two fronts: to unlink the Occupied Territories from their dependence on Israel and render them ungovernable by the Israeli regime, and to establish the indigenous structural underpinnings for a future Palestinian state.

The *intifada* started out as a struggle of an oppressed people to overthrow their oppressors. The dynamics of the situation were such that the *intifada* soon took on a momentum of its own and challenged the social and ideological underpinnings of the very people engaged in this resistance. The very act of resistance transformed the resisters. The situation was never static; Palestinians were in turn empowered and paralyzed. They acted upon their occupier, who was also transformed, and this transformation reflected back upon the resisters themselves. There is no single definition of the *intifada*; its meaning has been in constant flux, as have been its techniques, its priorities, its objectives, and its actors. Starting as a mass movement to end an occupation, it became a movement that in many respects shattered and rearranged the fabric of Palestinian society; sometimes for the better, sometimes for the worse, but never in entirely predictable ways. As for the occupier, the *intifada* was meant to separate, to unlink, and to break the chains of oppression. Ironically, the uprising bound Israel even more closely to the Occupied Territories. Israel was for the first time, and in a dramatic reversal of its role as unchallenged master, being acted upon from within. Israel itself was "shaken up," and responded accordingly. Each new countermeasure would elicit new responses from the Palestinians. Each community became locked within the other, held prisoner in a sense to the other's next move—transforming and being transformed at every stage.

The *intifada* highlighted both strengths and weaknesses in the Palestinian community. Though this process paved the way for major restructuring in some areas, it caused severe backlashes in others.

The Role of Mass Organizations

The popular and mass organizations that expanded in the 1970s formed the underpinnings of the *intifada*. These committees provided Palestinians with a heightened sense of their own power as direct actors. Younger men in particular (along with some women), who were noted for their political activism and organizational affiliations, became the symbols of the new authority in the Occupied Territories. As many more of the known nationalist leaders were arrested, detained, or expelled, younger activists emerged to replace them. Despite the imprisonment and detention of tens of thousands of people and the deportation of some 500 Palestinians, Israel did not succeed in totally suppressing this *intifada*. Palestinians in the Occupied Territories affirmed that the mobilization of the past decade had paid off. The *intifada* became a genuine people's struggle. However, it did not proceed without a price.

The grassroots committees were rent by factionalism and competition, which hampered the efforts of groups to coordinate their activities and to provide viable services and supports to the increasingly needy population. This situation was exacerbated as the *intifada* progressed; and by the second year of the peace talks (around 1993) it had reached such a critical level that civil society itself was threatened in the Occupied Territories.[4] Clearly factionalism was not the only problem. The aftermath of the Gulf War and the closure of Jerusalem, along with the rest of Israel, to Palestinian residents of the Occupied Territories left these areas close to being economically devastated. People were extremely frustrated with the peace talks and were on the verge of total despair. Both the regular PLO factions and the Islamic groups competed strongly to fill the vacuum.

The first years of the *intifada* started on a different note. Palestinian members of the grassroots committees found it relatively simple to adapt their roles in light of the new situation. Although they were not necessarily the organizations that were responsible for political and strategic decision-making, it was the grassroots organizations that were active at the community level. Among their responsibilities was the implementation of the instructions issued by the Unified Nationalist Leadership of the Uprising (UNLU).[5]

The functions of these Palestinian mass organizations are a clear indication of how structures of civil society provide a counterpoint to the power of the state—the kind of alternative "loci of power" to which Gene Sharp refers. During the *intifada,* these groups facilitated the provision of medical services, food, and relief to the residents of their communities. Throughout the first two years of the uprising they evinced a high degree of organization and solidarity that helped sustain an impressive level of Palestinian participation in the *intifada*. Their successes drew Israeli reprisals. The *Shabiba* (youth) organization was outlawed in March 1988, followed by the banning of other popular committees in August of that year. Stringent Israeli measures, such as widespread tax raids, curfews, and closing off whole communities, as well as other measures designed to put obstacles in the way of collective action, caused Palestinian participation at the community level to wane. By then, the problem of collaborators had become particularly acute and threatened to wreck the work of these popular groups.[6] The effort to expose and weed out collaborators, and along with them such "undesirable" elements as drug dealers and criminals, diverted energy away from the main struggle against the occupation. Mistrust, suspicion, fear, and ideological disputes over how to tackle the problem split efforts and alienated large segments of the community that might otherwise have been mobilized to participate in the national movement.[7]

Over the years of the *intifada* the functions of the grassroots committees and their branches in the Occupied Territories became noticeably more institutionalized. For obvious reasons they were unable to encompass all fields or meet the requirements of citizens at every level of community life. Nevertheless, they provided real and viable alternatives in some vital sectors. As overt demonstrations and stone-throwing confrontations gradually receded in the Occupied Territories, restructuring within the Palestinian community proceeded behind the scenes.[8]

Specialized committees spread throughout the villages, cities, and refugee camps of the Occupied Territories to administer almost every aspect of life under the *intifada*. The role of such committees was especially pronounced with the cutoff of aid and funding to regular institutions after the Gulf War. Examples abounded of committee members, including women activists, who defied curfew orders and risked their lives to enter into closed areas. *Shebab* from various areas (particularly camps and isolated villages) organized neighborhood night watches and guard units to patrol their areas and alert residents to any impending attacks. Welfare and relief services were also organized by the popular committees for families whose members were out of work, imprisoned, deported, or killed. Specialized committees were organized, often by women and children, for replacing locks on shops that had been broken by Israeli troops. Members of Medical Relief Committees likewise violated curfews to enter into camps and other areas where residents were in desperate need of medical care, especially after long sieges or after particularly brutal confrontations with Israeli soldiers or settlers.[9]

Local committees were responsible for ensuring adherence to the instructions of the Unified Leadership, such as calls for strikes, boycotts, and refusal to pay taxes. The strike forces, the "popular army" composed mainly of young activists in various locales, played an active role in this regard. By the end of the second year of the *intifada,* however, the popular appeal of these groups had waned. The population was beginning to tire from the burden of strikes and civil disobedience, and by the third year of the *intifada* whole cities and villages were openly disobeying specific strike calls. Factional splits and infighting among the *shebab* units and other grassroots groups increased the tensions, as did the bullying methods used by the *shebab* against the local population. Such tactics alienated the Palestinian residents and cost the youth the support and respect they had commanded earlier in the *intifada*.

The *intifada* gave rise to the formation of committees within specific social sectors—for example, in education. Popular Education Committees were formed by ordinary citizens who were concerned over the disruption to their children's education caused by the prolonged closure of schools and universities. Parents and teachers organized lessons in private homes, churches, or mosques. Such meetings were banned by the Israeli authorities. It became a "security offense" to conduct classes at home, and books and other educational materials found at such sites were confiscated. These alternative groups gradually lost their appeal. As they were unable to do more than respond to Israeli measures, they proliferated when the authorities closed schools for long periods, but died down when schools were reopened.

Agricultural Relief Committees worked closely with residents to create "home economies." Palestinians were initially encouraged to take advantage of long curfews and the boycott of Israeli products to seek indigenous alternatives. They located empty plots of land in their neighborhoods and grew their own vegetables. These were their "victory gardens." They raised goats for milk, chicken for eggs and meat, and, occasionally, rabbits. They were also encouraged by their cooperatives to market their products locally in the Occupied Territories, so as to reduce their dependence on outside markets.[10] As time went on, Palestinians (city dwellers in particular) found that the cost of watering these gardens far outweighed the price of simply buying the produce they needed from the local market, and their activities in this area naturally declined.

Clearly, the organizational reshaping of the Palestinian community during the *intifada*, as well as the structures of a burgeoning parallel government, had a significant impact both on the Palestinian community itself and on the Israeli occupation regime. Though the emerging alternative institutions were never all-encompassing in any given sector, their successes could be measured by the extent to which they directly challenged Israeli authority in these areas. "Obedience" was transferred to Palestinian loci of power; the very idea that they could command the authority and respect of the population was a new phenomenon, both to Israel and the Palestinians. It meant that Israel had to resort to brute force and repression in order to reassert its control. A combination of factors resulted in the decline in organizational efforts. These included renewed factionalism, a surge in the number of collaborators, a peak in mobilizing capabilities, and deteriorating economic and social conditions after the Gulf War. However, the very fact that Palestinians had exhibited the will, solidarity, and sacrifice necessary to build these structures exposed the vulnerability of Israeli control in the face of determined collective action.

The Israeli crackdown on Palestinian activists intensified, and serious factional differences emerged over the objectives and the means used during the uprising. It was around this time that the struggle between *Hamas* and the more secular factions competing for a position of prominence in the Palestinian community became more overt. With each group issuing calls for different strike days, the general Palestinian population grew resentful and frustrated. They felt they had to adhere to all these calls, for fear of alienating one or the other of the factions. Disagreements and conflicts became more serious and divisive, and the UNLU was largely immobilized.

Disunity among the Palestinians in the Occupied Territories emerged from another direction, with its roots in the growing disillusionment over the pace of diplomatic activity by the PLO outside. While the *intifada* wore on and hardships multiplied, Palestinians could see no comparable advances on the political front. Quite to the contrary, a significant number of Palestinians began to view the PLO as having made too many concessions, with little to show in return. The earlier consensus over tactics had dissipated, particularly as some factions issued calls for an escalation of violence or for the scrapping of the "peaceful" efforts of the past. The August 1990 Iraqi invasion of Kuwait and the subsequent U.S.-led war against Iraq in early 1991 dealt a further blow to the *intifada*. The plight of Palestinians was almost totally overshadowed throughout this crisis, leaving them to feel that they had been abandoned by the world. This perception was expressed in the popular enthusiasm and support for the Iraqi president, Saddam Hussein, when few outside the region could appreciate the depths of despair and anger that had triggered these responses.[11] Undoubtedly, pinning their hopes on Saddam Hussein harmed the Palestinian cause in more ways than one. Most significantly, Palestinians were deflected from the efforts espoused and established initially in the *intifada*—those of seizing the initiative and taking matters into their own hands in order to effect change.

At the local level, the widening rifts in the Palestinian community could also be attributed to the strategy adopted by the UNLU to decentralize its authority, so that the local leadership of each area would decide on how to interpret the general directives in a manner best suited to that particular setting. As Daoud Kuttab wrote early in the *intifada*, "While the Israelis may be able to succeed to some extent in blocking regional or national coordination, it is almost impossible to break up the efforts of the local committees spread out over the entire Occupied Territories."[12] The Israeli authorities, however, managed to penetrate local areas as well, and to disrupt the functions of the committees. Palestinians were confronted by a dilemma: Centralized authority would make them vulnerable; decentralized authority would risk splitting the national movement and destroying national consensus and unity. Decentralization took on particular urgency in view of intensified and repressive Israeli measures. Such measures were designed to cut off the Occupied Territories from the outside world and from each other, into separate and isolated communities in both the West Bank and Gaza Strip. Though, in theory, had they retained the initiative, decentralization would have worked to the advantage of Palestinians, in reality decentralization resulted in a breakdown of consensus. This occurred between factions in each community, between communities and their local leaderships, and within the factions themselves. The resulting fragmentation of efforts allowed Israel to further split the national movement.

A severe Israeli crackdown against individual communities isolated them and preempted collective responses. One tactic was the massive tax raids. Israeli military personnel, accompanied by tax officials, would appear in force in a given community and proceed to levy enormous taxes against individuals, businesses, and property. Millions of dollars worth of savings, confiscated goods, machinery, and household items would be collected from the Palestinians. The Israeli authorities apparently believed that such measures would create enough hardship to demoralize the population and break their will to continue the *intifada*. In the absence of a clear leadership, distinct goals, realistic tactics, and secure social supports, such tactics were successful. More and more people tired of the *intifada* and of the abnormal conditions they had to endure. Many Palestinians simply wanted to keep a low profile and normalize their lives as best they could.

One event that highlights the dilemmas concerning civilian resistance was the 1989 tax revolt in Beit Sahour, a village of about 12,000 people located near Bethlehem in the West Bank. For about six weeks during September and October 1989, Beit Sahour launched a total tax revolt against the Israeli occupation regime. Throughout their revolt, the people of Beit Sahour raised the slogan "No Taxation Without Representation." The village was placed under total siege by the Israeli army. Food and medical supplies were stopped, telephone lines were cut, and prolonged curfews were imposed. In the ensuing raids by army and tax officials, the residents were stripped of over US $1.5 million worth of goods, including personal belongings, furnishings, factory machinery, cars, and other items. Many residents were beaten and arrested.[13] The villagers persisted in their resolve, until, at the end of October 1989, media exposure and an international outcry finally forced Israel to lift the siege and to call off the raids. A number of factors—the village's history and composition, its geographical layout, proximity to Israel, access by the media and Israeli peace groups, level of education, and others—convinced the local UNLU that such an act of civil disobedience would be both appropriate and feasible in this setting. Though Beit Sahour set a precedent, total tax revolts were not adopted by other Palestinian communities.[14]

The events of Beit Sahour raise significant questions with regard to strategic planning and political unity. Although the reluctance of other communities to emulate Beit Sahour could be attributed to the specifics of their particular location, leadership, and social composition, other reasons can be located in the response of the Israeli authorities. Israel apparently realized that Palestinians could be determined, steadfast, and willing to sacrifice and work collectively for a goal, particularly when the punishment was indiscriminately meted out against a whole community. Perhaps these same Israelis realized the power of collective nonviolent action as it consolidated resistance within the community and at the same time back-fired against Israel. The impact of such a Palestinian initiative could be witnessed by the outpouring of international condemnation over Israel's prolonged siege of the village. From then on, the Israeli authorities con-ducted their tax raids selectively, in the form of lightning strikes against individual communities. By preempting the power of the civilian population to organize a collective response, the Israeli forces have since taken much of the initiative. Palestinians then had to grapple with the question of how to regain the initiative, perhaps by calling for tactics more commensurate with the ability of the population to carry them out.

Despite the problems already outlined, mass organizations and popular committees contributed to enhanced solidarity and cohesiveness within Palestinian society. This solidarity was evident in the early phases of the uprising, and it derived from the very experience of having resisted the occupation and having gained a sense of empowerment. The pervasive civilian character of the uprising and the participation of the population in all its sectors and at all levels, along with the deliberate choice of largely nonviolent means of struggle, contributed toward a feeling of euphoria and excitement among Palestinians. They had taken matters into their own hands and had risen against a very powerful opponent.

Ironically, Israel itself contributed to the forging of these bonds of solidarity among Palestinians. No sector of Palestinian society was immune to Israeli violence, repression, and dispossession. People felt that they had nothing to lose. The depth and strength of community bonds were revealed in the way they began to transcend traditional boundaries and distinctions. The early stages of the *intifada* depicted a true people's struggle. Class lines were blurred, as were distinctions between different age groups, gender roles, religious factions, cities and villages, the West Bank and Gaza Strip, and indeed, to some extent, Palestinians holding Israeli citizenship and those within the Occupied Territories.

Many incidents during the first few years of the uprising underscored this solidarity. There were merchants and businessmen who conformed to calls for strikes by agreeing to open and close their shops according to the hours designated by the Unified Leadership. With the exception of East Jerusalem, shopkeepers and consumers alike generally respected the call to boycott Israeli products and no longer bought or sold these items.[15] At the outset of the *intifada,* landlords desisted from demanding rent for their premises from merchants. Welders voluntarily contributed their time and labor to replace locks on shops and doors broken by Israeli troops. As the uprising wore on, however, class distinctions reappeared to cause divisiveness and tension among Palestinians.[16]

In a reversal of traditional modes of behavior in Arab society, the youth—*shebab*—the heroes of the *intifada,* won the respect of their elders. Each generation had apparently set aside traditional notions of authority and obedience within the patriarchal family, to respond to the higher call of the national cause. The instructions of the youth were usually obeyed by the residents of a given community without eliciting undue resentment or antagonism. A request to close a shop or to go home and park the car during strike days was usually followed. As the *intifada* wore on, excesses and transgressions occurred on all sides. For example, a shopkeeper would operate his business from his home on strike days, or youths would behave arrogantly and inconsiderately toward other residents. The bonds of solidarity that had characterized the early months of the *intifada* began to unravel. As conditions worsened and repression at the hands of the Israeli forces intensified, the youth began getting out of control and were no longer heeding any authority, partly because of the failure of the leadership to articulate a coherent strategy for the *intifada,* in which the *shebab*—indeed all sectors of Palestinian society—could play a defined role. Perhaps the leadership assumed that permitting the *shebab* to organize themselves as they pleased and permitting their use of limited or occasional violence would be a tactical measure that could later be circumscribed or reversed, as occasion demanded. However, with no clear specification of what any escalation of violence could accomplish in the first place and the failure to integrate the *shebab* fully into a cohesive strategy, the shortsightedness of such assumptions was soon made clear. By the opening of the Madrid Conference in October 1991, the problem had grown to such proportions that Palestinian inhabitants were expressing actual fear of masked youth. The *shebab,* on the other hand, had organized into opposed groups of "popular army" units, uniformed, masked, and "armed" (mainly with knives, stones, and sticks). They tended to show off by parading in the streets and demonstrating. In many cases, members of different factions settled their scores through violence and the use of firearms. Older Palestinians seemed to be at their wits end, not knowing how to contain the violence or how to prevent complete anarchy.

The double-edged nature of the uprising is perhaps most clearly demonstrated in its impact on Palestinian women. Their participation radically challenged and transformed traditional social relations and behaviors within Palestinian society. Palestinian women proved themselves to be especially brave and active during the *intifada,* both within their own committees and alongside men in the demonstrations, sit-ins, and other forms of protest and resistance. Their participation has been lauded as another example of the primacy of the national cause over and above class, gender, and other issues. Still, the changing role of women posed a significant challenge to the authority of the traditional Arab family and the prevailing notions of patriarchy, obedience, and family honor. The literal meaning of the word *intifada* as a "shake-up" is eminently revealed in this sphere.

The main source of the growing backlash against women's activities was the extreme religious factions. Most Palestinians initially dismissed pronouncements by *Hamas* and other fundamentalist groups as simply another normal and temporary reaction to the occupation. In the Gaza Strip especially, pressures against women soon became too pervasive to ignore. There, the paradoxical situation of women was particularly acute and the backlash most severe. The more extensively and actively women participated in the national struggle, the more did men, particularly followers of the extremist religious factions, demand that women once again be confined to their homes. They insisted that women be bound by patriarchal authority and restricted to their traditional duties as wives and mothers. Outside the home, women were commanded to dress conservatively in long dresses and scarves (or veils). Women who violated this code were punished; rocks were thrown at them, and they were harassed, attacked, and even beaten by men and youths. Equally serious was the attempt to redefine the woman's role, so that expressions of conformity to tradition and religion were themselves interpreted as indications of nationalist commitment. Women who challenged such understandings were labeled as deviating from the national goals—behavior akin to treason.[17] Women's Committees were quickly alerted to these threats, but were largely unsuccessful in their efforts to place this problem on the agenda of the nationalist leadership. Various analysts blamed the UNLU for its failure to address this issue at the outset—to nip it in the bud before it assumed uncontrollable proportions. One explanation was advanced that the UNLU did not appreciate the severity of the problem. Or else, people rationalized, the UNLU would prefer not to antagonize the religious factions that would play a pivotal role alongside the rest of the nationalist movement against a common enemy.[18] By the early 1990s, Palestinian women activists in the Occupied Territories decided that the issue could no longer be deferred and would have to be tackled immediately. Palestinian women had to protect their participation in the national struggle and ensure that the advent of a Palestinian state not only would culminate in ending an unwanted occupation, but also would pave the way for a more progressive, democratic, and participatory society, in which both men and women could realize their full potential.[19] It was then that Palestinian women became seriously engaged in articulating a women's agenda separate from the national cause.[20]

During the peace talks, *Hamas* and other religious organizations decreased their overt attacks against women's public participation. In this way they avoided directly antagonizing women and concentrated instead on a strategy that aimed at winning Palestinians to their side by providing needed services and aid. This technique paid off, even among women. Some women started espousing religious beliefs and practices and were encouraged by the same religious groups that had shown such disdain toward them in the first place.[21] Even female activists in some of the women's organizations began to circumscribe their public behaviors by pointing to the need to respect tradition and religion in their communities. The peace process complicated matters by introducing other issues of concern to women. The formation of a technical team for women, the Technical Committee for Women's Affairs (also known as Women's Issues Committees),[22] to oversee women's issues split the traditional grassroots movements and created different sectors of women's activities divided along class and factional lines.[23]

Nonviolent Resistance and the Campaign of Civil Disobedience

Whether nonviolent resistance could itself put enough pressure on Israel to withdraw from the Occupied Territories was one question that preoccupied Palestinians during the *intifada*. The other was the impact of nonviolent struggle on the Palestinian community engaged in this resistance.

Palestinians were serious about their consideration of nonviolent methods. This seriousness was evident in their call for a campaign of civil disobedience in January 1988. Palestinians referred to "civil disobedience" as the essence of their struggle and as the focal point of their uprising.[24] The immediate issue that provoked this call for civil disobedience was the threatened expulsion of four Palestinians from the Occupied Territories. Palestinians linked their demands for a halt to these expulsions with warnings that they would boycott Israeli cigarettes and other products. They subsequently issued more demands, and their "civil disobedience" was extended to comprise a variety of methods and techniques that were tried at different times during the uprising.

One leaflet, distributed early in the *intifada*, captures the essence of this civil disobedience campaign. Listed in this leaflet were calls for a number of nonviolent acts. These included shouting and wailing to prevent Israeli soldiers from entering people's homes, seeking arrest by the hundreds in order to overcrowd and paralyze Israeli prison systems, wearing the Palestinian *kuffiyeh* (headdress), blowing car horns at designated hours, and talking to Israeli soldiers in public places so as to affect their morale.[25]

A general survey of the methods of resistance employed by Palestinians during the *intifada* shows them to fall into the three main categories of nonviolent action defined by Sharp and others to comprise protests, noncooperation, including the civil disobedience campaign, and efforts to establish alternative institutions.[26]

Palestinians in the West Bank and Gaza Strip experimented with a variety of protest actions. These ranged from nonviolent demonstrations, sit-ins, marches, displaying the Palestinian flag, and mock funerals to more violent stone-throwing confrontations and use of gasoline bombs. Palestinians initially intended these to be "expressive" measures that underscored their rejection of the occupation and their determination to struggle until it is terminated. Indeed, regardless of the level of violence employed, these acts of direct protest and confrontation highlighted their plight and generated sympathy worldwide for the "children of the stones." Palestinians proved to be inventive and imaginative in devising new protest methods to challenge Israeli army control in the occupied areas. The deliberate selection of nonviolent techniques was corroborated by the findings of a survey of the communiqués that were issued during the first year and a half of the *intifada,* conducted by the Palestine Center for the Study of Nonviolence.[27]

One telling example of nonviolent protest took place in the Old City of East Jerusalem early in the *intifada.* One night, after shattering street lights in the immediate vicinity to ensure total darkness, young Palestinians lay in wait for Israeli troops. When the soldiers stormed the area, fully armed and apparently intent on chasing them, dozens of young boys blew their whistles, the shrill sounds piercing the night air and echoing from all directions. The soldiers panicked and tried frantically to capture the young boys. The latter, more familiar with the terrain, easily eluded the soldiers. Finally, the troops left the site, angry and scared.[28] In another incident, the villagers of Jumain, near Tulkarm in the West Bank, were reported to have held a demonstration carrying olive branches in one hand and the Palestinian flag in the other.[29] In that incident, Israeli troops remained well outside the village and observed the action without intervening.

Throughout the uprising, Palestinians remained intent on building the structures that would establish their independence from the occupation regime. The *intifada* assumed the form of a larger campaign of civilian resistance, one in which Palestinians supplemented civil disobedience with acts of noncooperation and the establishment of indigenous organizations. Palestinians were instructed in a variety of methods of noncooperation, such as general strikes, resigning from the institutions of the occupation regime, withdrawing their labor from Israel, boycotting Israeli goods and products, violating curfews, and refusing to pay taxes. It is interesting to note that Palestinians generally linked the escalation of these techniques to a series of specific demands and objectives that were issued in various communiqués. Many of the communiqués bore the signs of growing understanding of the operation of nonviolent techniques. Apart from the official appeals issued by the Unified Leadership, Palestinians issued a number of other statements. Although the long-term goal remained an end to occupation, there were a number of intermediary goals that were raised at different stages of the *intifada*. For example, in December 1987 a ten-point statement was issued called "Points for Consideration."[30] Its demands included the following:

> "Stop the torture of prisoners and release those taken during the
>   *intifada*."
> "Cancel the deportation rule and allow those who have been
>   deported to return."
> "Withdraw the soldiers from populated areas and stop the
>   harassment of the inhabitants of the refugee camps."
> "Stop the policy of house demolitions and give permits for house
>   construction."
> "Cease the closure of educational institutions and allow
>   academic freedom."
> "Stop unfair tax collection."

Also in January 1988 a 14-point statement was issued in English that was signed by the Palestinian Nationalist Institutions and Personalities from the West Bank and Gaza Strip. This statement reiterated some of the demands made earlier and urged the convening of an international peace conference, with the participation of all the parties involved, including the PLO. Other items included calling upon Israel to abide by the articles of the Fourth Geneva Convention and pertinent United Nations Security Council resolutions.[31]

Although Palestinians announced from the start that they were prepared for a total civil disobedience campaign, these earlier acts of noncooperation concentrated mainly on the achievement of a limited set of goals. It was not clear then whether Palestinians understood that they would not be able to carry out their civil disobedience to the point of complete disengagement from Israel. Nevertheless, they did attempt to move toward more extensive severance of their ties to Israel. Moreover, in spite of the absence of adequate indigenous supports, they no longer expected Israel to solve their daily problems.

One example of Palestinian efforts at noncooperation was the Beit Sahour tax revolt mentioned earlier. Noncooperation in this area would highlight the illegitimacy of tax regulations and amendments to existing laws in "occupied territories." The Israeli authorities quickly countered the effect of such noncooperation by instituting a particularly harsh system whereby permits to travel, operate cars and businesses, receive identity cards, and the like all hinged upon proof of payment of taxes. In the light of these restrictions, Palestinians concluded that their society would be virtually immobilized and rendered totally vulnerable to Israeli repression should they decide to emulate this example. Such action would exact a higher price from them than any gains they could extract from their opponent.

The idea of withdrawal of Palestinian labor from Israel (in the form of a general or permanent strike) was another method of noncooperation used by Palestinians. Its impact was also questionable, because Israel was soon able to accommodate by employing newly arrived Soviet Jewish immigrants and others.[32] Palestinians could not build enough viable indigenous productive ventures of their own that would enable them to totally forgo their jobs and sources of income in Israel. They became very vulnerable to Israeli countermeasures as they discovered that they were not in a position to choose whether or not to work in Israel.

The establishment of alternative institutions was perhaps one of the most exciting developments of the *intifada.* This took on various forms, as in the creation of specialized committees in the towns, villages, camps, and neighborhoods in the Occupied Territories. The initial establishment of the "home economies" and the expansion of the services of Medical Relief Committees, Agricultural Relief Committees, Voluntary Work Committees, Women's Committees, and Popular Education Committees are also examples of such efforts.

Palestinians created different alternatives to the civilian administration. They were quite proud to declare "liberated areas" (a street, a camp, a neighborhood, even a whole village) where they raised the Palestinian flag and renamed streets. Such areas were cleared of both collaborators and the army presence, the latter being kept at bay for a time. In creating their own institutions, Palestinians hoped to combine adequate supports for their community in the short term with efforts that would gradually pave the way toward more permanent alternative authority structures in the long term. The transformation of local committees into the political structures of a parallel government has historical precedent, such as the American colonial movement against the British (1765–1775).[33] There remain, however, many important differences in the colonial contexts of the two struggles. In the American case, one of the first moves toward the formation of local committees and alternative authority structures emanated from the growing disillusionment of Americans with the governing British colonial apparatus. As in the situation of Palestinians during the *intifada,* Americans took the initiative into their own hands to resist elements of colonial rule. Beginning with various acts of protest and noncooperation, they found themselves almost accidentally forced to create alternative institutional means to organize their defense. Ronald McCarthy argues that these organizations functioned as parallel institutions, quickly replacing and superseding the legal and political systems set in place by the British. In time, the new popular system of authority became entrenched as a parallel government.

A central factor determining the authority of the parallel political structure is its ability to command the obedience of the people. Whether in the experience of the American colonial movement or in the Palestinian *intifada,* it is insufficient to simply question the legitimacy of the opponent's government. The corresponding right of the alternative nationalist organizations to command authority and allegiance must be recognized by the people in question. As McCarthy points out, the parallel government must institutionalize this authority into "regular and lasting bodies with their own procedures and personnel as well as sources of support."[34] This is a point well taken in view of the expected role of the PLO in establishing some type of governing entity in the areas slated for "self-rule." Palestinians may not automatically take this "authority" for granted, and the governing entities may find their legitimacy challenged should they initiate policies that appear unpopular or unduly repressive.

In their own attempts to create parallel authorities during the *intifada,* Palestinians were encouraged to rely solely on these structures and obey their authority in lieu of those of the military administration. They anticipated that in the long term the Occupied Territories will become ungovernable and Palestinian independence will have been achieved de facto in these areas. For a variety of reasons this expectation was premature. Palestinians were soon to discover that breaking away from Israel could not and would not be complete, and that the creation of alternative institutions had faltered. Dissonance increased between the high morale and sense of empowerment that they had experienced through protest actions and the reality on the ground. Critical economic and social sectors existed where Palestinians were especially vulnerable to Israeli control. The Israeli authorities were then able to exploit the lag in the momentum of the uprising to impose severe economic and military reprisals. Tax raids forced Palestinians to resume paying taxes. Thousands flocked back to their jobs in Israel when they found no alternatives in their own communities. Others rejoined the civil administration in a variety of functions. These apparent setbacks highlighted for Palestinians the gap between their willingness to engage in protests, noncooperation, and civil disobedience, and their corresponding understanding of how these methods operated in practice, especially in terms of goals that could realistically be expected and the time it would take to achieve them.[35]

One of the essential characteristics of the *intifada* that highlights the Palestinian experience of nonviolent action was the apparent fearless attitude evinced toward the Israeli occupier, especially in the early months of the uprising.[36] It is almost an axiom of nonviolent struggle that the success of such a movement requires the shedding of fear by the victimized population. As Sharp points out, fear of sanctions—punishment—operates as a powerful deterrent against direct action and ensures the compliance and obedience of a population to an existing regime.[37]

There are countless examples of fearlessness among Palestinians in their confrontations with the Israeli military. Perhaps most indicative was the way Palestinian women, traditionally the target of so many stereotypes, exhibited tremendous courage, to the point of placing their own lives at risk for the sake of their families and communities. Many observers have been impressed by their fearlessness and dignity—how they taunted Israeli soldiers as they walked by, how they rushed to surround soldiers who tried to take away their sons and menfolks. They would scream, shout, bite, and beat at the soldiers with bare hands while they struggled to drag away the youth from the soldiers' grip. In many cases they succeeded in freeing these youths. In one example, in the Gaza Strip, a Palestinian woman came upon two soldiers who were preparing to strike a nine-year-old boy they had just captured. She saw the fear in the boy's eyes and rushed to protect him. The soldiers then threatened her, one pointing a gun at her chest, the other at her back, demanding that she release the boy or else they would shoot. She challenged them fearlessly, "Shoot."[38] In another example, a 14-year-old youth in East Jerusalem was surrounded by police who had come to arrest him. Women from the community quickly surrounded the soldiers and struggled with them until they succeeded in releasing this youth.

Dozens of stories recount what happened when youth fleeing soldiers entered the nearest house to hide. There, the women, and indeed the entire families involved, ran the risk of being beaten or otherwise punished if they were caught sheltering a wanted youth. Yet families responded fearlessly and devised ingenious ways of hiding a youth. In one instance, a woman successfully hid a boy underneath her long traditional gown, and the soldiers who barged into the house looking for him left empty-handed. In another instance, a woman quickly undressed a fleeing lad and shoved him into the bathtub, making it appear as though he was being bathed in his own home by his own mother. He also escaped arrest. Whole communities have risen together to protect or free their fellow citizens. In one example that occurred in El-Bireh in the West Bank in February 1988, Jewish settlers from a nearby settlement entered the town in several cars and tried to kidnap five young girls from an Arab school. The townspeople quickly surrounded the cars and fought to prevent the settlers from taking away the girls. They finally succeeded in having three of the girls released before the settlers drove off with the other two. In another instance, dozens of Palestinians in Ramallah successfully prevented Israeli soldiers from arresting a priest.

No discussion about the fearlessness of the Palestinians would be complete without including some of the stories of bravery among Palestinian youth. One cannot but admire the courage of these young Palestinians who have daily courted death in their confrontations with Israeli soldiers and police units. The *shebab* have been particularly susceptible to Israeli violence. They courageously faced clubs and bullets; they were injured, maimed, and imprisoned. The daring of these young men is especially moving, since many have known that their names appeared on the "wanted" lists of special Israeli units apparently created for the express purpose of killing them.

There are many stories of fearlessness and courage among Palestinian children, kids barely five or six years old who unflinchingly faced Israeli soldiers. In one story that was being told everywhere during the first two months of the *intifada,* a six-year-old Palestinian boy was caught throwing stones. He was roughly questioned by the soldiers who demanded to know who had put him up to this. The boy replied, "My brother Mohammed." The soldiers, armed and in full gear, demanded that the lad lead them to his brother and proceeded to drag him away to his house. Very cautiously, the soldiers surrounded the house, then broke in, calling for Mohammed. Mohammed appeared to face the soldiers; he was three years old.[39]

Despite such tales of fearlessness, Palestinians have not been totally immune from fear. Many may be permanently scarred by the extent of violence perpetrated against them. Young Palestinian children have been especially vulnerable, and there are indications of severe traumatization among youth. Preliminary research has indicated that Palestinian children were exhibiting typical symptoms of fear: bed-wetting, uncontrollable crying, loss of appetite, nightmares, aggressiveness, and the like.[40] The long-term implications of such severe psychological distress remain unclear, but it has certainly been an issue of mounting concern to Palestinian families, educators, and psychologists alike in the Occupied Territories.[41]

These examples of fearlessness illustrate the double-edged nature of the *intifada.* The ways in which it has strengthened and transformed the Palestinian community in the service of the national cause have been counterbalanced by repercussions from the violence against the inhabitants. Palestinians discovered that fearlessness is not enough, that their determination to resist has to build on stronger foundations that will enable them to persist and endure the harshest of reprisals. It was perhaps this realization of indeed how vulnerable they were that persuaded many among the Palestinians to largely abandon indigenous initiatives and direct their attention to the peace talks to achieve the goals they desired.

The Impact of the *Intifada* on Israel

Describing the effects of the *intifada* on Israel requires a look at three broad sectors: the Israeli military, the Israeli public, and the government in Israel. The dynamics of the uprising caused each to be affected in different ways, whether directly or indirectly, or involving different combinations of social, economic, and political elements.

It is not possible to provide a detailed examination here of Israeli society and the body politic. However, there are relevant social distinctions that have implications for Palestinian strategic thinking, especially in considering intersections between class, ethnicity, religion, and ideology in Israel. One area is the complex interweaving of religion in Israel, between orthodox and secular Jews of different political persuasions. Ethnic distinctions exist between Israeli Jews and Israeli Palestinians, who also vary by religion. Then there are the ethnic origins that distinguish Ashkenazi (Western) Jews and Sephardim (Jews of Eastern origin), as well as ideological differences between Israeli settlers in the Occupied Territories and the inhabitants of Israel proper. Interspersed within this general picture are the myriad social distinctions within each sector. These include the class affiliations of different groups, the variety of political parties of both the left and the right that represent them, the peace groups of different persuasions and ideological convictions, the settler groups, and others. The political scene is dominated by the two major blocs of Labor and Likud, commonly referred to as the "left" and the "right," and a vast array of smaller political groupings on either side of the political spectrum. The Israeli army intersects at all these points. This is a citizen's army, in which every Israeli, with the exception of Israeli Arabs, Orthodox Jews, and a limited number of pacifists and women, is required to serve.

The political parties of the left include Israeli Arab parties (among them the Communists, now the People's Party) and the Progressives. Many on the left in Israel are genuinely committed to a "secular" view of the conflict. Some advocate giving up the Occupied Territories and establishing an independent Palestinian state side by side with Israel. Among the observant orthodox Jews can also be found a sector that is avowedly anti-Zionist, believing that the very establishment of the State of Israel is a violation of fundamental Jewish precepts.[42] The left in Israel has wielded relatively little political weight, particularly in the more extreme right-wing governments that have ruled Israel. Religious groups are sometimes lumped together with the rest of the orthodox parties, including committed Zionists, as they reflect the growing primacy of religious concerns in Israeli life. The rest of the Israeli public can be characterized as essentially Zionist and secular, and united in their common perception that whether for religious or other reasons, Jews have a basic right to the whole of the land of Palestine. Such views are commonly held by those who also describe themselves as "liberals" and centrists, and are expressed in the main political parties and groupings that exist in the country. For many of these people, the religious and ideological overtones of the Zionist claim to Palestine appear largely a matter of degree and not one of principle.

Whether for pragmatic or ideological reasons, some Israelis have come to accept that the Zionist venture should stop at the door of the Occupied Territories. These people are generally willing to trade "territory for peace." Among them can be found strong supporters of Palestinian self-rule in the Occupied Territories. For those farther to the right, the Occupied Territories are deemed to be part of the original "Jewish" homeland that Israel "liberated" in 1967 and that should henceforth never be abandoned. For these Israeli Jews, the seizure of the West Bank and Gaza Strip was simply a realization of the dream of "Eretz Israel," the land of Greater Israel. Even more to the right are those who apparently believe that the Zionist dream will not be complete until Israel possesses the whole territory stretching "from the Nile to the Euphrates." This entity would include modern-day Jordan, Syria, parts of Iraq, the Sinai desert, and parts of Egypt. Among the parties advocating some version of this view are Tekhiah and Tsomet, as well as the certain wings within the Likud bloc.[43] These include Likud supporters who believe that at the very least Israel should rightfully include "Eastern Palestine," that is, Jordan, as a part of the Israeli state.[44]

The victory of the first Likud government in Israel in 1977 paved the way for such views to gain prominence and, in effect, bestowed an official stamp of legitimacy on what were previously considered "extremist fringes." These trends were manifested in the emergence of openly racist groups such as Rabbi Meir Kahane's Kach party, and the ascension to power of representatives of settler groups, such as Gush Emunim (Bloc of the Faithful) that openly advocated settling in all parts of the occupied areas as a Jewish right and duty.[45] The ideological position of the Likud bloc also reflected the changing social composition in Israel and the growing number of Oriental and Sephardic Jews. Despite their declining and disproportionate demographic representation, Ashkenazi have dominated political and economic life in Israel since its inception. A history of discrimination, poverty, and struggle among Oriental Jews has caused resentment and anger, and it could explain the consequent funneling of their frustrations against another even more oppressed group, the Palestinians.[46] It was largely from the ranks of the Sephardim that some of the most vocal expressions of hatred and rejection of the Arabs emerged.[47] Many supported Likud, seeing in this and other right-wing parties a means of redressing some of the wrongs committed against them, even at the expense of subjugating another people and depriving them of their rights.

The return to Labor rule in 1992 did not reverse the power of the right in

Israel, in spite of popular support for a peaceful resolution to the Arab-Israeli conflict. Many Israelis disagreed over the "concessions" that would be required for such a resolution, and the Likud bloc continued to mobilize support against such moves. Since the 1980s the right wing in Israel has been backed by the rise of several religious groups, whose growing influence in the country was totally disproportionate to their actual numbers. Many of these aligned themselves with the Likud bloc and reinforced its position on issues pertaining to the Palestinians and the Occupied Territories.[48]

Subsequent governments in Israel in which the Labor Party participated (first as National Unity governments in the 1980s, then the return to Labor rule in 1992) helped to counterbalance and check some of the more extremist positions. However, settlement activity in the Occupied Territories never ceased, and the Labor Party itself agreed with the Likud on the need to establish a certain number of additional settlements in these areas.[49] Both parties have consistently rejected the principle of a two-state solution.[50]

The *intifada* stunned Israel. It was unprecedented, it was organized, and it was universal across the Occupied Territories. Most significantly, it revealed a dimension of Palestinian resistance that Israel had never before encountered in such a sustained and determined manner: it was largely nonviolent. In the opening weeks and months, Israel was put on the defensive, confused about how to respond, and straining to devise ways that would put an end to the uprising at least cost to itself. Israeli efforts concentrated on trying to contain the *intifada* through the well-tried means of violent repression and damage control. Israel's image abroad suffered. What was depicted was a rough and well-equipped army pitted against an unarmed civilian population. This image proved extremely powerful in awakening people to the Palestinian cause and to the fact that they were determined to struggle for it. It was Israel that was seen as using inordinate and unwarranted force to suppress this movement. Although Israel suffered some international censure, the real impact of the uprising should be judged in terms of its impact within Israel itself. The *intifada* succeeded in raising certain "costs" for Israel. Though these proved insufficient to cause it to withdraw from the Occupied Territories, they were serious enough to warrant careful rethinking of tactics and countermeasures.

Economic costs to the army were one facet of overall economic costs to Israel. Other economic costs involved construction activity, which decreased because Arab labor was withdrawn, and exports to the Occupied Territories, which sharply declined. For at least the first year of the *intifada,* tourism to Israel also dropped off significantly.[51] Ultimately, however, economic costs to Israel did not prove significant. The more serious impact of the *intifada* on Israel, especially during its first year or two, lay indisputably in the fact that it succeeded in transforming the "military" issue of "restoring law and order" and "controlling riots" into the fundamental political question of the occupation itself. It was this question that has since preoccupied the Israeli government.

The Israeli Military

Much attention has been paid to the impact of the *intifada* on the Israeli military. Various articles published in Israel and the United States early in the *intifada* pointed to growing demoralization within the Israeli army. Concern was raised over its role in suppressing a civilian population by force, when army training had always concentrated on learning to fight the armed forces of Israel's opponents. Likewise, distinct economic costs were entailed by maintaining a fully equipped, fully alert army in the Occupied Territories at all times. Regular army training programs were disrupted, and more spending on certain types of military equipment for the soldiers was needed for combating the uprising, all at the expense of other programs.[52]

The task of combating the Palestinian *intifada* did not rest solely upon Israel's military. The Israeli police, the Shin Bet (Israeli security service), and Israeli settlers all played a role in Israel's violent response to the uprising.

Israel's response to the uprising passed through various phases. These reflected the direct impact that this struggle had on Israel internally and the degree of damage to Israel's international standing. The violent means of repression used in the early months generated a swell of protest among Arabs and many Israeli Jews within Israel. Several demonstrations were held to protest excessive army violence. Protest was also forthcoming from the international community, including the traditionally cohesive American Jewish community. From the ranks of the latter came expressions of pain, shame, and in some cases outrage at what Israel was perpetrating in the Occupied Territories in the name of the Israeli and Jewish people. Some of this criticism and concern was deemed sufficiently serious as to warrant a change in tactics and responses to the *intifada*. By the third year of the uprising, the Israeli government had reconsidered its techniques. Incidents of Palestinian violence had also increased; there were more cases of firebomb-ings, more arson attacks, occasional stabbings, and the isolated use of firearms. Israeli policy had until then relied on raising the level of violence "permitted" by Israeli troops against Palestinian civilians.[53] New definitions expanded existing open-fire regulations, to allow soldiers to shoot directly at any "masked" Palestinian, regardless of whether there was a clear threat to the soldiers' lives. The military was also permitted to seal or demolish the homes of Palestinians where a family member was "suspected" of throwing gasoline bombs or stones.[54]

Israeli soldiers continued the policy of tossing tear gas canisters into closed spaces and crowded homes, resulting in the paralysis and even death of dozens of Palestinians. Though this claim has been challenged by the Israeli army, tear gas also caused countless miscarriages among pregnant women and contributed to a high fetal mortality rate and a number of other health problems.[55] In a report by Israeli army doctors in June 1988, they referred to army misuse of tear gas in the Occupied Territories, stating that it caused miscarriages among pregnant women. The same report noted the serious injuries caused Palestinians by the use of high-velocity bullets.[56] A report issued by Amnesty International in the first year of the *intifada* documented at least 40 deaths in the Occupied Territories that could be attributed directly to the effects of tear gas thrown into closed spaces.[57] The Israeli army disputed this claim, as it also challenged the findings of an American team of physicians, the Physicians for Human Rights. This team visited the Occupied Territories in early 1988 and documented the "uncontrolled epidemic of violence" by Israeli soldiers and police, who inflicted extensive beatings and smashing of bones, teargassing, and other types of violence against Palestinians.[58]

Several reports covered the incident that took place in the village of Salem near Nablus, where in February 1988 four youths were buried alive upon orders given by Israeli troops at the scene. This was not an isolated incident. In reports that never made their way into American newspapers, there are documented accounts of at least four other cases of live burials of Palestinians. One occurred in the village of Aroura near Bir Zeit, where three youths were allegedly buried in rocks; two other incidents are said to have taken place in Gaza, and one near El-Bireh in the West Bank in April 1988.[59]

The escalation in Israeli violence against Palestinians persisted despite mounting evidence that it was this very violence that was fueling the momentum of the *intifada*. In June 1988 a group of Israeli Knesset members issued a statement that unequivocally charged the army with a policy of routine and systematic beating and shooting of Palestinians.[60] A report in the *Boston Globe* on June 1, 1988, cited a senior Israeli government official to the effect that army violence was practiced indiscriminately against Palestinian civilians, even against those not directly involved in demonstrations. The Israeli military denied reports that soldiers had inflicted extensive physical injury among the civilian population. In the summer of 1990, in recognition of the damage the policy of violent repression was causing Israel, Minister of Defense Moshe Arens (who had replaced Itzhak Rabin) introduced new measures to suppress the *intifada*. This end would be accomplished by a heavy reliance on economic sanctions and other measures to preempt collective action. The decrease in overt violence took the Occupied Territories off the news. This situation did not last long. By the time the United States broke off its dialogue with the PLO, the daily hardships Palestinians faced were growing well beyond their ability to endure. Both Palestinians and Israelis interpreted U.S. moves as indifference to the Palestinian cause. This perception pushed Palestinians to support Saddam Hussein and led Israelis to adopt stricter measures against Palestinians. These included the prolonged curfews of the Gulf War, the increased use of Israeli undercover units, the firing of Palestinian workers from their jobs in Israel, and other tough measures that were adopted in the early months of 1991 and that persisted into the period of the peace talks. During 1992–1993 there were reports of the use of sniper fire against defenseless Palestinians (many children), the demolition of Palestinian homes by anti-tank missiles (especially in the Gaza Strip), and the continued use of undercover units to kill "wanted" Palestinians. Sustained army violence continued to operate alongside repressive economic and social measures.

Far from giving the impression that Palestinian action is irrelevant to the type of Israeli measures that can be used against them, the dynamics of the confrontations between Palestinian civilians and Israeli forces were often quite indicative of the impact of Palestinian action on the latter. Palestinian actions during the early stages of the *intifada* were puzzling, disturbing, and frustrating to Israeli soldiers, and the latter sought to respond accordingly.[61]

Meantime, high-ranking Israeli army officials were assuring the world that excessive brutality was the "exception" and not the rule, and that soldiers had received explicit instructions to shoot only when their lives were in immediate danger and to beat only those Palestinians who were directly involved in violent demonstrations or in resisting arrest. Other Israelis admitted that the exception had become the rule.[62] The contrast between a violent army and unarmed civilians was becoming increasingly difficult to ignore or justify.[63] As Shlomo Avineri, a professor at the Hebrew University, warned, "An army can beat an army, but an army cannot beat a people."[64]

As the *intifada* wore on, the authorities in Israel moved to limit and censor media coverage, especially television. The media were faulted for being antagonistic to Israel.[65] A dispute arose between army and government officials. Each placed responsibility on the other for its method of dealing with the *intifada*. While some in the government, including various Likud ministers, argued that the *intifada* was essentially a case of riots and disturbances that could be quelled by force, high-ranking officials in the army were arguing that the root of the problem had to be addressed politically.[66] Both reservists and military officers began questioning the role of the army in quelling the civilian uprising in the Occupied Territories.[67]

A significant phenomenon that emerged in the early stages of the *intifada* was active civil disobedience by Israeli soldiers who refused to serve in the Occupied Territories. This was a courageous act of defiance by Israeli reservists, coming especially in a society that frowns upon conscientious objection. The Israeli army has always been considered the "sacred cow" of the state.[68] At first reports merely signaled the "frustration" of Israeli troops: "70 per cent of Israel's soldiers were angry and frustrated by a Palestinian uprising in the Occupied Territories."[69] As early as January 1988, however, some 160 reservists had announced their refusal to serve in the Occupied Territories. By the seventh month of the *intifada,* this number had risen to at least 600. It is indicative that in signing their "proclamation," the initial group of officer and reservist "refuseniks" referred to the "absence of a political solution," and not simply the degree of violence, as the reason for their refusal.[70] As one Yesh Gvul activist said at the time, "If 10,000 reservists would say that they won't take part in the occupation, then the Government would have to sit down and come up with a political solution to the problem."[71] By March 1988, some 2,000 reserve officers were urging Prime Minister Shamir to "favor the way of peace."[72] Another report, published in April 1988, stated that 1,250 army officers and commanders had signed a petition that they sent to Shamir, calling for "Territories in Exchange for Peace." The article went on to say that Peace Now believes that "90 percent of the senior officers in the Israeli army are in favor of territorial compromise and the return of the territories in exchange for peace."[73] Some reservists were actually jailed for refusing to serve; however, a *Jerusalem Post* article points out that in reality, "hundreds" have refused to serve and have either been transferred to other areas within the Green Line or have simply produced medical exemptions or traveled abroad.[74]

Former Israeli generals also voiced their concerns. The Council for Peace and Security, which was established in May 1988, included in its ranks former senior officers and other leading army figures who wanted Israel to give up territories for peace. In one council meeting, a prominent general cautioned about new wars and said, "We must arrive at an agreement that the other side can live with. From this it is clear that we must give up most of the territories."[75]

As Zeev Schiff and Ehud Ya'ari point out in their book on the uprising, the *intifada* overturned prevailing notions of security.[76] A sizable number of Israelis regarded the Occupied Territories as crucial to their security, giving their state geographical depth and forming a buffer between them and the Arab world. Yet the *intifada* erupted in their own backyard, so to speak, and on land that was ostensibly under their control. Many Israelis were quite disturbed by this revelation, and were made to rethink prevailing concepts of security. Realization dawned among some that holding onto the occupied lands and controlling another people was not a guarantee of either peace or security. Those on the left in Israel could point the way to peace based on some sort of territorial compromise. Others would come to the opposite conclusion, arguing that the *intifada* proved that Israel should never relinquish the West Bank and Gaza Strip and should do its utmost to prevent the emergence of a Palestinian state. Most Israelis, however, ultimately agreed that some effective political measures were needed to contain the *intifada* and its consequences.

The Gulf War and its aftermath generated a different set of concerns. Iraq's launching of Scud missiles into Israel reinforced the view that territorial depth was indispensable to Israel's security. Some Israelis countered that modern weaponry, such as the Scud missiles, was not halted by geographic borders. Although the lines were not clearly drawn between left and right in Israel on this issue, nor between the army and the public, most Israelis apparently missed a point that Palestinians have tried to signal all along—namely, that a state of war remained possible because of the absence of a just solution. Efforts should, therefore, concentrate on eliminating the political reasons for war, at the heart of which lies the Palestinian issue. Ironically, the very presence of Palestinians in these areas may have protected Israel during the Gulf War, considering that even Saddam Hussein was not likely to deliberately bomb Palestinian areas.

Despite the impact of the *intifada* on Israeli forces, it did not result in widespread dissent within the army, nor did it precipitate a political crisis in Israel over the role of the military. Periodic reevaluation by Israel of its tactics in the Occupied Territories ensured that social distance was maintained between occupier and occupied. This distance prevented Israeli soldiers from coming to direct contact with Palestinians and developing empathy with the population. Deliberate and indiscriminate violence by Israeli soldiers, police, and others was encouraged by the attitude of commanders in the field and by the system of justice in general in Israel. Characteristically, a blind eye was turned to the degree of violence perpetuated against Palestinian civilians, and offenders were only rarely sanctioned. Such policies, in turn, signaled to young soldiers that it is permissible, if not indeed desirable, to harm, injure, or even kill Palestinians. For those who have come with preconceived ideas about Palestinians, or who have been insensitive to the Palestinian context, it has not taken much to incite them to participate in all manner of violations against Palestinians. This point has been amply documented by Israeli soldiers themselves, some of whom were clearly distressed by the actions of their colleagues.[77] Palestinians also contributed to widening the social distance between the two sides by escalating their violent attacks against Israelis. These attacks entrenched a sense of fear, suspicion, and, indeed, hatred of the Palestinians among the Israeli soldiers sent to patrol these areas.

The Israeli Government and Public

Since Palestinian encounters with Israeli civilians (apart from the settlers) have been relatively infrequent and indirect, the dynamics of their influence on the Israeli public and government operates differently than it does with regard to the army or other branches of the occupation authorities. The Palestinian uprising was intended to influence the Israeli public, so as to push it, in turn, to exert pressure on the government to withdraw from the Occupied Territories.

Whether or not consciously planned as such, much of Palestinian action during the *intifada* incorporated tactics that aimed at polarizing the Israeli opponent and widening splits in its society and government over the issue of occupation. Palestinians were aware that their chosen technique provided them with the ability to manipulate the struggle to their advantage. But for most Palestinians, the Israeli public and government constituted a secondary strategic target. No explicit strategy was formulated to affect these specifically, except insofar as they would be influenced indirectly by the pressure of the *intifada*.

There were growing and visible signs of polarization in Israel over the issue of occupation. This would very likely not have occurred had the *intifada* been perceived as a serious threat to Israel's existence. In the event, the uprising clearly contributed to the first political crisis in Israel that revolved directly around the Palestinian issue—namely, the collapse of the National Unity government in March 1990.[78] In June 1990, after two months of political wrangling, a new and narrow right-wing government was formed under the premiership of Itzhak Shamir of the Likud Party. This government remained in place through the opening phases of the peace talks, until new elections the following June ushered in the Labor-led government of Itzhak Rabin.

During Likud's rule, polarization in Israel over the issue of occupation narrowed. Israel had once again consolidated in a more or less unified front after the Gulf War. Israel had also gained the upper hand in the Occupied Territories. Immediate "costs" were found to be bearable. International censure had lost its edge, and Israel discovered it could indeed live with the *intifada*. The huge influx of Soviet Jews into Israel, along with the anticipation that they would eventually replace Arab labor, allayed latent fears of rising economic costs. The Israeli authorities accelerated settlement activity in the Occupied Territories, and Israeli forecasts predicted that the demographic balance would be changed in its favor in a much shorter time. For these reasons, many Jewish Israelis who had been somewhat ambivalent about accommodation with Palestinians in the first place or who had advocated such a stand mainly out of concern for the Jewishness of the State of Israel abandoned the Palestinian issue altogether. Such positions were underscored by the policy of the United States, which continued to give Israel massive amounts of foreign aid and which refused to exert any pressure on Israel to halt settlement activities in the Occupied Territories. The message to Israel was that it would continue to get away with the denial of Palestinian rights. If no "costs" or sanctions were to be incurred, then most Israelis could simply forget about the Palestinians and concentrate on their own problems.

Many Palestinians directed their nonviolent acts into participation in different joint Arab-Israeli efforts to promote peace. They hoped that such means would expose the discrepancy between Jewish values and beliefs—in fundamental human rights, democracy, and the "benevolent occupation"— and the realities on the ground in the Occupied Territories. Perhaps Palestinians anticipated that Israeli Jews would be goaded into their own acts of civil disobedience against their government. For many Israelis, however, such expression of dissent, through direct violation of "illegitimate" laws, was premature. Such acts would likely become acceptable only if Israel's existence as a democratic society was at stake.

Joint Palestinian-Israeli meetings to promote peace have taken place both inside and outside the Occupied Territories. Official Israeli reaction was often negative. Contacts with the PLO were proscribed by the official "Prevention of Terror Act." This act, amended in 1986, was finally repealed altogether in January 1993.[79] For many years, however, it seemed Israelis had no need for such a law. They could take refuge in the image of Palestinian "intransigence" and the various denigrating stereotypes of Palestinians and the PLO. However, once successive Palestine National Council resolutions had sanctioned meetings between PLO figures and "democratic forces" in Israel, Israel had to move quickly to enact laws to prevent such meetings from taking place.[80] Inside Israel and the Occupied Territories, Israeli officials often appeared willing to sacrifice democratic principles and civil rights, and to do everything possible to discourage, even outlaw, contacts and cooperation between Palestinian Arabs and Israeli Jews.[81]

Of the thousands of Palestinian administrative detainees held without charge during the *intifada* (many in the Ansar III camp in the Negev Desert), several were arrested primarily because of their contacts with Israeli Jews. Palestinians noted a pattern: A doctor from Gaza invites Israeli doctors to tour the Shifa Hospital and is later arrested and sent to the desert camp.[82] Four months after some 15 Palestinian writers and journalists met with their Israeli counterparts to sign an agreement concerning coordination of efforts against the occupation, they were summarily thrown into prison. These writers were "accused" of having contacts with Israeli writers.[83] Palestinian psychiatrists would invite their Israeli counterparts to the Occupied Territories to observe the effects of the *intifada,* only to be thrown later into Ansar III. Mubarak Awad, director of the Palestine Center for the Study of Nonviolence, was banished altogether from his homeland on June 12, 1988. He had been vocal and influential in rallying Israeli Jews to the cause of nonviolent resistance and the search for a just peace. In this capacity, Awad seemed to pose a threat to Israeli control.[84] It is widely believed that the repeated detentions of Faisal Husseini, director of the Arab Studies Society in East Jerusalem, had much to do with his regular meetings and contacts with Israeli Jews.[85] A similar experience befell Mamduh Aker, a Palestinian physician who was jailed and placed in solitary confinement during 1991. His case was later adopted by Amnesty International, in recognition of his efforts to mediate peace between Israelis and Palestinians.

Palestinians were also deterred in other ways from establishing contacts with Jews. In at least two incidents during the early months of the *intifada,* Palestinians were actually punished for trying to protect Jewish lives. One of these occurred in April 1988 in the village of Beita. News reports at the time were filled with stories of how some of the Palestinian villagers took the settlers into their own homes to protect them from stone-throwing youth, even after two of their fellow villagers and a young settler were killed, the latter shot accidently by a fellow settler. In response, six Palestinian villagers were expelled, at least 13 houses were completely demolished, and an additional 17 or so were badly damaged. Later it transpired that one of the homes destroyed had actually belonged to one of the Palestinian villagers who had protected the settlers. Palestinians interpreted this as an attempt to provoke them into simply hating Jews and to make them react violently. This response would in turn justify Israel's intransigence and violence toward Palestinians, and legitimize all sorts of stereotypes of the Palestinian terrorist and of the impossibility of peace. In another incident in May 1988, two settlers approached a village near Bethlehem on motorbikes and began behaving aggressively toward the Palestinians. They were taken into the homes of some villagers and protected there until the army came. At that point, the army punished the villagers who had sheltered the settlers. It was they who were beaten and their furniture and other household belongings destroyed.[86]

In spite of these events, neither Israelis nor Palestinians committed to peace were deterred from establishing joint solidarity groups. One sector of the Israeli public that was distinctly affected by Palestinian resistance was the Israeli peace camp. The *intifada* jolted the peace movement out of a lethargy that had lasted virtually since the 1982 invasion of Lebanon. Among more liberal scholars and within the peace movement in Israel there was a discernible sense of horror and shame at the conduct of Israeli officials during the uprising.[87] Sometimes this seemed to derive from concern over what was perceived as an erosion of Jewish ideals and over the damage to Israel's image abroad, rather than concern over the fate of Palestinians in the Occupied Territories.

Joint committees existed for years. The Committee to Confront the Iron Fist is one such group. This committee operates as an umbrella group for a variety of other groups. Since it was formed in the early 1980s, it has concentrated on protesting the severity of Israeli rule in the Occupied

Territories.[88] Other committees are organized around more specific issues. The Committee for Solidarity with Birzeit University and the Committee Against the War in Lebanon are two examples. Another is the Family Reunification Committee, sponsored by the Palestine Center for the Study of Nonviolence. This has been pressing for the right of Palestinians who were forced out in 1967 to rejoin their families in the Occupied Territories.[89]

In a number of well-publicized cases, Israelis have directed their energies to the legal and human rights of Palestinians. Various Jewish-Israeli lawyers, notable among them the two female lawyers and activists Lea Tsemel and Felicia Langer, have both been victims of repeated slander and threats in Israel because of their work. Yet they have persisted in defending Palestinian prisoners and in challenging orders to demolish houses and deport Palestinians. During the *intifada*, many Israeli lawyers from the Association of Civil Rights in Israel defended Palestinians and voiced their growing sense of unease at the incompatibility between occupation and civil rights.[90] Other prominent Israelis, such as Israel Shahak of the Israeli League of Human and Civil Rights, a Holocaust survivor himself, have spent years in tireless and careful documentation of Israel's practices against Palestinians in the Occupied Territories and in documenting repeated violations of human rights and international law in these areas.[91]

The significance of these efforts is that they bring into focus Israel's claim to democracy and respect for the rule of law. The fact that democratic principles have been nonexistent in the treatment of Arabs under occupation is one aspect of this situation. For many of these Israelis, the defense of Palestinians has been linked, directly or indirectly, to the struggle for democracy within Israel itself. One instance was the West Jerusalem–based Alternative Information Center, run by Michael Warschawski, which was raided by the Israeli authorities in February 1987 and then closed down for a time. Its publications, documents, and equipment were all confiscated, and Warschawski himself was detained. Through its newsletter and other publications, this center has long been engaged in critically examining Israeli policy in the Occupied Territories, "to make public facts that are 'alternative' to the image Israel strives to project."[92]

Since the *intifada* began there have been other instances of closure of Israeli publications. On February 18, 1988, the authorities shut down two Israeli journals, the Hebrew *Derech Hanitzotz* and its Arab counterpart, *Tariq A-Sharara*. The editors were accused of having links to the Popular Front for the Liberation of Palestine (PFLP).[93] It was reported that the organization behind these journals, Nitzotz/A-Sharara, was involved in solidarity work during the *intifada*, collecting funds, medications, and food for Palestinian villagers. According to the Jewish publisher of the paper who was arrested and for a long time denied access to a lawyer, the Israeli authorities were trying to "create the atmosphere of a heavy security crime" to overshadow the violations of press freedom.[94]

An editorial in the *Jerusalem Post* of May 11, 1988, sums up the case quite succinctly:

> A thick fog of secrecy is enveloping the entire case. If the authorities do not wish the conclusion to be drawn that the real issue here is not truly state security but the democratic right to air unpopular ideas considered dangerous by the government, then let them promptly lift that fog.

This incident underscores the continuing dilemma that has often confronted Israeli Jews: Could they continue to believe in the essential democratic character of Israel and work within the law to initiate change? Would the restrictions become so harsh that these laws would need to be challenged? As for Palestinians, what could they or should they do, either directly through their *intifada* or indirectly through other efforts, to underscore such concerns? A telling statement on the operation of Israeli democracy comes from an Israeli journalist who refers to this quotation by a High Court judge: "The essence of a Jewish state is to give preeminence to Jews as Jews. Anyone who asks, in the name of democracy, for equality to all its citizens—Jews and Arabs—must be rejected as one who negates the existence of the Israeli state as the state of the Jewish people."[95]

Convenient scapegoats have always existed inside Israel to deflect pressures within. The Israeli authorities have used these to turn the tables against Israeli Jews and others who dared to speak out about their own democratic rights, let alone those of the Palestinians. Israelis have been constantly fed the same refrain: Palestinians are terrorists and a mortal threat to their existence. Jews who criticized the mistreatment and repression of Palestinians under occupation would themselves be suspect. Those who articulated Palestinian rights to self-determination fared even worse. "National security" could always be invoked to silence debate about the violation of press and other freedoms. One example occurred before the *intifada,* in July 1987, when a group of 225 American (including American-Jewish) academics, spoke out on behalf of an Israeli who had been fired from his job at the Ministry of Education and Culture. This Israeli, Gideon Spiro, was a member of the Committee to Confront the Iron Fist. He had written letters to Israeli newspapers critical of the invasion of Lebanon and the violation of human rights in the Occupied Territories. He wrote about the Palestinian right to resist, "While I would prefer to see nonviolent resistance, Gandhi style, I cannot condemn the Palestinian's use of violence when they are being oppressed by violent means."[96] In a petition to the Israeli president, the American group expressed its concern about the violation of democratic principles and civil rights, including freedom of speech and writing. They urged,

> You used your power of pardon in the case of members of the Jewish underground, who were convicted of sabotage and conspiracy to murder innocent Palestinians. And not so long ago, you pardoned a number of senior members of the General Security Service. These officials admitted to being implicated in killing two Palestinian bus hijackers after their capture, forging documents, and bearing false witness before government investigatory committees in order to cover up the murders. These officials can continue in their work, and they are not disqualified from any other government service. It is unthinkable to us that such crimes can be pardoned while criticism of the government can be punished—and punished so severely.[97]

In other joint efforts Israeli Jews have worked alongside Palestinians in such activities as planting trees or reclaiming lands. One such venture took place in January 1986 in the village of Qatanna in the West Bank. This was later publicized in the film *Courage Along the Divide*.[98] In this incident, Israeli officials from the Ministry of Agriculture, Nature Reserves, and other agencies uprooted some 2,000 olive trees from lands owned by the villagers. In response, the Palestine Center for the Study of Nonviolence organized more than 100 people, including Palestinians, and Jews from the Israeli Chapter of the International Fellowship of Reconciliation, to plant new olive trees where the others had been uprooted. The Israeli authorities appeared on the scene, began tearing out these new seedlings as quickly as they were being planted, and ordered all the participants to leave. Under military law, the planting of fruitful trees without a permit is a punishable offense.[99] Although the Palestinians were not successful in their efforts, their activities highlighted the potential of joint undertakings, particularly where constructive nonviolent action was taken against the occupying regime.[100]

The *intifada* clearly provided the impetus for greater coordination and cooperation between Jews and Palestinians. Contacts between Israeli and Palestinian writers and journalists, both prior to and during the uprising, culminated in the convening of a joint press conference on June 13, 1988. This joint committee, originally formed in 1985, was called the Israeli and Palestinian Writers and Artists and Academics Committee Against Occupation and for Peace and Freedom. According to a newspaper report, the main topic addressed at this conference was the need for a just peace and a halt to repressive Israeli practices against Palestinians and intellectuals.[101]

Israeli women have been particularly active during the *intifada*. One group that organized continuous vigils was Women in Black. Once a week, participants stood on street corners in West Jerusalem and other major

Israeli cities, silent, sometimes holding placards, and protesting the occupa-tion.[102] Delegations of Israeli women from the Movement of Democratic Women in Israel, the Council for Israeli Palestinian Peace, the Committee to Stop the Occupation, the Women's Organization for Political Prisoners, and others frequently traveled to the Occupied Territories to express solidarity with the Palestinians and meet with Palestinian women and various commit-tees. Together, these women have sent memoranda of protest to the United Nations and other human rights and women's organizations.[103]

Israeli peace groups that had earlier been criticized for not coming out more forcefully in support of Palestinian nonviolent activities felt especially vindicated by the *intifada*. Yet, as one article reminded its readers, Palestin-ian resistance during the *intifada* was essentially the same as their resistance throughout the occupation; "Why doesn't the Israeli left know this?" the writer Beth Goldring asks.[104] She criticizes the arrogance of Israelis who take it upon themselves to decide how Palestinians should resist as a precondition to securing Israeli support. She suggests that if Israelis are "truly interested in nonviolence," they could support "already existing Palestinian nonviolent efforts" and put "effort into confronting the massive disinformation campaign that keeps most Israelis, and foreigners, ignorant of the Palestinian situation."

In a very similar vein, Israel Shahak criticizes Peace Now and other left-wing groups for their acquiescence to the terms of discourse set by the Israeli authorities. Shahak maintains that nonviolent methods have long been practiced by Palestinians in the Occupied Territories, but that these are defined as "rebellion" by the Israeli authorities. As for the left and peace groups, they "are unanimous in refusing to support the Palestinians when the whole population actually employs nonviolent methods and by their silence they actually support their oppression."[105] Shahak charges that the same indifference applies to organizations in the West that praise nonviolent methods in theory, but are "silent when Palestinians who try to practice what they say are cruelly punished for it."

In Israel, demonstrations, rallies, and marches organized by the peace groups early in the *intifada* were attended by tens of thousands of people. On June 4, 1988, in a march and rally that was held in Tel Aviv to mark 21 years of occupation, an estimated 10,000 people participated. Slogans called for an end to occupation, for Israeli-Palestinian peace, and for bringing the soldiers home. This particular demonstration was organized by a coalition of about 20 groups. More than 50 Israeli groups and organizations in all were said to be involved in the campaign to end the occupation. These drew their support largely from the "grassroots" and were distinguished from traditional organizations such as Peace Now. Writing in the *Middle East International,* Peretz Kidron explains that Peace Now "remains largely dormant, principally due to its reluctance to challenge the Labor Party."

Instead, concerned Israelis have been flocking to more militant and active groups.[106]

One such organization whose formation coincided with the *intifada* was The 21st Year.[107] A central focus of this group's activities was to achieve an Israeli withdrawal from the Occupied Territories. Its "Covenant for the Struggle Against the Occupation"[108] outlines the group's philosophy and objectives. This covenant notes that "by accepting the terms and norms of political conduct set by the regime," Israeli society "implicitly collaborates with the Occupation." The 21st Year proposes direct political action against the occupation based on a "refusal to cooperate." Part of this noncooperation would be social: the refusal to participate in "any celebration, ceremony or symbolic occasion" connected with the occupation. Members of The 21st Year declared their refusal to travel to the Occupied Territories "uninvited by the local Arab inhabitants." Their economic noncooperation would take the form of refusing to participate in the exploitation of Palestinian labor, and to "publicize and boycott" all institutions, products, and the like whose "Palestinian employees are denied human dignity and decent working conditions." Another course of action proposed by the group is to be "physically present" to protest and stop the "coercion, humiliation, and beatings" of Palestinians in the Occupied Territories.[109] Some of the political actions suggested bordered on civil disobedience. The group makes clear its determination "not to obey any military command ordering us to take part in acts of repression or in policing in the Occupied Territories." Another important focus of this group's activity was the military; it involved instructing Israeli youth and soldiers on the choices they have available should they refuse to serve in these areas.[110] One activist in this organization summarizes these efforts as geared to "raising the price of the occupation."[111]

What is significant about The 21st Year and other groups such as Yesh Gvul (There Is a Limit) is the central place occupied by the army in their political action campaigns. Unlike Palestinian action in this regard, these organizations are in a position to work directly within the military. However, their ability to influence soldiers and other Israelis is likely to vary depending on the predominant type of resistance in the Occupied Territories. Should it be perceived mainly as the struggle of a civilian population against an occupying army, Israeli demoralization—and hence the effectiveness of Yesh Gvul, The 21st Year, and others—could increase. Conversely, an escalation in violent attacks by Palestinians, even when restricted to attacks against the Israeli military, may cause the opposite reaction.

Even within the ranks of staunchly Zionist groups, disaffection with the occupation was on the increase. A group called End to Occupation also made its debut during the *intifada* and included among its ranks some dedicated Zionist supporters. Their participation reflected concerns that

Israel was being harmed by its continued occupation of the West Bank and Gaza Strip, and, accordingly, members of this group perceived that it was in Israel's long-term interest to give up these territories. Some of their concerns, it should also be acknowledged, stemmed from their fear of the "demographic threat" posed by the presence of a large Arab minority in their midst.

In another vein, particularly since the *intifada,* Israeli authorities targeted another group, the Israeli Arabs. By trying to sow seeds of dissention and suspicion in their midst, the authorities would direct the population's attention away from the Palestinians and their plight. It was both inevitable and understandable that Israeli Arabs, the Palestinians of Israel, were among the first to express sympathy and support for the *intifada.* Their outrage at the extent of Israeli violence used to suppress the uprising led them to establish support groups and send food and aid to the Occupied Territories. Israeli Arabs also organized marches and demonstrations within the Green Line. In such cities as Haifa and Nazareth these demonstrations were attended by tens of thousands of people. According to news reports, such numbers were unprecedented in Israeli history. The Israeli authorities immediately interpreted this activism as disloyalty to the Israeli state. Thus Israeli Arabs exercising their democratic rights of freedom of expression were portrayed as showing their "true colors" of hostility to Jews and Israel. Several were placed in administrative detention for their activism. Some were beaten, a significant number of their houses were destroyed (allegedly for building without permits), and there were even reports of reimposing the British Emergency Regulations of 1945, which were abolished for Israeli Arabs in 1966 but remained in force in the Occupied Territories. Singling out this Arab minority in Israel as the new scapegoat would deflect attention from real issues concerning the plight of Palestinians under occupation. Concerned Jews and Arabs could, therefore, pool their energies to work for a just peace and counteract such a ploy.

Following the Gulf War, many Israeli peace groups experienced a decline in membership. They found their own interests, indeed their very motivation and commitment, tested by what they perceived as a Palestinian betrayal. Although some joint efforts were later revived, these did not attain the same momentum of earlier years. Some Israeli activists simply became complacent. In their view, their political interests were being officially represented and protected by the participation in the Labor-led government of *Meretz* (the coalition of leftist and progressive groups, including the Citizens Rights Movement, the Democratic List for Peace and Equality, and the Progressive List for Peace). There was no longer any need to risk being seen as undermining the political process. Similar inertia existed on the Palestinian side. Attention and energy were diverted to the Washington talks away from events on the ground in the Occupied Territories.[112]

*   *   *

The *intifada* has arguably been a double-edged sword. Although its main target remained essentially the Israeli occupation, there is no question that in the course of resistance, Palestinian society itself was being transformed. In its initial stages, the *intifada* reorganized and empowered Palestinians toward greater self-sufficiency, increased unity and solidarity, greater participation in the administration of their own affairs, and an undeniable determination to continue the struggle. While most writings on the *intifada* have extolled its virtues, we cannot overlook the fact that there has been a backlash. The repercussions within the Palestinian community have been enormous, if as yet incompletely analyzed. Over the years of the uprising Palestinian planners learned that resistance could not continue to be an exercise in trial and error, whereby a selection of techniques and methods are tried and abandoned, just to see if and how they work. Instead, they realized that the occupation would be a prolonged affair, and that they had to prepare for that eventuality.

The early phases of the uprising illustrate clearly the dynamics of active resistance against the Israeli occupation. Periods of activism and euphoria were followed by periods of stagnation, weariness, and paralysis. The launching of the Palestinian *intifada* contributed to changing the image of Palestinians where it seemed to matter most, in Israel and in the United States. From their portrayal as a violent people, bent on armed struggle and "terrorism" against Israel, Palestinians were more likely to be perceived as a people with a national cause. As the *intifada* wore on, news of the Occupied Territories receded from the headlines. The plight of the Palestinians was largely forgotten until Iraq's occupation of Kuwait in August 1990 and the Gulf War in January 1991 brought the Palestinians back to the forefront of the news. Their apparent "cheering" for Saddam Hussein placed Palestinians on the losing side in the war and maligned them and their intentions. Their actions were presented as "proof" that the PLO should be totally discredited and barred from any future negotiations. It was as though support for Iraq would automatically disqualify Palestinians from the pursuit of their legitimate national rights—a double standard that was not lost on them.

After the Gulf War, Palestinians woke up to another harsh reality. They realized that they would essentially have to rely on themselves. Although this was an underlying motive in their launching of their *intifada* in the first place, somehow, even then, the implications did not seem to sink in. True, Palestinians had taken matters into their own hands. They were empowered and gained strength and energy in their confrontation with Israel. They developed the attitude that they could seize their independence, nonviolently, with or without Israel's "permission." Perhaps they thought that their struggle would create sympathy and pressure to act; they thought surely America would reexamine its policy, and surely the Arab states would rally to support them. If all else failed, then surely the PLO, with all its apparent political concessions, would be invited to participate at the negotiating table. Instead of these predicted outcomes, Palestinians in the Occupied Territories saw their struggle and sacrifices resulting in even worse conditions of daily life for themselves and their families and in more stubbornness on the part of Israel. They found themselves even farther, if possible, from the realization of their political goals. Their *intifada* turned into factional infighting. Conflicts erupted over the appropriate roles of women in the struggle; there was violence among youth, religious extremism, and a paralysis in thinking and planning over how to deal with Israel.

It was in part these very doubts, concerns, and misplaced optimism that led Palestinians to join the peace talks. Many Palestinians were of the opinion that Israel would not have been willing to negotiate in the first place had it not been for the *intifada*. Palestinians also realized that they were at a disadvantage. Arab states would join anyway; the PLO was in serious financial and organizational disarray; and the institutionalization of the occupation on the ground had proceeded apace and was rapidly reaching a point when it would be irreversible.

Palestinians initially felt they had been given a new lease on life by the peace process, and they waited for results. As these talks faltered, Israeli repression intensified. The very fabric of Palestinian society seemed to be tearing apart at the seams. It appeared that Israel had gained the upper hand and that Palestinians were the ones who had to attempt "damage control." Palestinian thinkers realized that negotiations had to proceed from a position of strength; that is, negotiations in Washington had to be grounded in institution-building and alternative resistance within the Occupied Territories.[113] These hopes, however, did not materialize. Many Palestinians inside the Occupied Territories blamed the PLO for its autocratic and centralized style of control and its veto over local initiatives. Others would point to the polarization in the Palestinian community resulting from disagreements over the peace talks and would warn of the impending fragmentation of their society. It was in this atmosphere that in the summer of 1993 the PLO and Israel negotiated their secret deal for "Gaza and Jericho first" and for interim self-rule to begin in these areas.

Chapter Five will return to the question of strategy, to examine whether Palestinians can develop the means to cope with the task of reorganizing the Palestinian community on firmer grounds, while still affecting the occupation regime to induce it to withdraw completely from the Occupied

Territories. These undertakings and the strategy that organizes them would need to address developments generated by the peace talks and the immediate requirements of self-rule. Before turning to these issues, Chapter Four will examine theoretical and conceptual concerns underlying strategic formulation.

Four

Nonviolent Civilian Resistance: Theoretical Underpinnings

As was pointed out in an earlier chapter, analysis of both the *intifada* and the general feasibility of nonviolent civilian resistance derives from the strategic or "practical" school. This perspective defines a nonviolent struggle as a "war," albeit one that is waged without lethal weapons. Instead of aiming to change the heart of the opponent or to convert the enemy to one's point of view, nonviolent action rests on changing the balance of power between the resistance and the opponent. The aim is to prevent the latter from exercising its power, and to force it to reach an acceptable accommodation with the goals of the resistance. Such action is not without "principles." Underlying even practical nonviolent struggle is a clear preference for avoiding bloodshed and for preserving human life. Implicit in this is the premise that the solution to the Palestinian-Israeli conflict should be based on mutual rights to sovereignty and independence for both peoples—a two-state solution. Another consideration guiding the selection of such action is that given the asymmetrical relationship between Palestinians and Israel, the resistance cannot employ "power" equal to that of their opponent. Therefore, instead of being engaged in a futile struggle to destroy Israel's power structures, Palestinians would be struggling to defeat Israel's political will. Wielding power in this way is entirely possible through nonviolent civilian resistance.

Nonviolent Civilian Resistance

At first glance nonviolent civilian resistance may appear a contradiction in terms. The assumption, at least in the literature on the subject, is that the two are synonymous: Civilian resistance presumes nonviolent struggle, while nonviolent resistance assumes a strong civilian (versus military) base.

Among the many definitions of civilian resistance is that of William Gamson, who refers to it as a movement that utilizes "direct action to protest, counter and oppose the actions or policies of others."[1] In a similar vein, Paul Wehr describes civilian resistance as "that weapon which denies control of a state's social, political and economic institutions to the oppressor."[2] Elsewhere, Wehr provides an example based on the Norwegian case. He explains that under Germany's occupation during World War II, Norway was a "classic case of nonviolent resistance."[3] He describes the political, social, voluntary, and communication institutions and structures that were mobilized against the occupying regime. In his view, such resistance was possible and effective because of "the self-limiting and goal attaining characteristics of the methods used." Of these methods he cites three:

> "Minimal use of violence by the civilian population."
> "Focus on protecting their institutions, not liberating already occupied territory."
> "Providing control through creating unity by way of existing structures and networks."[4]

Protecting and reinforcing national institutions so that they cannot be used by an invader, is, therefore, crucial to this undertaking.

Other definitions highlight the nonviolent component. Gene Sharp, whose extensive writings on the subject are well known, depicts the dynamics of nonviolent action through mass mobilization of a civilian population "against invasion forces and occupation regimes."[5] Among the twentieth-century struggles he cites are strikes and protests preceding the Russian Revolution (1905), Gandhi and the nonviolent struggle in South Africa (beginning 1906), India (1930–1931), selected struggles against the Nazis (in Norway, the Netherlands, and Denmark), resistance in Guatemala (1944), struggles in Czechoslovakia against Soviet occupation (1968), and the preludes to the American civil rights movement in Montgomery, Alabama (1955–1956). These examples indicate that in certain settings, including foreign occupation, nonviolent action is both possible and effective; and in the view of the observers who document such resistance, it is a powerful and viable alternative to violence.

Social or civilian-based defense (CBD) embodies similar principles. Sharp refers to civilian defense as "the use of prepared nonviolent resistance to defeat domestic usurpations and foreign invasions."[6] Clarifying the distinctions between civilian defense and the civilian resistance discussed previously, Sharp underscores the role of civilian defense strategies as an alternative to warfare in "national defense." He writes, "Civilian-based defense is an application, in a refined and developed form, of the general technique of nonviolent struggle, to the problems of national defense."[7] Other writers have long been preoccupied with nonmilitary alternatives to defense. Addressing the needs of smaller European countries, these writers have been concerned with developing viable defense strategies that would minimize the threat of warfare and the potential for nuclear annihilation.[8] Essentially, civilian-based defense envisions that the population of a given country or community would be organized within their respective social-structural or institutional settings on the basis of two guiding principles: deterrence and defense.

Deterrence assigns the civilian population the responsibility for developing the appropriate institutional structures that would deter, or as Sharp says, "dissuade," (foreign) aggression.[9] They would create indigenous loci of power that would make it clear to a potential aggressor that it would pay a high price for its invasion.[10] Preexisting national institutions could readily be activated and mobilized in the nonviolent resistance struggle. These include local governments, trade unions, and professional, cultural, and religious associations. Traditional institutions could also be mobilized. Clans and tribes, customary cultural symbols, and established indigenous institutions, such as religion, could function as alternative "loci of power."[11] An aggressor would realize that subduing the population and inducing their cooperation would be difficult, as the people in question would already be organized in settings that provide a counterweight to a would be aggressor. The *intifada* operated precisely on such principles; since the 1970s, community organizations have expanded, increased their membership, and otherwise mobilized in readiness for the mass civilian uprising.[12]

In instances where deterrence fails, the conquered population would resort to civilian-based defense to deny the occupier its political will. Civilian-based defense acknowledges that an aggressor may rely on the superior military might at its disposal to proceed with a planned aggression or occupation anyway. The civilian population may be unable to forestall such actions. However, once "territory" is occupied or conquered, the aggressor would find it exceedingly difficult to win the cooperation of the people. It is this cooperation that would be required to install and operate the controlling regime. If obedience is not forthcoming, or indeed if resistance is mounted, then the occupier may find itself in a "weaker" position, whereby "costs" multiply in proportion to the force necessary to impose its rule.

Much of the research into civilian-based defense has been undertaken in various Scandinavian countries (specifically Sweden) and in Europe. The impetus behind this investigation came from the threat of worldwide nuclear conflagration, especially under conditions that existed throughout the Cold War. Many smaller countries felt trapped between the interests of the two superpowers, the United States and what was then the Soviet Union. In response, several countries opted to investigate a means of defense that would give them some measure of control over their own destinies. They chose this course instead of relying on conventional weapons or on their alliances with more powerful regimes to protect their security.[13] What is significant is that such defense creates conditions whereby a struggle is not necessarily fought on the opponent's terms.[14] Even if the struggle is not won, neither is it lost entirely. The opponent, therefore, is at a distinct disadvantage. Social defense may serve to demoralize an enemy and increase the costs of its control and suppression.

The mechanisms of civilian-based defense are important for the Palestinian case. On the one hand, throughout the proposed interim period, an "autonomous" Palestinian entity in the West Bank and Gaza Strip may well be vulnerable to renewed occupation by Israel, as well as to invasion by an Arab army (should some perceived provocation arise). Palestinians would need to devise ways to deter such aggression in the first place or, if it does occur, to defend against it and resist it. These preparations would need to be undertaken while Palestinians are still engaged in the struggle to end all vestiges of Israeli occupation and while they are moving from self-rule to complete independence. It is envisioned that the autonomous Palestinian entity (or entities) would have no military power beyond that of a local police force responsible essentially for maintaining internal law and order. Palestinians must, therefore, rely on the institutions and structures of civil society that exist or could yet be created to fashion the underpinnings of their resistance. Much as they did throughout the *intifada,* Palestinians can build on the institutions and organizations within their society to deny the occupier its political will. Once again, the underlying premise is that the "power" of the people rests in their ability to defeat the political will of their opponent rather than defend "territory" as such.

Another reason for considering the potential for civilian-based defense in the Palestinian case is that the same Scandinavian countries that have been involved in research and planning around civilian-based defense are those whose good offices helped broker the Israeli-PLO agreement for interim self-rule and mutual recognition (specifically Norway). These countries are well positioned to lend their expertise to Palestinians in the Occupied Territories. They may help Palestinians prepare for and engage in civilian-based defense, in order to protect themselves through the uncertain interim phases ahead.

The Issue of Power

The dynamics of nonviolent action, whether referred to as nonviolent civilian resistance, social defense, or civilian-based defense, cannot be appreciated without referring to the issue of power. Various analysts have often faulted Sharp and others in the field for their failure to investigate the structural roots of power systematically and for failing to locate these appropriately in their theories of nonviolent action. In its barest outlines, Sharp's theory of power hinges on obedience—on the question "Why do people obey?" In his view, "power" is located in both the rulers and the ruled. In order to be able to wield "power" effectively, the nonviolent technique depends upon the oppressed and ruled people "withdrawing their consent" from their ruler or opponent. They would do so by refusing to obey and cooperate with the regime in question.[15] Sharp argues that, for a variety of reasons, people tend to automatically obey their rulers, their governments, and their oppressors. As he explains, one reason for this tendency may be fear of sanctions (punishment), but there are other reasons as well. Some relate to tradition or habit, or to the feeling that people have a "moral obligation" to obey. Other reasons may include perceptions of self-interest and identification with the authority figure.[16] It is, however, when this compliance is withdrawn, when people question or challenge the legitimacy of the power of the ruler—its "authority"—that the essence of the power relationship is transformed. The withdrawal of consent becomes paramount in resisting the "power" of oppressors.

The technique of nonviolent action depends precisely on people becoming aware of their own power.[17] When they refuse to obey and when they take direct action to consolidate their own position against the opponent, their people power can throw the power of the opponent off balance. The locus of the power of the people, then, lies not in their ability to change the oppressor's social structures but in their ability to challenge, even defeat, the political will of their opponent.

As it stands, Sharp's theory of power relies heavily on individual and "voluntaristic" behavior,[18] when in reality social power is deeply rooted in social relationships and patterns of social behavior that are institutionalized over time and are pervasive throughout society. Power is located in the social structures in which these patterns exist and are reproduced. In any given society, social class arrangements are the more likely manifestations of this distribution of power. Social classes intersect in turn with different ethnic, religious, and other sociocultural elements of a given society.

People's "obedience" to rulers, therefore, is not so much an element of free personal choice that can be reversed at will, but a characteristic of the way society is organized. Instead of asking, "Why do people obey?" the more appropriate question could be asked in reverse, "Who is being served?" or, even more accurately so as to reflect structural, as opposed to individual realities, "Why do power relationships persist?" Once framed in this way, the sociostructural context that organizes and institutionalizes power relationships can be unmasked.[19] Similar social patterns would also explain the origins and perpetuation of the system of colonial rule in the occupied West Bank and Gaza Strip.

As earlier chapters indicated, this colonial rule is characterized and dominated by distinct relations between the colonizer and the colonized. These are reflected in the processes of marginalization, dependency, and integration outlined earlier. Once "power" is located in established social patterns and structures and unmasked as such, then identifying avenues for countering this power becomes possible and meaningful. Social movements, including resistance to colonial rule, originate in precisely such situations where the structures of control have become so pervasive as to totally dominate the lives of the oppressed. At some point, this domination is exposed for what it is, its sources are unmasked and discredited, and resistance to it can then be undertaken.[20]

We must now make the transition (or leap) from a structural theory of power to a type of action that can withstand or challenge this power, and to make a compelling case for the effectiveness of nonviolent civilian resistance in this scenario. Our theory of power dynamics has to account for at least three factors, in order to be credible for this type of strategy.

The first consideration is the conceptual compatibility of this technique with a structural theory of power. If indeed Sharp's theory of "withdrawal of consent" is unsatisfactory because it fails to analyze the structural roots of power in society, then a convincing theory of power must make these necessary links. It should be able to connect the general premises surrounding the geneses of social and revolutionary movements to a viable and coherent strategy of nonviolent resistance. This perspective should account for such factors as the roots of social movements, the "power" and resources available to the opponent and the resistance, and the means available for changing power relationships.

A second consideration is that the theory of power must unmask the sources of power in a given context. This unmasking is indispensable to any process of strategic formulation. Beyond the question of "violent" or "nonviolent" techniques, this issue is fundamental to the very selection of a particular strategy. The sources of the opponent's power must be identified, whether these be structural, ideological, or a combination thereof.[21] Once these sources of power have been unmasked—that is, once the structural underpinnings have been identified and exposed in terms of who, precisely, they exist to serve—then the task of strategic formulation can proceed. Sources of power (of both the resistance and the opponent) can then be taken as reference points to guide the resistance. These are essential in deciding such strategic issues as where to secure the weak points of the resistance, where to mobilize and organize most effectively to wield power, and where to locate and develop "alternative" loci of power.[22] Similar identification must be made for the opponent, as well as its political, social, economic, and ideological sources of power and the avenues that are available to the resistance to target these sources of power.

From the Palestinian perspective, identification of sources of power of both the resistance and the opponent would proceed initially, to be followed by a strategy that is based, at one level, on decentralized and diffuse loci of power. This development seems inevitable, in order to counter Israel's hegemonic control over the occupied areas effectively. Such a conceptualization of "power" in the Palestinian community leaves open the question of a future role for the PLO in the Occupied Territories, especially during the interim stages of autonomy. At this time, the PLO may be reconstituted as another political force on the ground in the Occupied Territories, and would henceforth be expected to work from the inside to resolve the final status of the West Bank and Gaza Strip. Its relationship to other parties and organizations in these areas would have to be worked out so as to ensure the appropriate degree of decentralization and independence of action, both within the community and against the occupying regime.

In view of the asymmetrical power relationship in this setting, a strategic wielding of power against the Israeli opponent may have to take the form of attempts to defeat the political will of this opponent, rather than to destroy directly its structures of colonial control. This observation brings us to the third consideration underlying the significance of a theory of power to strategic formulation—that understanding the location and operation of power will contribute to a more convincing assessment of the viability of the method of nonviolent civilian resistance. Frequently dismissed out of hand as a naive, unrealistic, and nonviable option (a dismissal that commonly rests on an incomplete analysis of power in many of the writings on the issue), this method could indeed be reconciled with a more comprehensive and rooted view of power and analyzed in various comparative contexts. If traditional "structural" theories of power lead resisters (or analysts of social movements) to conclude automatically that war or guerrilla warfare are the only means of toppling such power, our task is to assess whether the same theory of power is amenable to the opposite conclusion—namely, that nonviolent struggles are neither exotic nor naive, and may offer comparable successes.[23] The cases of South Africa and India are informative.[24]

South Africa

The South African situation provides interesting parallels with the Occupied Territories. Here too was a settler colony, in this case dominated by white South Africans. Blacks formed the demographic majority but were oppressed, discriminated against, and denied equal rights in their own country. Similarities in the setting are complemented by parallels in the specific factors that contributed to various types of struggle and to some of the outcomes in each instance. Without suggesting an identical situation, some general comparisons with the Occupied Territories can be made.

Briefly, prior to European colonization, both South Africa and early Palestine were characterized by precapitalist social formations—largely peasant-based agricultural economies. The impact of colonization was to introduce in each instance the beginnings of capitalist structures and relations of production, which either destroyed or seriously transformed indigenous formations. The impact was not only structural; in each case, the settler group was primarily European, ethnically distinct, and motivated by ideologies that justified their supremacy and dominance. Thus, in South Africa, early European settlements were established on farming lands expropriated from black South Africans. These Africans were pushed in turn into poor and congested "Native Reserve" areas, to be exploited as a migrant labor force for the South African economy, for example, in the mining industry.[25] In both the Occupied Territories and South Africa, therefore, the ethnically segregated labor structure became a major point of contention in the respective struggles and a focal point of resistance.

Moreover, both Israel and South Africa subsequently faced the contradiction between taking measures that further destroyed indigenous social formations and having to assume the increased costs of maintaining the native population. In the Occupied Territories, this process took its most extreme form in the Gaza Strip, and it was a compelling reason for Israel to consider withdrawing from this area and for transferring "costs" to the Palestinians. By the late 1940s, the situation of blacks in the reserves had so deteriorated that the South African government decided on institutionalized separation, intended to preserve the profitable migrant labor system without increasing costs for whites—hence, the system of apartheid and separate development. The Bantustans, Bantu homelands, or black states, as these reserve areas were called at various times, were to enjoy a degree of autonomy, and the central government of South Africa was no longer responsible for them.

In both the Occupied Territories and South Africa, the structural conditions were similar enough to give rise to comparable struggles. One significant feature shared by these two struggles was the precedence of national (or in the case of South Africa, racial) origins over and above class issues. Even though labor was traditionally the "vanguard" of the resistance movement in South

Africa and became increasingly so in the Palestinian case, especially after the *intifada,* the struggle was distinctly anticolonial in each case. In another parallel, in both South Africa and the Occupied Territories, the resistance movement was dominated by an organization that in varying degrees existed outside the area, whose leadership lived largely in exile. This statement does not do justice to the complexity of the situation, especially in South Africa, where many organizations proliferated to resist apartheid, of which the African National Congress (ANC) was perhaps the best known internationally. However, what this comparison does underscore is the difficulty of strategic formulation in each instance, as well as the difficulty in achieving consensus and unity between and within various groups.

Another parallel worth noting is in the mode of resistance. As in the Occupied Territories, the decades of struggle against apartheid were characterized by mainly nonviolent action: Strikes, boycotts, protests, institution building, and other forms of civil disobedience and noncooperation dominated resistance activities. As William Pomeroy notes, the initial strategy of the South African liberation movements in the 1950s was consciously nonviolent, "It was only after exhausting every possible nonviolent means that its component groups . . . (ANC, CP, Indian Congress, trade unions) . . . decided on the armed action."[26] He maintains that "serious" armed struggle did not begin until 1967, in response to increased intransigence and repression by the government. As the South African Communist Party explains, the government closed all "legal and peaceful channels of protest and resistance," leaving the South African people with no other recourse but to use violent and illegal methods to make their case heard.[27]

Taking into account the different international and regional contexts of each of the two struggles, it is interesting to note that in the case of South Africa, it was the black South African people who first launched "spontaneous" violent resistance, which was later adopted and steered by the leadership. Among the Palestinian people, the situation was reversed; PLO action outside the Occupied Territories concentrated on guerrilla warfare, while inside the people launched their largely nonviolent *intifada,* on which the leadership later capitalized. Without weighing the effectiveness of one or the other mode of struggle, this example certainly illustrates that nonviolent action can have a distinct impact against an oppressor. In South Africa, the decades after the 1960s were characterized by the shifting back and forth between various methods, but nonviolent resistance increasingly predominated during this period. By the 1980s, the South African people had regrouped and mobilized inside differentiated sociopolitical structures that were extremely effective in putting pressure on the central government. Black South African trade unions were an example of this success, and it could be said that this type of increased mobilization in different civilian sectors contributed significantly to the demise of apartheid in the 1990s.[28]

India

The struggle of the Indian people against British colonial rule provides a strikingly different example of resistance against colonialism.

Unlike South Africa, early Palestine, and later the Occupied Territories, the British colonizers were not attempting to establish a settler colony in India. Nevertheless, the Indian people were subjected to harsh and repressive colonial rule as British imperial strategy aimed at exploiting Indian resources and benefiting from cheap products and profitable trade routes. Conditions prevailing in India in the early part of the twentieth century were characterized by the general inability of the masses of poor people to mobilize resources for an all-out guerrilla war. Moreover, in conformity to colonial strategies of "divide and rule," the British exploited existing social divisions to coopt certain groups into service with the colonial regime, as government officials and as members of the police force.

In view of the distinct circumstances operating in India, an effective struggle against colonialism had to assume forms different from those outlined earlier. Out of his experience in South Africa very early in the twentieth century, Mohandas Gandhi carried back with him to India a strategy for nonviolent revolution—*satyagraha* (a combination of "truth" and "power"). It is not clear whether Gandhi's strategy incorporated from the beginning a goal of total independence and liberation. It was clear, however, that his method was to be used as a form of political "*jiu-jitsu*" about which Sharp writes, both against Indians who exploited other Indians and against the British.[29] One aim was to draw attention to the injustice and hardships of British rule, as well as to "convert" the British into accepting the Indians as equal partners in negotiations for some form of self-rule. Only after continuous violence and repression on the part of the British did Gandhi and others become firmly convinced that the British must go.[30]

Gandhi's program of *satyagraha* incorporates several of the methods of nonviolent action and nonviolent civilian resistance examined earlier. It may be described as strategy that combines direct action with constructive work, and in this way it parallels closely the actions taken by Palestinians in their resistance against occupation.[31] Indians aimed to expose the extent of British violence and to establish that its colonial rule could not proceed without the "consent" of the people, which in this case would be withdrawn. This strategy suggests another parallel with the Occupied Territories. One area where the Indian struggle was unique, however, was in the ideological underpinnings, especially those that espoused principled nonviolence. Gandhi firmly believed that any strategy of revolution had to consider both means and ends. The same conceptualization had to build toward a nonviolent revolution that would pay back in the future in the form of a strong independent nation that valued human life and preserved a peaceful existence. Gandhi hoped to mobilize the

Indian people primarily by setting a personal example and by appealing to shared Indian values and beliefs.

Clearly Gandhi had a major impact both on the British and on Indian society itself under British rule. However, it is not clear that one can go so far as to conclude that it was the Gandhi-led nonviolent campaign that finally "shook British power in India and ended with negotiations between equals," as Sharp asserts.[32] Colonialism does not give away something for nothing, and in this instance there were many other considerations underlying the British decision to leave India. While some of these may indeed be linked to concern over increased "costs" of colonial domination, others had to do with the weakening position of the British Empire as a whole during that period, as well as with its assessment of strategic interests in Asia as well as other parts of the world at the time.

Nonviolent Action

A few final observations may be made concerning the technique of nonviolent action and how it operates within a strategy of civilian resistance. First, as we said earlier, and as the *intifada* clearly demonstrated, nonviolent action is direct, active, and dynamic. It is neither passive nor submissive. It is, therefore, quite distinct from "pacifism." Sharp explains that the essence of nonviolent action lies in wielding power in all its dimensions—political, economic, and social—intended to put the opponent "off balance." He refers to this process as "political *jiu-jitsu*," whereby nonviolent action causes the violence of the opponent to be exposed and to rebound against itself.[33]

We cannot say that nonviolent action will always be successful. Nor can we guarantee that the opponent will not use force, even terrible brutality, in response. But we can say that nonviolent action is a technique for challenging and displacing loci of power, and for shifting this locus from the hands of oppressive rulers to the hands of the people being ruled. What is exciting about nonviolent action is the dynamic process whereby power relationships change, as well as the endless possibilities that are introduced by such action.

People engaged in nonviolent resistance may gradually come to realize that they do not have to "put up with it" and that they can, as individuals and groups, or indeed as a society, organize effectively to challenge an opponent. This action is itself empowering and generates a sense of self-esteem, dignity, and responsibility. Sometimes people become conscious of belonging to a community with a shared purpose. By using direct action to highlight their plight and make the world aware of their cause, the oppressed may also win international sympathy and support. It should be conceded, however, that armed struggle has sometimes achieved the same effect.[34] Conversely, action that could be equated with passivity in the face of hardship may also evoke sympathy in certain instances, as in scenes of millions of starving children in Africa. It should also be conceded that, regardless of how nonviolent the struggle, the world may remain indifferent to a cause, or may indeed remain positively hostile. This is particularly the case if that cause has suffered from years of ignorance or misrepresentation.

Some of the dynamics outlined here operated in Israel and the Occupied Territories during the *intifada*. Unlike war and violent struggle—where the options appear to be win, lose, or stalemate until the next round— nonviolent struggle introduces several nuances to the outcome. Changes occur that may have a lingering or permanent effect on all parties concerned. These influences may be psychological, in the sense that there may be new and different perceptions of the "enemy." They may be social, as they rearrange relationships within and between people in both communities. They may be economic, in terms of generating new forms of productive relationships. And they may be political. In the political case, the power relationship may be such that the opponent does not necessarily have to experience a "change of heart" or be convinced of ending its control or rule (although nonviolent action does offer some possibility of such outcomes). Instead, the impact of nonviolent struggle may be to bring the opponent to a point where it simply cannot sustain its previous rule. The cause may be a combination of financial, moral, political, or economic considerations, in addition to pressures from other states or through international public opinion. In the event, the people of the area in question simply become ungovernable, and the opponent is then forced to back down.[35]

In his work, Sharp identifies three major categories of nonviolent action that are then divided into 198 specific methods.[36] The three broad catego- ries—nonviolent protest and persuasion, nonviolent noncooperation, and nonviolent intervention—have already been referred to.[37]

Each of the different methods and their subclasses operates differently with regard to its effects on both the nonviolent actors and their opponents. These effects also depend on how specific methods are organized within a particular strategy or struggle.

Without going into detail about the individual techniques, there is one that is pertinent to the Palestinian struggle, namely, civil disobedience.

Civil Disobedience

The method of civil disobedience can be located within the range of methods of noncooperation. It involves "a deliberate, open and peaceful violation of particular laws, decrees, regulations, ordinances, military or police institu- tions, and the like, which are believed to be illegitimate for some reason."[38]

Civil disobedience, therefore, is a refusal to obey or comply with laws that are regarded as unjust. It could reach the point of rejecting the very legitimacy of a given authority structure and its right to institute laws; that is, it could constitute a rejection of that regime as a whole.

Civil disobedience has operated within a variety of social contexts. In some instances, the basic legitimacy of the system itself is not questioned, but civil disobedience is launched to achieve gains that people feel are rightfully theirs. One example is the struggle of blacks in the United States for equal civil rights and for an end to various forms of segregation and discrimination.[39]

In other instances, as in cases of colonial rule, civil disobedience denotes "illegal" protests and struggles against what is often viewed as an illegitimate authority.[40] Resistance in these instances is especially problematic because virtually any kind of protest could be declared "illegal." Such a situation prevailed in the colonial occupation of the Occupied Territories. Despite the popular characterization of the *intifada* as a campaign of civil disobedience, this designation is rather misleading. Civil disobedience is only a single aspect of a total campaign of resistance, one that also incorporates protests and demonstrations, the establishment of alternative indigenous institutions, and other forms of noncooperation, all of which have been widely used during the *intifada*.[41]

In an article that was published in 1984, well before the *intifada*, Mubarak Awad, former director of the Palestine Center for the Study of Nonviolence, describes in detail how several methods of nonviolent action could be applied to the Occupied Territories.[42] He reviews the range of methods that can be used, from protests to noncooperation to the establishment of alternative institutions. Awad insists, however, that civil disobedience is perhaps the one method that requires the most careful planning and preparation. Another instance of the use of nonviolent resistance in the region occurred in the Golan Heights in 1982, again well before the *intifada*. There, the Druze residents of the Golan launched a determined nonviolent campaign against Israel's annexation of this area.[43]

Nonviolent Discipline

Among the many elements that may determine the success or failure of nonviolent action is the degree of nonviolent discipline. Sharp maintains that in order to achieve maximum effectiveness, nonviolent methods should be employed in total abstention from any form of violence.[44] Although other analysts disagree, Sharp's insistence is based on a number of considerations. Some of these can be illustrated as they pertain to the Palestinian case.

First, maintaining nonviolent discipline may help to reduce casualties.[45] Although this is by no means an iron rule of nonviolent action, the use of force aimed to kill is difficult to sustain and justify when the opponent is facing nonviolent resisters. We have witnessed how during the Palestinian *intifada* many Israelis were taken by surprise by the persistence of relatively nonviolent demonstrations. Israeli government officials found themselves shifting back and forth in growing confusion and perplexity over effective tactics for suppressing this uprising.

Another consideration is that in a situation where the military balance is unequal, such as that which exists between the Israeli forces and the Palestinians under occupation, maintaining nonviolent discipline helps to keep the initiative in the hands of the resistance. The struggle will then be fought on its terms rather than those determined by the opponent.

Maintaining nonviolent discipline may help win sympathy and support for the resistance. Public opinion may be split within the opponent's camp, or international public opinion may be mobilized on the side of the oppressed. Resorting to violent means would only highlight the violence itself and the need to combat it, and deflect attention away from the underlying political cause.

Another factor Sharp cites in emphasizing nonviolent discipline is the tendency of nonviolent struggle to attract "maximum" participation.[46] In contrast, in military or guerrilla warfare, only a small portion of the population generally is actively engaged in confronting an opponent. Other advantages include the fact that a larger number of people involved in nonviolent resistance would make it more difficult for the opponent to know where to strike back. Its troops would be spread thin and in constant motion from place to place. There would be no specific target against which the opponent could launch a decisive counterattack. Although the whole civilian population would then be at risk of severe punishment, this kind of resistance is difficult to control and suppress. Nonviolent struggle allows the whole community to unite, mobilize, participate and gain strength. It would thus derive experience, responsibility, and a sense of power from its actions against the opponent.

Mechanisms of Nonviolent Resistance

There are four broad mechanisms through which nonviolent resistance operates. These are conversion, accommodation or persuasion, coercion, and disintegration.[47]

Both Sharp and George Lakey agree that conversion is achieved when the opponent comes to appreciate the point of view of the resistance and becomes convinced of the justice of its cause. The opponent may even begin to identify with the suffering of that group.[48] A number of factors may affect the conversion process. The opponent may be influenced by the willingness of the group to endure suffering for its cause—as, for example, in India.

Here, the opponent, or members of its group, may grow to respect the disciplined nonviolence, unity, and determination of the actors. However, such feelings could be hampered by the nature of the social setting and by prevailing beliefs and attitudes about the grievance group. Thus perceptions of a colonized people by the colonizers may differ quite markedly from the ways in which diverse ethnic groups, races, or classes view each other in a "democratic" setting or in a setting in which social values are shared.[49]

The second process, accommodation, or, in Lakey's terminology, persuasion, involves a willingness on the part of the opponent to make certain adjustments and to grant concessions to the resisting group.[50] The opponent is not necessarily convinced that the resistance has a just cause but acts on the basis of other considerations, such as a need to cut losses or reduce costs. Lakey explains that at this stage nonviolent action causes the opponent to regard the actor as a "nuisance" rather than a threat, and on this basis is persuaded to make certain concessions.[51] Based on our earlier analysis of power relationships, what is happening here is that the nonviolent resistance has begun to affect the political will of the opponent, though it may not yet have achieved any significant impact on its social structures.

A third mechanism, nonviolent coercion, is indicated when the opponent is simply unable to sustain its rule and control in its current form. On this Sharp writes, "The demands of the nonviolent group may also be achieved against the will of the opponent, that is, he may be nonviolently coerced."[52] The idea is to cut the "sources of power" of the opponent by refusing to obey or assist the authorities, and by direct use of human and natural resources to create alternatives to the opponent's power. There are a number of other factors underlying the dynamics of nonviolent coercion. These include, among others, the relationship between the opponent and the resistance and the influence of third parties, especially the international allies of the opponent. Such elements have relevance to Israel and the Occupied Territories, and they are discussed in a later section.

Finally, a resistance can work against the opponent through a fourth mechanism—disintegration. It is worth mentioning Sharp's definition to underscore the fact that this mechanism exists potentially in any given conflict but need not constitute a conscious strategic aim of a resistance movement. Disintegration is indicated by the total collapse of the opponent's system of government.[53] It comes about when the opponent's sources of power are undercut to the point that remaining avenues of coercion are rendered inoperative. It is an extreme case, one comparable to a zero-sum game in which, as a result of nonviolent action, the opponent's system of rule disappears altogether.[54]

The Palestinian struggle in the Occupied Territories has incorporated elements of conversion, accommodation/persuasion, and coercion. However, the explicit Palestinian objective of a two-state solution indicates that, whether strategically or consciously, disintegration as a mechanism of change has been precluded and disavowed in this conflict. One could argue that the articles of the Palestinian National Charter that called explicitly for the dismantling of the "Zionist entity" were an example of a movement seeking the total disintegration of the opponent's system of government. However, this charter was largely superseded by subsequent resolutions of the Palestine National Council. Later, as part of the "mutual recognition" between the PLO and Israel in September 1993, the relevant articles of the charter were formally renounced by Arafat. Technically speaking, "disintegration" at this stage seems more applicable to the resistance than to the opponent, since it was the PLO that was required to basically renounce and forgo the guiding premises and policies of all the preceding years so as to qualify for the "gains" it made in negotiating for autonomy.

To note these changes in the PLO is not to suggest a tactical measure designed simply to reassure Israelis. What they do signify is that the Palestinian struggle is distinct from other anticolonial movements in its willingness to settle for something less than the "total" collapse of a colonial regime. Many Israelis and their supporters would counter that even to suggest that their settlement in the land of "Palestine" is a case of colonialism (whether in a classic sense or as a settler colony) is misleading. From the point of view of the colonized, however, the situation is rather clear-cut. Either colonialism exists or it does not, and if it is the latter, then the whole colonial apparatus must necessarily be dismantled.[55] Yet the Palestinian national movement aimed instead in recent years to end the occupation of the territory of the West Bank and Gaza Strip without challenging or dismantling the Zionist system as a whole. As far as Palestinians are concerned, this fact constitutes a clear affirmation of their recognition of Israel's existence, as an entity that is legitimate, separate, and distinct from their own.

No mechanisms of social change through nonviolent action are immune to the countermeasures that are available to the opponent. The Israeli occupation regime can employ several options to preempt or dilute the effect of Palestinian direct action. This is another reason why it is essential that nonviolent methods, or indeed any form of civilian resistance, be articulated within a whole strategic formulation. A strategy will simultaneously assess the strengths and weaknesses of the resistance itself and the resources at its disposal, as well as take into account the countermeasures available to the opponent.

Strategy and Nonviolent Civilian Resistance

We need to clarify several assumptions implicit in our discussion of strategic formulation. The first of these concerns the venue for the implementation of a strategy of resistance. In our formulation, the Palestinians on the ground in the West Bank and Gaza Strip comprise the main actors, placed as they are in a direct relationship with the occupation regime. Though this situation may change with the implementation of autonomy and the institutionalization of the PLO as a direct actor within these areas, this civilian population remains the key to strategic formulation. A strategy of resistance by civilians in the Occupied Territories, therefore, has to rely on the power of the civilians themselves to effect change, and this strategy should be organized around their ability to wield such power. As Palestinians themselves have discovered over the long years of occupation, armed or guerrilla struggle is not a viable option. A central premise, therefore, is the development of a strategy of civilian resistance that does not require the force of arms to be effective. Palestinians already have a precedent for this in their *intifada.*

In our preliminary review of civilian resistance and armed struggle, we suggested that the first steps toward strategic thinking involved (1) to determine the essence (locus) of power of the resistance and ways to enhance that power, and (2) to identify and undermine the sources of power of the opponent.

During different phases of the struggle, strengthening the resistance can begin prior to, or coexist simultaneously with, efforts to undermine the opponent. This task requires what we referred to earlier as identifying and targeting the "centers of gravity" in each camp: strengthening one and undermining the other.[56] These "centers" would likely vary in both the resistance and the opponent, depending on the conflict at hand. The strategy of the offense (initially taken to be the opponent) would likely be to try to direct a swift and decisive blow to the center of gravity of the defense (the resistance). Conversely, the aim of the resistance would be to wear down and undermine the identifiable sources of power of the opponent. Nonviolent struggle keeps the initiative largely in the hands of this resistance, to which the opponent is then forced to respond. By selecting this technique of struggle, the resistance is defining its own center of gravity or source of power. If the opponent does not succeed in destroying this "power" with the first blow (highly unlikely in this case), the resistance is then in a position to consolidate its defense and engage in a prolonged struggle to undermine the opponent.[57]

Analysts such as Boserup and Mack, referred to earlier, strongly contest prevailing strategic theory, particularly that which postulates that the "defense" should react and "mould itself after the offense."[58] On the contrary, they assert that strategic theory is not a sequence of scenarios and countermeasures. Strategic planning should not involve anticipating and waiting for the initiative of the offense while simply trying to "protect" itself from that superior force at each stage. Instead, the essence of nonviolent civilian resistance is to enable the defense itself to select the terms of struggle.

This view approaches Sharp's idea of political *"jiu-jitsu,"* where the rug is swept from under the feet of the opponent, so to speak. In this type of resistance, the center of gravity will necessarily be located in the will, the power, and the unity of the people participating in the defense. It is to this unity that the resistance must direct its attention and resources.[59]

Linking these ideas to concepts derived from civilian resistance and social and civilian-based defense, we have a scenario whereby the "center of gravity" of Palestinians, their locus of power, rests in the Palestinian people themselves, and in the elements that lend "power" to their population. These essentially comprise their unity, mobilization, organization, leadership, and determination. It is not primarily territory or lands but their own power that they must defend. Israel, the stronger power militarily, remains in a position to conquer or reconquer territory. But its forces cannot "conquer" forever a people that is unwilling to cooperate.

During the first phases of the struggle, the resistance concentrates on directing its forces and energies internally, in order to prevent the opponent from destroying its unity and strength. There are several specific nonviolent methods that consolidate the resistance that were relevant to the experiences of the Palestinians early in the *intifada*. These include the boycott of Israeli goods and the general strikes. At this stage, while the resistance is not yet fully developed and prepared, the use of nonviolent methods to try to deny the opponent its political "purpose" may even be counterproductive.[60] The opponent may feel provoked and threatened enough to strike back violently and prematurely at the resistance, in a way that the latter is not yet in a position to withstand. Once the unity and strength of the resistance have been tested and found to endure, then a second phase can be launched. Nonviolent methods are then used by the resistance in the "counterattack." Here the aim is to target the sources of power or the centers of gravity of the opponent. Theoretically speaking, a Palestinian struggle directed against the political will of the opponent indicates the operation of nonviolent action even in situations characterized by gross structural inequalities and asymmetrical power relationships. Practically speaking, the dynamics of nonviolent action cause the "power" of the opponent to be neutralized and rendered ineffective, consequently backfiring against itself.

What is needed next is to identify specific sources of the opponent's power that can be manipulated to the advantage of the resistance. Any given conflict, as Boserup and Mack point out, is constrained by certain "inhibiting factors." These are political and ideological elements that are usually assumed to be working in favor of the opponent, but ones which can also be used strategically against it. In such cases the means of struggle are designed to split the unity of the opponent and expose any contradictions that exist within its own camp.[61]

The specific utility of nonviolence as compared with other means of defense lies in its double feature of at once giving rise to a wide range of "contradictions" in the ideological fabric of the enemy camp, and at the same time denying the enemy the justification, the ideological license for violence, which a violent response would have provided. These are of course only the two sides of the same coin. The more the enemy resorts to violent repression, the more he widens the contradictions in his own camp until he either reaches a limit beyond which he cannot go, or else, in Clausewitz' words, his "extreme effort would be wrecked by the opposing weight of the forces within itself."[62]

*   *   *

There are obviously many factors pertaining to a given struggle that also affect the outcome. The effective use of the technique of nonviolent resistance may be one, but there are others. These include the specific social setting, leadership and organizational structures, the degree of mobilization, the nature of the opponent's power and its objectives, the extent of international support, and last but not least, the existence of a coherent strategy. The following chapter pulls together the various themes and strands explored throughout this study, to uncover the specific elements that go into strategic formulation. It examines in particular how the task of developing a strategy of nonviolent civilian resistance may be accomplished in the Palestinian case, to afford the Palestinians some possibility of liberating themselves completely from Israeli rule.

Five

Assessing Strategic Directions: Prospects for a Strategy of Nonviolent Civilian Resistance

The defeat of Iraq at the end of the Gulf War in 1991 lent new urgency to strategic thinking regarding the future directions of Palestinian resistance. Most Palestinians, whether inside or outside the Occupied Territories, agreed on one thing—that the *intifada* should continue. By the summer of 1993, however, all but a few of the active groups in the Occupied Territories had turned to simply monitoring the discussions in Washington and waiting for these negotiations to produce results.

The expected outcome of these talks envisioned no more than limited Palestinian self-rule in certain populated areas of the West Bank and Gaza Strip, with the final status of these areas to be deferred for five years. The secret agreement reached between the PLO and Israel in the summer of 1993 did not radically depart from this framework. What changed was that Palestinians were to be afforded immediate self-rule in the Gaza Strip and Jericho (whose geographical limits were not immediately specified). This "autonomy" would later be extended to the rest of the Occupied Territories or, more accurately, to the Palestinian population of the Occupied Territories. East Jerusalem and its environs ("Greater Jerusalem") would be excluded, as would all Israeli settlements and authority over lands and resources.[1] This agreement, widely lauded as a "first step," left the Palestinians with much to do to ensure that they could eventually realize their independent statehood in these areas.

It is because of these developments and their implications that this chapter reevaluates the type of resistance established by the *intifada,* to analyze how similar forms of struggle could be incorporated within a broader strategy of resistance. Another theme of this chapter is to formulate a strategy in a manner that would build on options proposed by Palestinians and draw these together into an effective, coherent whole. We can recapitulate the three premises that underlie our analysis:

1. The location of the greatest concentration of power on the part of the resistance (the Palestinians) that can be pitted against the power of the opponent (Israel) rests within the Occupied Territories themselves.
2. The most vulnerable area of the opponent (Israel) that can be identified and exploited in this struggle remains its political will. This can be targeted through each of the different sectors of the Israeli body politic, including its army, society, and government, as well as its international allies.
3. The most effective technique of struggle to maximize the power and strength of the resistance and undermine that of the opponent is nonviolent civilian resistance.

The Palestinian Resistance

The first task is to identify the strengths and weaknesses of the Palestinian community within the Occupied Territories and to determine the particular loci of power that can be mobilized for effective resistance against the Israeli occupation.

Throughout the years prior to the *intifada* it was never clear whether the Palestinians of the Occupied Territories would play more than a rather passive role in their own liberation.[2] These Palestinians were to remain as a thorn in Israel's side, a reminder that the Palestinian "problem" would not conveniently go away. Gradually, Palestinians moved from a type of static *sumud* to a more dynamic program of development and mass mobilization, and were more immediately involved in the struggle for their cause.

Contrasting some of the earlier short-term "strategies" and tactics with the modes of resistance adopted during the uprising would highlight the evolution in Palestinian thinking about strategy. Some of these tactics of resistance are discussed in the following sections.

Causing Israeli Retreats

Palestinian resistance against the Israeli occupation has always included an element of unrelenting daily pressure against the occupation forces. In the "defensive" phase of the struggle, as Palestinians prepare themselves for a full-fledged strategy, sustained action at this level enables them to pinpoint the loci of power at their disposal. Action that causes Israeli "retreats," regardless of how limited or short-term, helps Palestinians determine how and where to take the offensive against Israel. When incorporated into an overall strategy, the aim of this tactical measure is twofold. First, it encourages greater mobilization and increases direct action in the resistance camp. It demonstrates that Palestinian action can indeed achieve results. Second, it constantly wears down the opponent's political will by forcing Israel to confront the political issues surrounding the Palestinian cause and the Arab-Israeli conflict. One advantage of this tactic is that it does not seriously threaten the actual power bases of the opponent so as to cause the latter to lash back prematurely against the resistance. Palestinians have used such methods as protests and hunger strikes by prisoners in Israeli jails with some degree of success. Though these acts did not erode Israel's "centers of gravity," by making their way to the attention of the international media, they did on occasion succeed in bringing to bear local and international pressure to force Israel into limited retreats. Concessions included improving prison conditions and desisting in the administration of electric shocks to prisoners.

Palestinians realized that they could exploit splits and contradictions in the opponent's camp. They were also aware that the Israeli reaction, in the form of granting certain concessions, did not involve any real power retreats. As Palestinians learned, the opponent will try to deliberately wield these concessions at certain stages in the struggle, in order to destroy the unity and purpose of the Palestinian resistance. The "carrot" end of the "carrot and stick" approach has been used by Israel to try to wean away some sectors of the Palestinian population. During the *intifada,* the Israeli authorities manipulated precisely such techniques to stall the momentum of the resistance and destroy the Palestinian consensus. For example, they granted family reunifications and approved more building permits. Palestinian strategists need to keep in mind that Israeli strategy may combine actions at more than one level. Apparent "retreats" on minor issues may mask long-term strategic gains on others. For example, while the peace talks were proceeding in Washington between 1991 and 1993, Israel was reportedly offering Palestinians a number of minor concessions in the manner just mentioned, to give Palestinians greater control over their daily lives. However, the same Israeli authorities were also forging ahead with land confiscations and settlement building, as well with measures that caused the economic strangulation of whole Palestinian communities. Because of the serious disruptions to Palestinian lives, Israeli "retreats" have often been eagerly clutched at as a welcome relief. Israel may then manipulate such retreats politically, to indicate which groups it is willing to regard favorably and at what price.

Improving the Quality of Life

Some sectors of the Palestinian community have always argued in favor of immediate improvement in living conditions. In their view, this would enhance their *sumud* and enable Palestinians to withstand pressures to emigrate. Others have argued that such measures would only deflect them from the goal of total liberation.

The idea of improving the quality of life gained renewed attention in October 1983 when U.S. Secretary of State George Shultz presented an American proposal on the issue. Up to that point, Palestinians in the Occupied Areas had generally not differentiated between *sumud* and liberation, in the sense that the former was a necessary and interim strategy for the achievement of the latter. The new proposals, however, appeared to preclude altogether the option of ultimate liberation and concentrated instead on "accommodation" to the "reality" of the occupation. Proposals for the "improvement of the quality of life" aimed at developing several institutional areas in the West Bank and Gaza Strip with the support of American and Jewish funding. The expectation was that better standards of living would establish vested interests that would in turn forestall "radical" tendencies among the oppressed Palestinians. The best that Palestinians could hope for would be "self-rule" in the context of overall Israeli sovereignty. As Meron Benvenisti pointed out, financial allocations of the U.S. Agency for International Development contributed more to the "pacification" and personal prosperity of Palestinians than to the "community development" of the areas under occupation.[3] The Likud Party, then in power in Israel, opposed even limited measures to liberalize its policies in the Occupied Territories, and further steps had to await the new National Unity Coalition. In 1985 and 1986 news again circulated in the Israeli and foreign media about plans for "autonomy." These called for appointing Palestinian mayors and for raising standards of living in the Occupied Territories.[4]

The "quality of life" argument was largely discredited by Palestinians, and plans to implement it were soon superseded by the events of the *intifada*. Even then, there was little articulation of how, concretely and specifically, these or any *sumud* tactics could be incorporated in the struggle for final liberation. Since virtually the same proposals for self-rule were floated once again as part of the agreement negotiated between the PLO and Israel in 1993, it is worth revisiting the issue. For many Palestinian thinkers, improvement of the quality of life could not be judged separately from an overall program of development. Such a comprehensive program would establish Palestinian self-sufficiency in such areas as education, health care, municipal services, and economic enterprises, and it would enhance the creation of Palestinian alternatives to the occupation regime. In a context where the administration of this "autonomy" would be Palestinian rather than Israeli, improvement in the standards of living would likely be warmly received as an expression of internal Palestinian development and, as such, perhaps would be more difficult to link directly to any Israeli plan for "pacification." Palestinian strategists would, therefore, face a dual task. On the one hand, they would need to maximize this opportunity to raise the standards of living of the people, so as to strengthen Palestinian institutions for the long haul ahead. On the other hand, they would have to guard against pacification becoming a permanent solution.

Development

Palestinians came to regard a long-term strategy of development as an indispensable component of a their overall resistance. The first task of a development program would be to strengthen indigenous institutions and create unity. Palestinians realized that targeting areas at risk was especially vital. Through hard experience, Palestinians learned that it was impossible to sustain high morale or even a basic level of mobilization and participation without the necessary social supports for the people to fall back on.

The launching of the peace talks changed the focus of development efforts in the Occupied Territories to some degree. International donors (especially nongovernmental organizations, or NGOs), converged on the scene with huge sums of money to invest. Factional groups, even individuals, competed for funding. There was no real planning or coordination of investment strategies.[5] News that Israel would ease restrictions over the implementation of certain projects and permit the opening of branches of Arab banks in the Occupied Territories was combined with expectations that the World Bank would become involved in Palestinian "development." All these events made the idea of investment in these areas much more attractive. Technical teams were established early in the peace talks, ostensibly to provide data to delegates in the bilateral and multilateral negotiating teams.[6] According to critics in the Occupied Territories, however, these teams soon transformed themselves into "mini-ministries," in which members of the factional groups supporting the peace talks jockeyed for position in the forthcoming "autonomy." Members of factions that had reservations about the talks were largely excluded from these teams. Resentment was felt by many people, especially long-term activists in the grassroots movements.[7] No matter how these trends unfolded, they did not start out quite that way. The aftermath of the Gulf War was regarded by many Palestinians as a "transitional period." This period, as Salim Tamari explains, would allow Palestinians to think constructively on what lay ahead.[8]

As these developments were taking place, Israel was itself devising new strategies to preempt Palestinian development efforts and to weaken their resolve. The leniency shown by the Israeli authorities toward development in certain service sectors and municipal functions (particularly during the peace talks) coexisted with more severe economic strangulation in other spheres. The Israeli authorities continued to institute measures that would exploit conflicts in Palestinian society and target Palestinians at their weakest points. Permitting certain factions to receive funding, preventing Palestinian laborers from working in Israel, and continuing to expropriate lands all gave added urgency to collective Palestinian efforts beyond any interim stages.

Clearly, long-range development planning remains indispensable if Palestinians are to assume responsibility for their resistance. Palestinian strategists would need to look beyond improvement of standards of living during an interim phase, into the kinds of development programs that would link these efforts to the struggle for complete independence. To accomplish this purpose, three interrelated issues would need to be addressed:

1. To secure the weakest links of the Palestinian community.
2. To develop and strengthen indigenous loci of power.
3. To consolidate and cement the unity of the resistance.

Securing the Weakest Links of the Palestinians

As a consequence of intensified Israeli repression at different levels, one of the most vulnerable areas of the Palestinians has been a collective, national-scale economic endeavor. Productive sectors were progressively weakened by the lack of funding and by the cutoff of remittances and other sources of aid after the Gulf War. Over the years, the weaker links of the Palestinian community whose needs had to be addressed expanded to include whole populations, especially among Gaza Strip residents.[9]

It is not necessarily the group that is most dispossessed that would be most vulnerable to Israeli policies. The Israeli authorities have taken great pains to create vested interests among certain sectors of the population, people who would be at a disadvantage should the *intifada* or similar disruptions to their normal life persist. These could include landlords, merchants, bourgeoisie, workers, officials in the civilian administration, and others. Israeli policies have also singled out students and youth as a group receiving special reprisals.

During the *intifada,* some steps were taken to prevent these weaker links from being unduly exploited by Israel. Successive communiqués issued by the Unified Nationalist Leadership of the Uprising (UNLU) expressed commitments and guarantees to families of striking workers that they would be supported and protected. Merchants were praised for their continued adherence to strike calls. Landlords were commended for their national stand and their refusal to collect rent for their shops and buildings.

Palestinians learned that securing the weakest links of their population would necessitate not only the development of appropriate social structures, but also the instilling of a national spirit. This is the area where the need for unity and cohesion was dramatized. It is difficult to find an English equivalent to convey the Palestinian understanding of this phase. "Development" was part of it. The rest was rooted in the very meaning of the word *intifada* and in the nuances and shared cultural meanings this word conjured up among the Palestinian people. It had something to do with a rebirth of Palestinian dignity, identity, and will.[10] Palestinian resistance would ultimately be built on real people. They are the foundations of its strength, persistence, and power. At the same time, they are potentially its greatest source of weakness. A viable strategy, then, must secure the elements that enhance the "power" of the people, whether these are economic resources, support networks, or ideological consensus.

Palestinians have retained their commitment to the national cause. However, over the years they watched their resources dwindle, then disappear entirely. Their children lived in constant fear and danger; the people hungered and found no food; mothers, daughters, and sisters were beaten and threatened; homes and means of livelihood were destroyed before their very eyes. When their lives became ones of total misery and dispossession, Palestinians found it increasingly difficult to continue to uphold an ideal.

Developing Indigenous Loci of Power

A related component of a civilian resistance strategy is to direct development programs toward the establishment and strengthening of Palestinian loci of power. The aftermath of the Gulf War underscored Palestinian vulnerability in this regard.

In education, industry, agriculture, and medical services, Palestinians sensed the need to create their nation, not simply in opposition to Israel, but for themselves. This turning inward and rebuilding a Palestinian community on firmer ground was what initially differentiated the *intifada* after the Gulf War from its earlier manifestations. Palestinians reassessed strategies and tactics of the uprising, and emerged with new directions for change and resistance. Some of these initiatives could also point the way to future strategic thinking. Beyond ideas for internal development, Palestinians would be planning for the long-term goal of liberation.[11]

Palestinians could continue to tap into their tradition of mass mobilization and organization within "alternative" institutions and sectors. It is this tradition of civil society that has enabled Palestinians to remain engaged in a methodical social defense against the encroachment of the colonial state.

Consolidation of the Unity of the Resistance

A third imperative underlying Palestinian resistance is to ensure unity. Although cohesiveness and consensus over a given course of action may be generated through successive confrontations with the opponent, Palestinians realize that this approach alone is insufficient and that it renders them vulnerable to Israeli countermeasures. Factionalism remains a problem, both internally and with regard to relations with the PLO. Some of these differences may or may not disappear should Palestinians be granted a credible degree of autonomy. Other differences may instead be exacerbated by the perception that by accepting the autonomy plans, *Fatah*—Arafat in particular—has "sold out" and has endangered the ultimate goal of total liberation. Many ideological differences, both inside and outside the Occupied Territories, were fueled by financial concerns.[12] The bankruptcy of the PLO affected in turn the institutions of the Occupied Territories that were dependent on outside support. Questions about appropriate strategy that earlier preoccupied various factions seemed moot in the face of financial disaster.[13]

The debates about strategy and unity in the aftermath of the Gulf War suggested the outlines of a two-pronged approach. One view was that the main task facing Palestinians was basic survival and waiting for a more favorable "balance of forces" outside to pursue a just peace. Palestinians emphasized the need to bridge factional differences and to coordinate with the PLO. This would be a "defensive" phase, characterized by internal reorganization, retrenchment, and strengthening of indigenous loci of power. While "waiting," Palestinians would also be engaged in known acts of resistance, unlinking from Israel, and establishing the ungovernability of these areas; that is, a more "offensive" posture would exist within this same strategy.

The second strand was concerned mainly with the role of the PLO. It would work with the international community and the United Nations to impose some type of UN mandate over the occupied areas. This strategic focus was not necessarily divorced from the task of rebuilding and recreating Palestinian society.[14] An indication of how the two strategic strands diverged was evident in the directions in which efforts at Palestinian development and resistance were heading. It was one "strategy" if Palestinians were simply struggling to stay on the land until more amenable conditions emerged for a political solution. It was quite another if restructuring would allow the PLO to declare an actual government there at an opportune moment. Each of these choices would identify different loci of power, and different weights would be given to the inside and the outside. Each choice also determined which tactics and mechanisms would be required for dealing with Israel in both the short and long term. With hindsight, and in light of the 1993 PLO-Israeli agreements, the inferences from these respective strategic foci become even more intriguing. This period became characterized by an increased channeling of energies toward the peace process outside and by a centralization of control by the PLO in Tunis. In many ways, indigenous efforts were subverted by what were perceived as autocratic decisions by Arafat himself—a development that seriously hindered local mobilization capacities.

Serious questions concerning the direction of future strategic thinking and planning are suggested by these developments. As "power" is removed from diverse sectors within the Palestinian community and increasingly centralized within the PLO itself, options for resistance become more circumscribed and dependent on that same PLO. A long-term strategy for final independence would need to weigh the advantages and disadvantages of centralized and decentralized loci of power. If the PLO succeeds in reconstituting itself as a political entity on the "inside," it may be expected to wield "power" alongside institutions already on the ground in these areas. However, the PLO's institutionalization in these areas may also result in the creation of vested interests that would prevent it from functioning as a dynamic force of change. In the event, Palestinians may find themselves in a position where they would need to organize the institutions of civil society to mediate against or counter the power of that same political structure, as well as against continued Israeli rule over these areas. The implications for civilian resistance and social defense are complex and are not elaborated here.[15]

Undermining the Opponent—Israel

Israel has identifiable "centers of gravity" that Palestinians could target to defeat its political will. Should Palestinian action be successful, Israel may be forced to seek some different kind of accommodation with the resisting group.

As we have seen, a number of political and ideological factors characterize Israel's relationship to the Palestinians and complicate strategic formulation. As Palestinians learned to their dismay and frustration, these "inhibiting factors" have long rendered suspect almost any action on their part.[16] Palestinians need to determine, therefore, how and when such elements can be manipulated effectively within a strategy of resistance.[17]

It has been not only ideology and politics that separate Palestinians and

Israelis, but also the ways in which these processes have been internalized into the psychology of the occupier. Israelis reacted in part to the Palestinians themselves, but also to what Palestinian action forced them to confront about themselves. Many Israelis seemed to resent Palestinians for making them conscious of what Jews could do to other people. Some resorted to denial—"Jews could not do that" (engage in excessive violence)—or to rationalization—"Palestinians are terrorists" (and the violence is thus justified). Others were clearly horrified, and more determined than ever to end the occupation. Regardless of the specific reactions involved, Palestinians proved that Israel was vulnerable, that their action had an impact on Israelis. A qualitative change had taken place. During the uprising Palestinians began to pierce the collective armor of Israel, so to speak. Their civilian resistance did more than simply express or establish "disengagement" in some form; it made many Israelis question reality as they knew it. This element underlies some of the polarization that occurred.

Palestinians have exploited and could continue to manipulate the degree to which Israel is prepared to use force and physical violence against them. Excessive brutality by Israeli soldiers against Palestinians could in the long term be circumscribed and controlled by the actions of Palestinians themselves, though such control may not be achieved in the short term.[18] A violent resistance will likely provoke a violent Israeli response. Many Palestinians believed that Israelis often provoked Palestinians into precisely such actions in order to justify the use of force to crush the whole movement.[19]

As the Israeli authorities scrambled to respond to the *intifada,* they clearly exposed Israel's vulnerability to actions taken by Palestinians. This exposure was significant because it indicated that Israel had to actually take Palestinians into account, if only to decide how to repress their movement.[20]

The Israeli Military

As a sector that is in direct and daily contact with Palestinians, the Israeli army plays an important role in the strategy to undermine the opponent. In an earlier chapter, we examined how Palestinians have tried to affect the morale of soldiers patrolling the Occupied Territories.[21] Palestinian noncooperation, protests, and other actions could demonstrate that the army is not in control, and that the only way it can maintain "law and order" is not through the willing cooperation of the people, but through the increasing application of brute force.[22] As long as they can influence the army, Palestinians can have direct access to Israeli society itself. The "attack" against the army, therefore, would be two-pronged: To split ranks internally, and to establish the refusal of Palestinians under occupation to submit or cooperate with Israeli rule. This tactic would remain feasible for the few years during which the Israeli army would be "redeployed" in the Occupied Territories in conformity to the interim self-rule plans.

Palestinians' confrontations with troops have most often taken the form of stone-throwing demonstrations. Few attempts were made to approach soldiers as human beings, even if such actions were possible given the context. The image of the "violent" Palestinian largely persisted, even though these same Israeli forces were likely well aware that they were using inordinate violence against civilians. Some may have rationalized their behavior by believing that given the chance, Palestinians would stab them, throw gasoline bombs at them, or shower them with deadly stones. Collective punishment, the use of sniper fire, shooting from helicopters, and other methods were designed to keep a distance between the Israeli army units and the Palestinians, and to prevent soldiers from developing empathy with their enemy.

As long as Israeli troops continue to patrol Palestinian communities, Palestinians can keep up the tempo of demonstrations, particularly those that use nonviolent methods, in order to increase "costs" to the army. For example, by constantly alternating the locations of mass demonstrations over different areas in the Occupied Territories, Palestinians could keep Israeli troops on the move, distracted and exhausted, while relieving the pressure from communities that fall under prolonged sieges. Palestinians will be aiming indirectly to demoralize the Israeli soldiers and police, and to have them call into question the morality and legality of following orders that condone violence against civilians. Their continued struggle would also express the determination of a fearless yet peace-loving community that wants to live in its own state, in coexistence with an Israeli state nearby.

In the short term, particularly during the interim phase, one focus of Palestinian strategy could be to address the issue of settlers. Palestinians actions could be designed to cause a "rift" between Israeli settlers and the army. The aim would be to expose the dangerous power wielded by settlers who have been intent on staking their own claims to the land. Many Israeli settlers have behaved as vigilantes, taking the law into their own hands and rampaging throughout the occupied areas. The army has often turned a blind eye as settlers have been given free rein to kill and injure Palestinians. Various reports claim that some Palestinian deaths documented during the uprising could be attributed to settlers.[23] They posed a threat not only to Palestinians, but also to Israeli efforts to seek a lasting peace.[24] Exposing the settler's agenda may likely require support from sympathetic groups and peace organizations within Israel that would work alongside Palestinians on the issue.[25] Splits between the forces engaged in monitoring security in the interim stage may collide with the forces of those settlers and others who are bent on keeping the situation heated up.[26]

Israel is both vulnerable and sensitive to issues of army violence. Palestinians can use this knowledge to create more confusion and demoralization within army ranks in the short term, and to precipitate questions about the settler presence and army control in the long term. While it is important for Palestinians to call into question the army's involvement in an essentially political problem, their direct access to Israeli society via the Israeli army may move onto a different plane under interim self-rule. Palestinian efforts to bring the political issue to the attention of the Israeli public would also likely take different forms.[27] Palestinians may need to act simultaneously within distinct loci of power (currently existing or yet to be formed) both to check the power of their own political leadership and to sustain the momentum of the struggle against Israel's control of the Occupied Territories. Palestinians would need a defined strategic focus, as well as the necessary social supports, in order to avoid being mired down by the tasks and politics of the moment.[28]

The Israeli Government and Public

Palestinians have long been aware that there will be no movement to address their rights to independence and sovereignty unless and until Israel is convinced that it simply cannot continue to govern these areas. Palestinians differ in their assessment of the fundamental locus of power in this configuration—whether they should attempt to influence Israel directly, or whether action to pressure the United States is the key to greater flexibility on Israel's part. However, most Palestinians realize that their activities can have some effect on Israel. The *intifada* has demonstrated this fact quite clearly.

This uprising and subsequent regional developments have brought the issue of occupation to the direct attention of the Israeli public and government. Mark Tessler talks about a redrawing of the Green Line and the explosion of the myth of a "unified Jerusalem."[29] Israeli civilians were made painfully aware that the Occupied Territories were "another country," so to speak, in which they did not dare venture. Tessler insists that polarization in Israeli society did indeed occur, until the Gulf War and increased incidents of stabbings of Jews by Palestinians led the Israeli public to a more unified stand against Palestinians. The situation remained in flux, however, enough to allow divisions in Israeli society to be further exploited. Palestinians managed to introduce the idea of "disengagement." To them, this meant Israeli withdrawal from the occupied areas and the realization of their national independence. For the Israeli public, disengagement could take several forms, one of which was tried in March 1993, when Israel closed off the Occupied Territories and restricted the number of Palestinians working in Israel. As Hanan Ashrawi states, this resembled a form of "ghettoization."[30] In the summer of 1993, the Israeli government evinced its willingness to experiment with more liberal interpretations of "disengagement," in the form of interim self-rule.

Increasing dissent and polarization within Israel would become especially complicated once autonomy is implemented, because many Israelis could become complacent in their view that a "solution" has been found. Meantime, others on the far right would perhaps be struggling to overturn the whole deal, and both the right and left in Israel may become involved in an internal struggle that would deflect them from attending to Palestinian concerns. Likewise, Palestinians would be concentrating on normalizing the situation, and as they rebuild their economy and society, they would have little energy and incentive left over to pursue long-term goals. Their own leadership may or may not discourage them from contacts with their Israeli counterparts or from engaging in the kinds of civilian struggles that could have an impact on Israel. Should the ruling authority be centralized in the Occupied Territories, the "power" and influence wielded by alternative groups in these areas may be diminished, perhaps even suppressed. Palestinian strategists need to keep in sight long-term goals and assess how and where their efforts to affect the Israeli society and body politic can advance their long-term goals.

In examining what they can do to increase polarization within Israel in their favor, Palestinians may direct their resistance to target Israel at its weak points. They may seek to "convert" Israelis by persuading them of the justice of their cause. Or, they could try to reach "accommodation" by forcing Israel to cut "costs" and abandon the occupied areas. Finally, they could "coerce" Israel, however unwilling it is, to withdraw completely from these areas. While some measures to affect Israel can be undertaken directly by the Palestinians themselves, others may rely more on the impact Palestinians can have on third parties, such as the United States and other international players.[31]

Sympathetic and supportive Israelis—beyond the traditional peace groups—may also be invited to expand actions to end the occupation or move toward a complete peace settlement beyond autonomy. Palestinians and liberal Israelis have long been engaged in activities that test Israeli democracy. Building upon such initiatives and devising new ways to affect Israeli society are important. Though different initiatives would be needed in the case of "autonomy," one example is described in the next paragraph.

In the spring of 1987, Hanna Siniora, editor of the *Al-Fajr* newspaper, made a bid for a post in the Jerusalem municipality in the planned elections.[32] Various Palestinians condemned the move, charging that it would legitimize the Israeli occupation of Jerusalem and would amount to an abdication of Arab sovereignty over the city. Jewish Israelis, particularly those of the Likud Party, found the possibility threatening enough to propose a new law "barring anyone from participating in municipal elections unless they are an Israeli citizen and have sworn allegiance to the State of Israel."[33] Geula Cohen, a Knesset member from the right-wing Tehiya Party, went so far as to call for the repeal of the law allowing Jerusalem's Palestinians to vote in municipal elections.[34] Siniora's Israeli lawyer, Avigdor Feldman, had this to say: "As long as Jews are in control of the legislative process, they will not allow Palestinians inside the system."[35] This incident remains significant in light of the proposed autonomy plan. Jerusalem Arabs could be allowed to elect members of the Palestinian Council that is to administer the self-rule plan. However, their votes would still not make them eligible to elect Palestinian officials for the Jerusalem municipality itself. Palestinians can use the opportunity of elections as a means of pushing the limits of Israeli democracy.[36] Comparable efforts could test the Israeli system and its proclaimed support of the right of people to continue to work "within the law," an opportunity that has not generally been available to Palestinians.[37]

A critical degree of polarization in Israel has, in the short term, been preempted by Rabin's agreement with Arafat over limited self-rule. However, Palestinians learned important lessons over the years of resistance that may yet point the way to further efforts. Palestinians realized that their adherence to a largely nonviolent civilian resistance enabled them to polarize Israeli society on its strategic, yet most vulnerable, points. The most effective Palestinian strategy has been to establish Palestinian noncooperation with the Israeli regime. This was expressed both in the actions of Palestinians against Israeli occupation forces during the uprising and in the activities that indicated Palestinian attempts to separate and reduce dependence on Israel. As the autonomy phase begins, Palestinian noncooperation would have to assume different forms, less "offensive" and direct, and more "defensive" and indirect. "Defensive" noncooperation would be no less powerful and no less challenging to Israeli control, as it would clearly demonstrate that Palestinians simply refuse to be governed by Israel and refuse to submit. Regardless of the policies Israel implements and the "deals" that are struck with the United States, Arab states, or the PLO, the collective Palestinian rejection of permanent Israeli occupation would remain a trip wire to any political solution that does not address their rights.

Palestinians have also recognized that Israelis may not come to the point of acknowledging their rights until their "pockets" are affected. To this end, they worked to increase the direct costs of the occupation—for example, in tourism, trade, and costs to the military. Following the autonomy phase, incurring direct "costs" to Israel may no longer be feasible. Indeed, many Israeli politicians readily admitted that part of the motivation for this deal was to shift the responsibility (and hence potential blame) to the Palestinians and eliminate costs to themselves of policing the Occupied Territories. In the Gaza Strip especially, Palestinians themselves would have to address the abject poverty and desperation of the people.

The concept of raising "costs" would require reinterpretation and reformulation in a future strategy. Palestinian action during the *intifada* was clearly significant in Israel's calculations. Yet Israeli analysts insisted that the impetus to vacate the Gaza Strip and shift responsibility to Palestinians was the rise of Islamic fundamentalism in these areas, not any "civilian" resistance on their part. Likewise, the regional context also changed. There were clear signals that other surrounding Arab countries had already been or would soon be stripped of their "power." They would no longer be in a position to challenge Israel should it decide to keep lands and resources in the Occupied Territories while simultaneously dropping its responsibility for the Palestinian people there. Nevertheless, Israeli "strength" was accompanied by "weakness." Israel had clearly tired from its role in the Occupied Territories, particularly in the desolate Gaza Strip, and decided to cut losses before the situation grew too desperate for it to handle.

The Opponent's International Alliances

Palestinians understood that because of the complex ideological, political, and economic "investments" involved in Israel's occupation of the West Bank and Gaza Strip, it would very likely not withdraw completely unless it was made to. In order to achieve this outcome, Palestinian strategy also concentrated on influencing third parties, particularly Israel's closest ally, the United States. This focus remained in effect until the Oslo Agreements of 1993 that were negotiated "secretly" between the PLO and Israel.[38]

Over the last few decades, the effort to influence the United States was for the most part conducted indirectly. It was in this vein that the PLO attempted to work through various Arab states, in order for the latter to intervene directly with the United States. These efforts concentrated on trying to obtain a U.S. commitment to convene an international conference with the participation of all the parties, and to negotiate a settlement on the basis of United Nations Security Council Resolutions 242 and 338.

Most of these intercessions essentially floundered time and again on U.S. unwillingness to pressure Israel[39] and on Israel's refusal to abide by these UN resolutions.[40] Conflicting interests of various Arab states also played a part, as did the PLO's on-again, off-again relationship with the main Arab players, such as Egypt, Syria, and Jordan. A central stumbling block to any agreement in the view of the United States and Israel was always the PLO. Both parties refused to consider this organization as a major negotiating partner. This position was "justified" by the PLO's refusal, until November/

December 1988, to come out with a clear, public, and unambiguous acceptance of UN resolutions and recognition of Israel.[41]

Both the United States and Israel remained consistent in their categorical rejection of a separate Palestinian state. The United States, however, was the first to articulate publicly that Palestinians were entitled to certain "political rights."[42] The official position of both the United States and the Labor Party in Israel was based on a willingness to accept some kind of "territorial compromise" that returned parts of the Occupied Territories to Jordan.[43] Significant parts of these same positions were incorporated into the interim autonomy plan for Gaza and Jericho in 1993.

Other states, notably the Europeans and the Soviets, played important roles over the course of the Arab-Israeli conflict, but these are not elaborated here. It is important to note that the U.S. perception of the Cold War complicated the scenario. Israel was always considered a "strategic ally" to offset Soviet influence in the Middle East. This was especially the case when the Soviet Union, for its part, was backing what were considered "radical" Arab states such as Syria. Thus the whole Arab-Israeli conflict, particularly during the Reagan administration between 1981 and 1989, was largely viewed within the framework of U.S./Soviet relations and their competing interests in the region.[44]

The close relationship between Israel and the United States cannot be fully appreciated without considering broader U.S. strategic interests in the region. Of singular importance is U.S. access to oil reserves in the Middle East, which it would protect at virtually any price. As a strategic ally, Israel could afford the United States a potential military base from which to launch attacks against any Arab state in the region that threatened its interests. Israel would also be strengthened as a powerful state in its own right to check the spread of any "radical" movements that may pose a threat to combined U.S. and Western strategic interests in the region. These threats could take the form of indigenous nationalist movements or, as was the trend in recent years, the emergence of militant Islam. For many years, Israel had performed this strategic role alongside Iran, until the Iranian Revolution in the late 1970s brought down the shah's regime and removed Iran from this configuration.[45] Since then, Israel has emerged as the sole strategic ally of the United States in the region, and has continued to be generously supported by the latter.

Meanwhile, one after another of the Arab states seemed targeted for "neutralization" and the cancellation of any military threat they posed to Israel. This process started with Egypt and the signing of the Camp David Accords in 1978. After being diverted by a long civil war, Lebanon was attacked by Israel in 1982, and it has spent most of the ensuing years trying to rebuild its fractured country. Jordan never posed a serious military threat to Israel, and the regime's close ties with the West rendered it a minor player in the region. Iraq, on the other hand, was a distinct military power that for all intents and purposes was destroyed during the U.S.-led Gulf War of early 1991. Finally, there was Syria, the only remaining Arab regime to be brought into the fold. This aim would be accomplished either through agreements that could be reached during the peace process or, failing that, conceivably even through war. Both Saudi Arabia and the Gulf states had their interests securely in line with the West, and as such, with little military might and still less political will, were not considered likely sources of an armed confrontation with Israel. That left the Palestinians, who were always at the mercy of the various states in the region, and the weakest player in terms of military strength. Their fate and desires, therefore, were mostly inconsequential in the larger scheme of things. If the Arab states were not in any position to pose objections, then limited Palestinian rights within a framework of self-rule would have to satisfy them.[46]

During the *intifada,* Palestinians proved that they could neither be ignored nor be swept away under the guise of different Arab, Israeli, and U.S. solutions. The scrambling for appropriate strategies that would somehow "solve" the issue without necessitating substantial "concessions" on the part of Israel is evident in the various "plans" that have been advanced for self-rule and autonomy.[47] It was also the *intifada* that helped to generate more critical questioning among the American public concerning the U.S. government's largely uncritical acceptance of Israeli discourse on the issue and the unilateral support of Israel.[48]

The Issue of Democratic Principles

Public pronouncements in the United States invariably proclaimed America's commitment to democratic principles and to the rights of all peoples to freely choose their governments and leadership. A double standard has existed, however, vis-à-vis the Palestinians, one that both they and their sympathizers have struggled to expose. As far as Arabs and Palestinians were concerned, the Gulf War clearly underscored the existence of double standards concerning "occupation." This war brought home the perceived arrogance with which U.S. government officials dismissed any legitimate Palestinian claim to nationhood, while on the other hand intervening directly and sometimes illegally to establish the "rights" of various groups around the world in their anti-occupation or self-determination struggles. The support of the United States has been extended to such movements as the *Mujahideen* in Afghanistan struggling against Soviet occupation, the Contras in Nicaragua fighting the Sandinista regime, the Lithuanians in their struggle against the Soviet Union, and the prodemocracy forces in China, not to mention to the Kuwaitis resisting Iraq's occupation. In contrast, by 1993, the U.S. government was still maintaining that it did not support the establishment of a Palestinian state, in disregard of the wishes of some five million Palestinians worldwide. Palestinians as well as other supporters of a just peace in the Middle East have tried to make more information available on the history of the conflict, so that more Americans would be aware that the same standards by which their government purported to judge the rest of the world simply did not apply in this case.

There have been attempts to articulate the issue of democratic principles by highlighting the ordinary American's own stake in the issue. One such area is freedom of speech and assembly. The U.S. government is shown to have largely succumbed to pressure from the Zionist lobby and its beneficiaries in Congress, as evidenced, for example, in its decision to close down the Palestine Information Office in Washington in 1988 and in its unsuccessful attempt to close the PLO observer mission at the United Nations that same year.[49] Campaigns have occasionally been directed toward publicizing other aspects of the Palestinian-Israeli conflict. One approach has been to emphasize how the voice of Palestinians has regularly been stifled in the United States. Many Americans have been denied access to both sides of the issue and, for that reason, have not been able to make informed decisions.[50]

Issues of freedom of speech and assembly have been tackled in other ways. Arab-American organizations and other concerned groups have attempted to alert Americans to the processes at work in disseminating information about the Arab-Israeli conflict in the United States. One particular focus was on the influence wielded by the American Israel Public Affairs Committee (AIPAC) and other pro-Zionist and pro-Israel lobby groups. Such groups have exerted tremendous pressure on institutions, universities, and the media, as well as on the U.S. Congress and other governmental bodies, to suppress alternative avenues of discourse.[51] This kind of influence, however, would not have been possible if U.S. strategic and vital interests had not also been served by a close relationship with Israel.

Since the Israeli invasion of Lebanon in 1982, the pro-Israel monopoly over the media has cracked noticeably in the United States. Questions and doubts began to creep in concerning Israeli policy, its continued occupation of the West Bank and Gaza Strip, and the degree of Israeli repression there. Some information began trickling down on the Palestinian national cause, on the growing moderation of the Palestinian leadership, and on its willingness to join a peace conference and participate in the negotiations over a two-state solution. During those years, however, many signals emanating from the Palestinian community continued to be dismissed in the United States, where the popular image of the Palestinian "terrorist" and "rejectionist" largely persisted. Meantime, various European states were becoming quite informed about the PLO and its policies. As one news report observes, during the Palestinian *intifada,* Israel's image in the Western world suffered damage ranging from "substantial deterioration" to "total collapse."[52] As the same article maintains, quoting an Israeli Foreign Ministry official, "European governments have to find excuses for every move which might be construed as friendly, or even neutral, towards Israel. Every little thing is now a problem." Among the nations that reacted negatively in one way or another to Israel's conduct during the *intifada* were Poland, Greece, Ireland, the Soviet Union, Portugal, members of the European Community, Denmark, Norway, Holland, Sweden, France, Italy, Japan, and Canada.[53] It was only the United States that continued to hold out, barring the opportunity for an informed debate on the issue.

In the years since the mid-1980s, a number of books that challenge myths and misinformation about the establishment of the State of Israel have been published in English by Israeli and other Jewish authors. Often based on recently declassified Israeli archival material, many reiterated the same arguments that have long been made by Arabs and Europeans, supported by extensive documentation and long ignored, especially in the United States. These works documented the basis of the Zionist enterprise in Palestine and pointed to the deliberate dispossession of the Arab population, the expropriation of lands, the mass expulsions, the killings, the destruction, and the massacres, and, most importantly, they acknowledged the very existence of a Palestinian people on that land long before Zionist immigration started in the early part of the twentieth century. In the United States, *The Birth of Israel* by Simha Flapan, *The Birth of the Palestinian Refugee Problem, 1947–1949* by Benny Morris, and *The Palestinian Catastrophe* by Michael Palumbo are only three examples of such works that have not been reviewed and publicized to the extent they deserve.[54]

Several efforts have concentrated on publicizing the fact that the right to freedom of speech cannot be taken for granted in the Arab-American community. There are many documented instances of groups canceling appearances of Palestinian or pro-Arab speakers after receiving warnings and pressure from pro-Israel groups and individuals. On various occasions, the organizers themselves have refused to allow a Palestinian-American or Arab-American to address a given function or event.[55]

With regard to television, it was clear to many observers that each Arab invited to appear on a talk show would be met (for the sake of "balance") with a number of Israelis or pro-Israeli speakers.[56] This would not be the case if a pro-Israeli speaker was featured. Many Americans discerned that the interviewer would more likely than not allow the views of a pro-Israel speaker to go unchallenged, while the Arab speaker would be grilled and bombarded with questions designed to push him or her into a corner and "disqualify" the Arab and Palestinian position in American eyes.[57]

There has been a marked shift in the media in the United States since the *intifada.* Americans seemed more willing to air an Arab or Palestinian point of view, if mainly because the *intifada*—at least until the Gulf War—made it impossible to sustain a one-sided view of the conflict. Palestinian direct action caused the Israeli use of force to backfire against itself and alienate some of its traditional supporters in the United States. It was increasingly Israel that was being viewed as excessively violent, and Palestinians as the victims. Once the prevailing view of Palestinians had been challenged, a whole range of questions and doubts began to creep into other areas. These caused Americans to take a fresh look at the way Israel and the pro-Israel lobby in the United States manipulated and controlled the terms of discourse over the last 40 years.[58]

In the interim self-rule period, American sympathizers and supporters of a just peace in the Middle East will have a crucial role to play. Their work will be especially complicated in view of tendencies in U.S. official discourse to equate elections with democracy, and generally to substitute process for substance.[59] Should elections for some kind of ruling council actually take place in the autonomous Palestinian areas, one can predict that coverage of the ongoing occupation of these territories will largely disappear from the media. It will be assumed that elections constitute the appropriate mechanisms for establishing "parity" between the two sides, and henceforth these parties can be left to negotiate at their own pace. The asymmetrical situation of a people seeking total liberation from a colonial occupier will likely no longer be referred to. The challenge would then be to expose the absence of a free sovereign state for Palestinians, the continued marginalization of East Jerusalem Palestinians from the scene, and the disregard of the rights of hundreds of thousands of Palestinians languishing in exile elsewhere in the world.

The Media

The press and the issue of freedom of speech is a topic that deserves more lengthy discussion. In the United States, many organizations and groups have worked to expose the absence of factual reporting of events in the Occupied Territories. One writer summarizes the issues at hand quite succinctly by saying,

> And it isn't wise, in the long run, to make Americans afraid, in their own country, to speak their minds about a foreign country. They will eventually resent the colossal impudence of it. And the country on whose behalf the suppression was enacted will bear the consequences.[60]

During the *intifada* the foreign press was often banned from access to camps, villages, and towns by the random declaration of "closed areas" by the military. Journalists were sometimes only allowed to travel within a designated area under army escort, and were not allowed to approach Palestinians directly during these tours. Individual journalists and media personnel were beaten and harassed by the Israeli army.[61] As a result of various complaints, special instructions were issued to soldiers on how to treat the press in a more civilized manner.[62] This institution, a focal point in the American democratic system, was constantly being undermined by Israeli actions, particularly during the *intifada*.[63]

Several communiqués were issued in English by the UNLU during the *intifada* that outlined the short-term and long-term goals of the Palestinians. Palestinians have tried to make these available to the American public, to inform and perhaps influence their opinions regarding the Palestinian issue. For the most part, however, such documents did not come to the attention of the U.S. public, except as "interpreted" through the U.S. government or Israeli officials.[64]

Another area where Palestinians concentrated efforts on the media is the joint Arab and American efforts to make available to American citizens information on the extent of U.S. aid to Israel. This was seen as especially important at a time when Americans themselves were experiencing a severe economic pinch in many states across the nation, and were suffering from the lack of jobs, costly health care, unaffordable housing, inadequate welfare, and a host of other problems. At about $4 billion per year, Israelis are benefiting from American aid to the tune of about $1,250 dollars per capita per year, or $12 million per day.[65] The magnitude of this aid leads some observers to conclude that the United States is only giving lip service to its claim to support a solution based on UN Resolution 242, when its financial support has enabled Israel to free its own funds for the purpose of building and expanding settlements in the Occupied Territories.[66] The American government has also provided the instruments of repression that allow Israeli forces to kill and maim Palestinians and that enable Israel to persist in its violations of human rights and international law.[67] There are also laws pertaining to the United States itself that Israel has continued to violate. Many groups in the United States have made concerted efforts over the years to inform the American public on these matters. These include, for example, Israel's violations of the Arms Export Act and the Foreign Assistance Act. These laws restrict the sale of arms to countries found to be violating human rights or to countries using these arms for offensive rather than for clearly defensive purposes. Israel has flagrantly violated these laws—for example, in its use of cluster bombs during the 1982 invasion of Lebanon and its indiscriminate use of tear gas in the Occupied Territories during the *intifada*.

With the launching of the *intifada,* a number of activists and organizations in the United States began calling for a reevaluation of aid to Israel, perhaps even a reduction of such aid until the latter agreed to participate in negotiations. These efforts received hardly any coverage in the regular media.

Palestinians and various Arab and American organizations in the United States also worked through the media to portray the Palestinians as real people, and so break away from the traditional stranglehold of negative Israeli characterizations and stereotypes. This indeed had some impact during the *intifada,* a situation that persisted until the Palestinian issue largely receded from the news after the Gulf War. In an era where the U.S. media almost uncritically lauded the Israeli/PLO accords of September 1993, special attention could be paid to the potential victims of these agreements, especially the refugees of the earlier 1948 and 1967 wars, whose fate was not addressed in these agreements. Their individual stories and ordeals could be told—their lives in exile, and their desire to return to some part of their homeland in which to live in peace and dignity. Many are refugees, people without passports, without rights, and without a real choice for their futures.

Only one Palestinian deportee received extensive media coverage in the United States, though close to 70 Palestinians had been expelled by then. This lone case was Mubarak Awad, who was deported from the West Bank in June 1988. The media even reported disagreements arising between Israel and the United States stemming from his case. Awad also happened to be an American citizen, and he was portrayed in the media as a Palestinian "Gandhi," as though alone in a den of terrorists and inciters.[68]

Palestinians, Arab supporters, and sympathetic Americans alike have a role to play in ensuring that the Palestinians are not forgotten once autonomy is in place. As some observers have already warned, if the final outcome is not based on international law, or if it does not offer sovereignty for the Palestinians, there will be no lasting peace in the region.[69]

Human Rights and International Law

Nowhere is the denial of Palestinian rights and U.S. double standards concerning these rights more evident than in the studied neglect toward the implementation of international resolutions and agreements pertaining to the Palestinians.

One major area of concern has been Israel's refusal to recognize the application of the provisions of the Fourth Geneva Convention of 1949 (Relative to the Protection of Civilian Persons in Time of War) to the inhabitants of the Occupied Territories. Israel claims that the West Bank and Gaza Strip were not "occupied" from a sovereign state, since its view is that Jordan and Egypt, respectively, were not legitimate rulers of these areas.

Israel claims that it does apply the "humanitarian" provisions of the convention. Yet, as we have seen in earlier chapters, it has proceeded to violate virtually every one of these provisions. The use of collective punishment, the settling of Jewish Israeli citizens in these areas, the imprisonment of Palestinians in Israeli jails, the expropriation of land and property, and the expulsion of Palestinians from their homeland are all examples of violations of articles of the Fourth Geneva Convention. Of graver concern has been the escalation in the level of violence permitted against Palestinians and the growing number of Palestinian casualties during the *intifada*. On June 14, 1990, two prominent organizations in the West Bank, Al-Haq and the Palestine Human Rights Information Center, sent an urgent message to state signatories of the Geneva Convention demanding international protection for Palestinians in the occupied areas. In their letter and supporting documents, representatives of these organizations described Israel's extensive violations of human rights and international law. The letter is direct and succinct:

> Palestinians in the West Bank and Gaza Strip have full standing to claim from these governments the enactment of the protections granted in the Fourth Geneva Convention. In our view the choices for governments are limited: to acquiesce in the steady deterioration of the situation on the ground into insecurity and lawlessness, or, to effectively discharge their obligation to ensure respect for the Convention.[70]

It is significant that one of the worst periods of Israeli repression against Palestinian civilians coincided precisely with the eight or nine months of "secret" talks in Norway between Israeli and PLO officials. Ostensibly, the two parties were then negotiating in good faith over the future of the Occupied Territories. The level of Israeli violence against Palestinians intensified markedly, taking such forms as more frequent sniper fire against children, killing of alleged "wanted" youth, and demolition of homes by antitank missiles. These measures were accompanied by a virtual strangulation of the Palestinian community, as evidenced by the closure of the Occupied Territories from Jerusalem and the rest of Israel after March 1993. To many observers it appeared as though the Israeli government had decided to "soften" Palestinians and blunt the edge of their resistance in preparation for capitulation, and only awaited acceptance of its terms by the PLO.[71] Instead of focusing on these gross violations of human rights, the U.S. media in particular were pointing to Palestinian "violence" and "terrorism" that allegedly necessitated such drastic Israeli "responses." During the final weeks of the negotiations between the PLO and Israel, much was made of the PLO renouncing "terror," when, arguably, no organized terror attacks had been committed by the PLO for at least the preceding five years (since its first declarations renouncing such "terror"). Nothing was reported about organized and systematic Israeli-imposed terror against Palestinian civilians during this same period, nor about the massive bombardment of South Lebanon in July 1993. The goal of this attack, as was publicly admitted by Israeli officials, was to create a huge refugee problem in Lebanon in order to put pressure on the government there to rein in *Hizbullah*.[72] It is important to recall that while the PLO was commanded to renounce violence (and preferably the *intifada* as well), international law embodies principles that recognize the right of people under occupation to struggle for their freedom.

A powerful means of contrasting the U.S. position with the rest of the international community and its prevailing consensus regarding the Palestinian issue is to note the discrepancy in voting patterns in the United Nations. By looking at a few examples from General Assembly and Security Council resolutions, we may uncover some interesting facts. A consideration of UN General Assembly resolutions, which, in contrast to those of the Security Council, are not "enforceable" but simply express the opinions and positions of its constituent members, reveals overwhelming support for the rights of Palestinians. To illustrate, at the height of the Gulf crisis in December 1990, the UN General Assembly voted 144 to 2, to call for an international peace conference, and 141 to 2, to call on the Security Council to take action to protect Palestinians under occupation.[73]

Historically, the UN General Assembly has consistently taken a position that recognizes Palestinian rights to national self-determination; this position reflects the will of the international community.[74] One of the first of these resolutions was issued in the context of the very act of Partition of Palestine in November 1947 (General Assembly Resolution 181). In calling for the establishment of a Jewish state and an Arab state, this resolution implicitly recognizes the right of the Palestinian people to self-determination and independence. Another, General Assembly Resolution 2649 of November 30, 1970, mentions the Palestinian people explicitly, in their right to self-determination. Since then numerous resolutions have been passed that reiterate this same position—for example, UN General Assembly Resolution 3236 of November 22, 1974, which refers to the "inalienable rights of the Palestinian people" including "the right to self-determination" and "the right to national independence and sovereignty." This resolution also refers to the right of return for the Palestinians (first noted in UN General Assembly Resolution No. 194 [III] of December 11, 1948). The UN General Assembly has been critical of the United States for "preventing" the Security Council from implementing various resolutions concerning Palestinian rights.[75]

It is also revealing that this same United States, which put the UN to such effective use during the Gulf crisis, had long tried to negotiate peace in the

Middle East far removed from the mantle of the UN. Palestinians suspected this policy was designed to deliberately bypass their rights as enshrined in international law. Moreover, the same United States that refused to pressure Israel to join an international conference sponsored by the UN had itself agreed precisely to such a conference in 1973.[76] Both the United States and Israel would countenance negotiations with the PLO when it acceded to their terms.[77]

Over the years, numerous resolutions have been passed in the UN Security Council relative to the Palestinian issue. These have repeatedly been vetoed by the United States. In some cases, the United States simply abstains from voting. By so exercising its power of veto or abstention, the United States has deliberately prevented the implementation of the main articles of these resolutions. During the Gulf War in particular various analysts turned their attention to the UN, to compare the United States' voting record and its resolve in implementing the 12 UN Security Council resolutions issued against Iraq with the 40 or so that had been issued since 1967 on the Palestinian problem and remained unenforced. In one article on the subject, Norman Finkelstein compares five such basic areas in UN Security Council resolutions.[78] The first category, "aggression," shows that compared to two resolutions against Iraq, 11 have been passed that condemn Israel's aggression against Arab countries (four in this category were vetoed by the United States). The second area is "annexation," where the UN Security Council voted Iraq's annexation of Kuwait "null and void" (August 9, 1990). In August 1980, the UN Security Council declared Israel's annexation of East Jerusalem "null and void," and in December 1981 it declared the annexation of Syria's Golan Heights by Israel also "null and void."[79] A third category comprises "occupation." The UN Security Council voted on August 3, 1990, to condemn Iraq's occupation of Kuwait and call for its immediate withdrawal. Concerning the Arab-Israeli conflict, various UN Security Council resolutions repeatedly called for Israel's withdrawal from Arab territory (including three resolutions referring specifically to South Lebanon). The United States vetoed two such resolutions. "Human rights violations," the next category, has generated repeated UN Security Council resolutions condemning Israel for its violations of human rights, of which the United States has vetoed 14 in the last decade. One resolution was passed against Iraq on the issue, on August 18, 1990. The last category, "sanctions," concerns the two resolutions that impose sanctions against Iraq (August 6, 1990, and September 25, 1990). Regarding Israel, the United States vetoed a number of resolutions that call for sanctions and arms embargoes against Israel, in response to such issues as its annexation of the Golan Heights and its refusal to withdraw from Lebanon.[80]

Significantly, during the *intifada*, the United States vetoed a number of UN Security Council resolutions that were critical of Israel. According to a

1988 Special Report by the Middle East Justice Network, the United States vetoed five resolutions critical of Israel for its use of force against civilians. In 1989 it vetoed another five.[81] In May 1990, following the Rishon LeZion massacre of seven Palestinians by an Israeli, the United States was alone in vetoing a Security Council resolution that called for international protection of Palestinians in the Occupied Territories.[82]

Turning to Israel's violations of the human rights of the Palestinians under occupation, one area of special concern that Palestinians have tried to publicize is that of the brutality of the Israeli army toward young children in the Occupied Territories. There has been extensive documentation on the physical and psychological torture of children, on their horrible conditions under occupation, in jails and other conditions of detention, as well as on the numbers of young children killed by Israeli forces since the beginning of the *intifada*. As of June 8, 1993, the number of Palestinian children under 16 years of age killed was estimated at 232.[83] Little of this information reached the U.S. media, although the U.S. government continues to be aware of such violations. One report notes, "Children as young as 12 are not only detained and subjected to violent interrogation sessions, but many are held for months in appalling prison conditions, systematically tortured and mistreated, and then released without charge." The "hostile terrorist activities" for which many as young as nine or ten are arrested and mistreated, consist of nothing more than throwing stones, raising flags, burning tires, and the like.[84]

Israel's extensive use of collective punishment, both prior to and during the *intifada,* is another area of concern. Whole communities have been placed under prolonged and agonizing curfews; some of these have amounted to veritable sieges, during which electricity and water have been cut off and food and medical supplies barred. Another concern is the blowing up or sealing of houses for the suspected involvement of individual members in stone throwing or other forms of resistance. During the Gulf War the severe repression of the Palestinians was intensified when the Occupied Territories were declared "closed areas" and put under complete curfew, with all the suffering and problems that these measures entailed.[85] The closure of the Occupied Territories in March 1993 and the practice of missile-bombing houses (especially in the Gaza Strip) are further examples of collective punishment.

In 1989 a report by the U.S. State Department concerning violations of human rights around the world admitted that there was an increase in such violations in the Occupied Territories between 1988 and 1989. But it appears that many references to this effect were "deleted" from the final report.[86] It later transpired that before compiling the final report, Richard Schifter, then assistant secretary of state for human rights, refused to meet with Arab-American representatives and hear their views and evidence, while he reportedly remained readily accessible to pro-Israeli figures to discuss the issue.

Much evidence and documentation has been accumulating concerning Israeli misinformation during the *intifada*. Both Palestinians and international groups and organizations that have been monitoring events in the Occupied Territories have attempted to counter and challenge official Israeli explanations.[87] Some examples were cited earlier. They include documentation on the numbers of deaths and miscarriages due to the extensive use of tear gas, especially in homes and other closed areas. Other examples include the policy of crushing bones, applied liberally early in the *intifada*, reportedly under orders from Itzhak Rabin (then minister of defense), the unrestrained use of live ammunition, and the controversy over the actual number of those killed and injured, particularly among Palestinians who were not participating in any demonstrations or who were shot in cold blood by soldiers.[88]

Attempts to provide alternative information would help the American public realize that it should not be too quick to dismiss and invalidate Palestinian claims and documented evidence out of hand, as though the Arab view is necessarily biased and exaggerated, while the Israeli view is never so.[89]

Efforts to publicize Israeli violence against Christians and their churches in the Occupied Territories may sensitize the American public to be more discerning of other acts of repression and violence. These efforts are significant in view of the atmosphere of heightened awareness of "Islamic fundamentalism" and the casual stereotyping of all Arabs as potential terrorists. For example, there was little in the U.S. media, with the exception of the *Washington Report on Middle East Affairs*, that, to this author's knowledge, reported on Israeli army brutality toward Christian religious personnel in the Occupied Territories.[90] In one incident, Palestinian priests were reportedly beaten and otherwise mistreated, and these events were witnessed by many Palestinians and church officials in the West Bank.

There has also been little coverage in major U.S. newspapers on the mistreatment of American citizens in the Occupied Territories. This mistreatment has not been restricted to Arab-Americans, but has also affected others, including United Nations Relief and Works Agency (UNRWA) officials who visited or worked in these areas. In various incidents early in the *intifada*, several Americans reported being beaten by Israeli soldiers. When they protested to their consulate in Jerusalem, they were simply told that it was their fault for being among Palestinians. The response of the U.S. embassy in Tel Aviv merely noted that the cases in question had been raised to the U.S. State Department.[91] The U.S. response, blaming the Americans themselves for living among Palestinians, was reminiscent of the identical Israeli response in 1982, when it excused the bombing of Arab civilians in

Lebanon by saying that it was their fault for living among "terrorists." In the case of the Occupied Territories, the American media gave scant coverage to this potentially explosive issue of Americans being physically threatened, imprisoned, and even killed.[92]

Both concerned Americans and Arabs of various nationalities feel they have a continued responsibility to monitor violations of human rights in the Occupied Territories and to ensure that international resolutions, especially UN Security Council Resolutions 242 and 338, are implemented in their entirety. For all its shortcomings on the issue of Palestinian rights, the United States does retain a long tradition of democracy. This exists at the social level through the diffuse agencies of civil society that can be mobilized for different causes. The success of mobilization in this instance will likely vary according to whether a given issue is of direct concern to the American people. Mobilization may be difficult to accomplish in the short term, not least because of the dearth of balanced information available through the regular media. Another is that there are many issues of more immediate and pressing concern to most Americans, such as racism, inadequate health care, and unemployment. Yet, power structures in the United States that benefit from close relations with Israel may be forced to accommodate to the will of the people, should these constituents exert more pressure on their elected leaders to reverse the customary blind support for this state. One approach could be to highlight the common destiny, shared to one degree or another by all oppressed groups, that emerges as a consequence of U.S. policies both inside and outside the country. The struggles for an end to oppression and discrimination, therefore, would be that much more powerful if the groups concerned could pool their resources and coordinate their strategies at some level.

American Jews

There is nothing in the American Jewish community that could be described as monolithic or homogeneous with regard to its position on Israel and the Arab-Israeli conflict. However, supporters of a just peace in the Middle East have always been aware that their efforts to change U.S. policy toward the region are not likely to be fruitful unless they take into account the power and influence wielded by the organized membership of this community, particularly the active pro-Israel lobby in the United States and its supporters in Congress.

This area remains a charged and complex issue in American life. In recent years Palestinian efforts have aimed at breaking through the outward facade of cohesion in the American Jewish community and weaning away some of its influential sectors from a virtually automatic deference to Israel. Since the beginning of the *intifada,* policy differences between the two major parties of Likud and Labor in Israel have been reflected in the American Jewish community. Some believe that such contradictions in Israel legitimized dissent within the American Jewish community and allowed different groups to speak out against the "other half." This was highlighted during the premiership of Itzhak Shamir, when the right-wing government was viewed as responsible for Israel's intransigence and its excessive violence in the Occupied Territories.

The unrelenting and inescapable media coverage of the *intifada,* especially during its first year, also gave rise to more vocal and direct expressions of shame, anger, and dissent within the American Jewish community. Members of this community have also been supported by a number of other peace groups active in the United States. These groups, such as New Jewish Agenda and American Friends of Peace Now, were particularly active and vocal during the uprising, when they worked to highlight the need for negotiations and for a peaceful and just settlement in the area. As various reports indicate, since the *intifada,* American Jewish organizations and their supporters, like American Friends of Peace Now, have doubled their membership in the United States and Canada. Other Jewish groups sprang into action, lobbying with the U.S. Congress, for example, in support of PLO participation in the peace process.[93] Indeed it was several prominent American Jews who were instrumental in convincing Arafat, in November 1989, to pursue his declaration of independence, and subsequently, in December of that year, to announce the PLO's recognition of Israel.

The organized Jewish lobby continues to wield considerable influence in the formulation of U.S. government policy toward the Middle East. Concerned Americans have, over the years, exposed the extent of pro-Israel PAC money (from political action committees) that has been spent on reelection campaigns of sympathetic members of Congress.[94] However, the influence of the pro-Israel lobby in the United States could not have been so pronounced had U.S. interests not coincided so closely with those of Israel.[95] This is not to say that both countries' policies are identical: Indeed, there have been many points of disagreement over the years, over such issues as the U.S. sale of sophisticated weapons to Saudi Arabia and the building of Israeli settlements in the Occupied Territories (with funds freed from American aid). Still, pro-Israel forces in the United States exert considerable influence over policy makers, over the media, and over American organizations. Among their supporters are influential researchers at major Washington "think tanks," who are regularly consulted over Middle East policy.[96] Pro-Israel groups have played instrumental roles in shaping the debate around the Palestinian issue and in stifling opinions that are critical of Israeli government policy, or those that urge the recognition of Palestinian rights. Israelis themselves have occasionally observed that the leaders of

Jewish organizations in the United States have appeared more "hawkish" on issues pertaining to Israel than Israeli Jews living in Israel. Israel Shahak documents some evidence of this hawkishness and points to his own experience at the hands of sectors of the American Jewish community, which, he asserts, has tried to discredit him both politically and professionally.[97]

The role of Palestinians at this level is largely indirect. Through concerted civilian resistance, they may underscore the need for a just resolution to the Palestinian/Israeli conflict. However, the events of the summer of 1993 may have also paved the way for direct Palestinian involvement on the U.S. scene. President Clinton's announcement of a resumption of a dialogue with the PLO "legitimizes" a Palestinian voice and discourse on the issue. This introduction could be seized upon by all those concerned with the achievement of a just peace in the Middle East. This development also takes the edge out of the more extreme strands of the pro-Israel lobby in the United States, which must in turn accommodate to emerging realities.[98]

Reacting to the Palestine Liberation Organization

Over the years, the United States has been almost single-minded in its effort to keep the PLO out of any peace negotiations, to deny its claim to represent the Palestinian people, and to ignore its call for an independent state alongside Israel. In spite of the momentous events of September 1993 that culminated in the "mutual recognition" between the PLO and Israel, the trends of the past remain indicative of U.S. strategic thinking and of its fundamental approach toward the Palestinian people and their rights to national sovereignty.

Both "democracies," the United States and Israel, for a long time had their own brands of "antiterrorist" laws securely in place, one of the main targets being the PLO. Until December 1988, when Arafat uttered the formula that paved the way for a dialogue with the United States, the Anti-Terrorism Act of 1987 defined American policy in this area. This law made it a punishable offense to "aid, abet, provide services or funds to or accept funds from, represent, or act on behalf or direction of the Palestine Liberation Organization."[99] The act prohibited setting up in the United States any office for the PLO.[100] Although opening a front between the U.S. government and the PLO only a year later may be viewed as an improvement (despite the eventual "suspension" of the dialogue), even this limited "dialogue" was subject to a host of restrictions and conditions.[101] In an amendment to the conditions attached to the dialogue, the president of the United States was required to report to Congress every three months on whether the PLO was abiding by its commitments. Any "terrorist" act in which the PLO or its constituent organizations were directly implicated would constitute a breach of the agreement, and the United States would then be obliged to suspend this dialogue, as it eventually did, in June 1990.[102]

Meantime, contrary to what had been hoped for and expected by Palestinians, the U.S.-PLO dialogue did not pave the way for greater publicity of their cause and their recognized leadership. Many analysts surmised that this dialogue was deliberately designed to marginalize the PLO from the negotiating process altogether, by pushing it into a remote corner where discussion was legitimate but far removed from ongoing political developments in the area. In the wake of the signing of the September 1993 Israeli-Palestinian accords, it has yet to be seen what role the rehabilitated PLO would be allowed to play in the U.S. public arena and what official channels of communication would be opened to it in the United States.

Misinformation and ignorance about the PLO have existed for years. The violence attributed to the PLO and Arabs in general, along with their presumed propensity for settling disputes by murder, has been widely publicized. Such distortions and exaggerations have been fused into a single argument: that the PLO will never abandon an alleged intention of destroying Israel. The Palestinian tradition of seeking democratic change and the PLO's increasing political maturity over the years were buried under layers of labels and accusations. In light of the momentum created by the *intifada,* Palestinians and the PLO hoped that making all the "required" moves would place both Israel and opponents of the PLO in the United States in a position where they would be forced to negotiate with this organization.[103] The first PLO initiative at the time came in the form of a statement by PLO spokesman Bassam Abu-Sharif, of which the first excerpts appeared in print in the United States in the *New York Times* on June 22, 1988. This statement called for direct talks between the PLO and Israel. Almost immediately, the race for damage control began in the United States. Some reports confirmed that the U.S. State Department had already received a copy of the document and was considering whether it meant that the PLO had actually recognized "Israel's right to exist" and whether it constituted an "authentic" PLO statement.[104]

The strategic timing of this initiative was meant to coincide with the U.S.-Russian summit in Moscow at the end of May 1988. As such, it was clearly intended as a message to the superpowers that the PLO was ready for peace and as a means of pressuring the United States to discuss with the Russians a clear agenda for addressing the issue. In the event, apart from one U.S. State Department official's comment that the document was "the clearest, best-formulated indication of a willingness to meet with

Israelis or negotiate with Israel,"[105] no other official U.S. response was forthcoming.

Israel had also insisted that the PLO recognize its "right to exist" without guaranteeing that it would reciprocate by recognizing the PLO. The official Israeli response to PLO initiatives was to reject the idea of a referendum in the Occupied Territories, as well as any negotiations with this "terrorist" organization, regardless of the democratic wishes of the Palestinian people under occupation.[106] Other official Israeli reactions reiterated that Israel would only negotiate on the basis of the Camp David Accords, with Jordan and not with the PLO.[107] Then Prime Minister Shamir's reaction was that the document contained "nothing new,"[108] a curious observation in view of the fact that Israel had always complained that the PLO had never explicitly recognized the Israeli state. It is also curious that no one in the American media picked up on the irony. By early July 1988, however, some Israeli officials were allegedly praising the "important shift" expressed in the statement, and Foreign Minister Peres was described as referring to it as "interesting."[109] Beyond such pronouncements, the general trend toward inaction continued, because, as was supposed, elections were approaching in November in that year in Israel.

The momentum generated by this statement was not stilled. The PLO did indeed rise to the challenge by sustaining its political pressure. This process culminated, as noted earlier, in the declaration of Palestinian independence later that same year.

For Palestinians, the questions posed by developments in the region center on their assessments as to whether these signal a fundamental or merely a cosmetic shift in U.S. policy toward them and their national rights. In view of past trends and persisting U.S. strategic interests in the region, one could draw the conclusion that little of fundamental significance has changed and that Palestinians must prepare for a long haul ahead. For the United States, access to oil remains paramount (though this was not placed in immediate jeopardy by the Palestinian issue). Economic interests continued to predominate in other fields. The Middle East was a huge potential source for U.S. investment and for the export of U.S.-made goods. Much of this economic advantage could be increased once the Arab states ended their boycott of Israel. Companies investing in Israel could then tap into the Arab world, and both U.S.- and Israeli-manufactured goods could flow "freely" into the Arab world. Israel itself was experiencing an economic pinch; the *intifada* had created political obstacles to its ability to dump manufactured products into the Occupied Territories in the same quantities as before, and had placed obstacles in the way of the consumer ability of Palestinians to purchase such products.[110]

Immediate economic factors aside, it was both to the United States' and

Israel's advantage to "contain" radical movements that were antithetical to their own interests in the area. *Hamas* posed one such threat in the sense that, should it converge with comparable movements across the rest of the Arab world, it could seriously challenge U.S. hegemony (still largely protected by acquiescent and pro-Western Arab regimes).[111] One solution then, would be to eliminate these threats. The first step would be to neutralize *Hamas* by cutting off the Gaza Strip and placing PLO "security" forces in place to contain this movement. The next step would be to implement the PLO/Israeli agreement, in order to set a precedent for other Arab states. The way would then be clear for Jordan, Syria, and Lebanon to sign their own agreements or peace treaties with Israel. Part of ensuring that these states would honor their agreements would entail that each country assume responsibility for its "radical" elements, be these Islamic militants, disgruntled nationalists, dispossessed Palestinian refugees, or others.[112]

Many Palestinians have evinced concern that the Israeli-PLO agreements were simply measures to eliminate whatever "problem" they posed to the realization of wider American and Israeli interests. They fear that they will be kept busy with their own affairs under self-rule, while the pursuit of these regional interests proceeds unhindered. "Minority" civil and political rights for Palestinians could be tolerated by Israel, to a greater or lesser degree, depending on which party was in power there, and by the United States. However, it appeared to them that Israel would always require control over at least some of the strategic lands and resources, especially in the West Bank.[113] As it transpired in the aftermath of the August-September 1993 events, certain U.S. officials, including President Clinton, had been officially informed of the "secret" negotiations as early as January 1993.[114] Once again in retrospect, official pronouncements emanating from the United States during those months began to take on new meanings and increased Palestinian anxiety. For example, in June 1993, Palestinian negotiators in Washington were quite incensed to learn that the U.S. "document" that Secretary of State Warren Christopher brought to the region to try to break the impasse over the peace talks contained references to the Occupied Territories as "disputed," rather than "occupied," areas. Palestinians construed this wording as a departure from original U.S. positions on the status of these territories, including those articulated in the first letters of "assurances" presented at the outset of the Madrid conference. Looking back, some Palestinians interpreted this phrase as a hidden signal to Israel to proceed with the "secret" talks in Oslo, with the reassurance that the U.S. government would also back a deal that solves the Palestinian issue to Israel's satisfaction. In other words, the United States would not make a sticking point of international law, particularly UN Resolutions 242 and 338 in this instance. Moreover, if the PLO could be brought around, then the United States would be supportive.[115]

The Technique and Mechanisms of Nonviolent Civilian Resistance

In the existing unequal situation, in which Israel enjoys the military advantage—and in some circles, the moral advantage—Palestinians have had to opt for a technique that would afford them some initiative in determining the course of their struggle. The asymmetry of their chosen technique to that practiced by the adversary, especially during the course of the *intifada,* allowed the Palestinian nonviolent struggle to highlight the significance of the political issue of occupation over and above "military" and "security" considerations. Although in essence this argument would remain valid as long as the overall occupation of the West Bank and Gaza Strip continues, other elements would necessarily change. During the two to five years of interim self-rule, Palestinians can formulate and implement a civilian resistance strategy to improve the odds in their favor for a more equitable final outcome and for their independence.

A discussion of a nonviolent civilian struggle in the Occupied Territories would remain incomplete without considering the mechanisms that would determine the final outcome. As we noted earlier, the choice of mechanisms derives as much from the chosen means of struggle as from the ultimate objectives of the resistance. It then follows that the mechanisms are largely intrinsic to the strategy as well, as they are both defined and circumscribed by, and incorporated into a strategy of nonviolent civilian resistance.

The first mechanism seeks to convert the opponent into accepting the goals of the resistance.[116] This process would entail that Israelis be made to reevaluate their beliefs and attitudes toward the Palestinians, and come around to recognizing the legitimacy of the Palestinians' cause and their rights to an independent state. For various reasons, including the tradition of dehumanization of Palestinians and the demonization of the PLO, the realization of this process is rather unlikely in the conflict at hand. However, Palestinians and the PLO could build on their newfound legitimacy to attempt to reach Israelis at this level. Earlier sections analyzed the possibilities of "converting" parts of the opponent's public, particularly in galvanizing the peace camp in Israel and thereby increasing polarization in the opponent's camp, and in winning sympathy and support in the international community.

Clearly, however, the process of conversion cannot be expected to succeed completely, regardless of how disciplined the nonviolent movement in the Occupied Territories is and how extensive the sacrifices of Palestinians are. Animosities and fears run deep on both sides, and the nature of everyday interaction between Palestinians and Israelis (largely as soldiers against a resisting population) is not conducive to this process.

The second mechanism, accommodation, is the process whereby the opponent decides to concede some or all of the demands of the resistance, in order to cut losses or prevent additional "costs" from accruing.[117] In the case of the Occupied Territories, Israeli willingness to accommodate to emerging political realities has been hastened by its perception of the costs of maintaining the occupation and by the need to contain various types of "damage" or preempt more extensive "concessions" at a later date.

Israeli Prime Minister Itzhak Rabin has himself admitted that the Palestinians never posed a threat to the security of the State of Israel. Rather, he maintained that they constituted a threat to the "personal" security of Israelis.[118] The kind of "accommodation" entailed by the autonomy proposals would combine enhancing Israeli "personal" security with transferring some of the responsibility for maintaining internal "law and order" to Palestinian hands. Israel's demand that the PLO renounce the "violence" of the *intifada* only attests to the continuing impact of this uprising on Israel.

Israel has remained vulnerable to further erosion of its image abroad and to exposure of the contradictions inherent in its claims to democracy and respect for human rights. Attempts at damage control and accommodation make sense in this context. Clearly, self-rule or elections are not the kind of concessions that Palestinians are ultimately seeking. Yet these do provide the impression of movement and buy time for Israel as it proceeds with its settlement policy and its pursuit of peace treaties with the rest of the Arab world.

The type of accommodation sought by Palestinians is that Israel acknowledge the inevitability of full withdrawal from the Occupied Territories and establishment of an independent Palestinian state on these lands. When Israel is made to realize that the status quo cannot be reimposed and that force only makes the situation worse both for Israel and the Occupied Territories, then it would become anxious to seek a modus vivendi that would limit the damage without entailing additional sacrifices.[119]

The obstacles to the realization of Palestinian goals do not begin and end with Israel's imposition of an autonomy plan. Israel has several alternative political options that can be pulled out as needed, to accommodate to political changes inside or outside the region. Israel's options range anywhere from limited autonomy under permanent Israeli rule to the other extreme—the independent Palestinian state that is desired by Palestinians. Should one option fail, Israel could conceivably resort to the next in line. No matter how unpalatable at an earlier stage, this next option may be reconsidered at that time to achieve the necessary or unavoidable accommodations.

A study prepared in 1989 by the Jaffee Center for Strategic Studies at Tel Aviv University, which outlines six specific options open to Israel, is revealing of Israeli strategic thinking.[120] Since we are concerned with the mechanism of accommodation, we can dismiss the first option cited in the study, that of maintaining the status quo, as no longer viable. The fourth option cited in the report is the establishment of an independent Palestinian state. This goal remains largely outside the realm of the conceivable in most Israeli circles. Nor has there yet been sufficient pressure brought to bear on the Israeli state to force it to accommodate along those lines. The remaining four options are autonomy, annexation, unilateral withdrawal from the Gaza Strip, and a Jordanian-Palestinian Federation.

For various reasons mentioned in the Jaffee Center study—which can be summarized in one argument, that Israel cannot get away with it—annexation of the Occupied Territories is not viewed as an immediately viable option. Should Israeli perceptions change and conditions later be judged favorable for such a move, Israel may yet try to achieve it. For the duration of the 1990s, however, this expectation did not appear to be forthcoming.

For most of the last decade since the early 1980s, a Jordanian-Palestinian federation has formed the mainstay of the political platform of the Labor Party in Israel. The JCSS study seems to suggest that there may still be room for this to be realized, though the chances, at least until the eruption of the Gulf War, were remote. In the aftermath of the war, the intervention of the United States in the "peace process" may have been based on precisely such a platform. In contrast, both Jordanians and Palestinians continued to discuss their future relationship more in terms of a confederation between two independent states, following Palestinian independence, rather than as an imposed "federation" of Jordan and Palestine. Theoretically, such an option would always be preferred by both the United States and Israel over that of an independent Palestinian state. And it was once again floated during Rabin's rule. Such an arrangement may require Israel to withdraw from only very limited areas in the West Bank rather than from the whole of the Occupied Territories. It would then keep Jerusalem and all areas where "strategic" settlements are located. Jordan's concern has been compounded by what it perceived as an unresponsive attitude of the United States, whose position has coincided closely with that of Israel. The Palestinian-Jordanian journalist Lamis Andoni reveals that after the civil war in Jordan during 1970–1971, King Hussein was informed by American officials that the United States was prepared to "sacrifice" the Jordanian kingdom if "Palestinians" seized power. Andoni elaborates on this report to convey the concern of Jordanian officials in the early 1980s that "some in Washington would be ready to sacrifice the regime and accommodate the Israeli claim that 'Jordan is Palestine,' if this appeared the only way out for Israel."[121] Perhaps not coincidental was the revival of claims after the September 1993 accords that "Jordan is Palestine," signaling possible U.S. approval of this approach as a long-term solution.[122]

In view of the coincidence between U.S. and Israeli interests, the interim self-rule arrangements could indeed culminate in such an outcome. This sequence of events could be accelerated by a combination of "push" and "pull" factors. Palestinians in the autonomous regions could tire of economic distress, the slow pace of development, or political instability and flock to Jordan. Or the establishment of the expected "cantons" (autonomous Palestinian regions) could entail large-scale Israeli measures to evacuate and expel people from regions (including towns and villages) in the West Bank and Gaza Strip that lie outside the designated Palestinian regions. In the event, many people could be forced into Jordan. Both Jordan and Lebanon were warning about such future scenarios. Lebanon declared its categorical refusal to allow Palestinian refugees to remain there (where an estimated 350,000 continue to reside).[123] Jordan, on the other hand, was rumored to have begun restricting West Bank residents entering Jordan from keeping their Jordanian passports. The purpose may have been to deter them from settling permanently in the country. Israeli officials have already declared their opposition to any wholesale "right of return" of Palestinians, even to the autonomous regions. The only alternative left for many Palestinians may inevitably be Jordan.

The JCSS study lists another option, that of unilateral withdrawal from the Gaza Strip. The West Bank, however, would remain under Israel control in this arrangement. This option was overtaken by the events of August and September 1993 and by the plans for "Gaza and Jericho first." However, much of the essence of the plan remains unchanged. The underlying rationale for such a move is that the Gaza Strip does not constitute part of the biblical lands of "Judea and Samaria." It is, therefore, conceivable that withdrawal from this area would not entail the kinds of political risks within Israel that would be associated with a withdrawal from most or all of the West Bank. Moreover, the Gaza Strip does not possess the water and other resources on which Israel is dependent, and the settler population remains at a minimum there. Throughout the years of occupation, the extreme deprivation of the Gaza Strip, whose residents are mainly dispossessed refugees, has made it a powder keg waiting to explode, as indeed it did during the *intifada*. Israel ultimately reached the point of wanting to rid itself of this economic and political burden.

We have left to the end a discussion of the second option listed in the JCSS study: autonomy. Once again superseded by events on the ground, details of this option remain significant, as they point to areas where continued Palestinian action is required to move from the autonomy stages (in whatever forms) to final and total independence. The JCSS study distinguishes between different degrees of autonomy, ranging from limited or partial autonomy to more extensive or full autonomy, depending on the degree of control afforded the Palestinians over their own affairs. Regardless of the type of autonomy being proposed, lands and many of the resources of the West Bank and Gaza Strip, as well as responsibility for security, would all remain under strict Israeli control. Palestinians and the PLO have generally been willing to consider some kind of interim arrangement, as indicated in their negotiations throughout the peace process. By virtue of such arrangements, Palestinians hoped that autonomy would lead to full Israeli withdrawal and the establishment of Palestinian sovereignty on the land.

Regardless of the array of political and economic constraints and factors, both internal and external, that caused Israel to opt for some form of autonomy as a means of accommodation, Palestinians are still faced with the task of directing their strategy to ensure that the question of Palestinian national rights is not swept aside altogether. Given the very real threat of displacement of Palestinians in a final arrangement, they cannot afford to wait for Israel, either on its own volition or through U.S. and international pressure, to gradually concede their national rights. Some additional pressure, therefore, needs to be exerted on other fronts. Palestinians must find ways of incorporating in their strategy viable mechanisms for coercing Israel to withdraw completely from the West Bank and Gaza Strip. This is the third process by which the outcome of the struggle can be determined.

Nonviolent coercion refers to a situation whereby the opponent may want to pursue the struggle but simply cannot.[124] Precipitating such an outcome is the responsibility of other actors in the conflict as well, and it may lie outside the immediate realm of Palestinian control. Yet Palestinians can sustain their pressure on Israel and cause increased polarization both within the government and among the Israeli public on the issue of occupation. They can work to increase the strains between Israel and its close American ally. Other means may be used to involve the UN in the peace process or involve it simply in the protection of Palestinians under occupation. Palestinians can use their newfound legitimacy, through the PLO, to press their case for the implementation of international law.

There remain serious countermeasures that Israel can bring to bear against any type of Palestinian civilian action. These should be discussed in relation to the choice of mechanisms. We have examined some of the customary measures that Israel has employed, including physical violence, economic sanctions, other means of collective punishment, and human rights violations. There are also measures that may at first glance appear to be too improbable to contemplate, but which, upon closer examination, still merit serious consideration.[125]

Settling Soviet Jewish, Ethiopian Jewish, or other immigrants in the Occupied Territories is one way of increasing both the Jewish population of the state and their presence in the Occupied Territories. Though not a direct response to Palestinian resistance, it remains a countermeasure in the sense that it creates physical facts on the ground and virtually ensures Israel's permanent control of these lands.[126] Some Palestinians have dismissed the significance of massive Soviet Jewish immigration by maintaining that, "all things being equal," this only sets back the "demographic time bomb" by another decade or two, after which they—Palestinians—may yet become a majority to be reckoned with.[127] Palestinians would not likely want to remain complacent and await their fate, as though the status quo would remain unchanged.[128] Though Labor has been willing to give up some lands, it has never committed itself to a total halt in building settlements, some of which are seen as vital for "security" purposes. For Palestinians, therefore, the final picture could either resemble a series of autonomous Palestinian "cantons," possibly linked with Jordan, or, at best, an autonomous Palestinian "entity" and not the state they envision.[129]

These are not the worst-case scenarios as far as the Palestinians are concerned. However threatening, such processes will likely occur gradually and would theoretically give Palestinians the time they need to meet such challenges as they arise. The real danger, in the Palestinian view, emanates from the ever-present threat of mass expulsions. Some Israeli officials, such as Ariel Sharon of the Likud Party, have never hidden their position that Israel should never give up the Occupied Areas and that "Jordan is Palestine." Though such statements do not necessarily amount to an actual policy of "transfer," they do underscore that in recent years this idea gained newfound acceptability in some official Israeli circles. What increases concerns for Palestinians is that such a policy could be implemented more easily during wartime, when it could be legitimized in view of "security," or when peoples' attention is diverted elsewhere.[130] Israel Shahak has frequently warned of the possibility of war with Syria and has insisted that not only will Israel not return any of the Occupied Territories, but "there will be no autonomy."[131] In the event of a return to Likud rule, and were such leaders as Benjamin Netanyahu to gain power (he warned that he would not necessarily honor any agreements reached with the PLO), this threat to Palestinians may yet be revived.[132]

*   *   *

Ultimately, Palestinian strategy must be aimed at making the Occupied Territories impossible to rule. If Israeli rule by political means has already failed, Palestinian options for the future also need to make this rule impossible by military means. This is an undeniably difficult task in the short term. Palestinians have endured incredible suffering as a result of the violence and repression used against them during the *intifada,* and as a result of the almost total collapse of their economy after the Gulf War.

Many Palestinians have been engaged in reevaluating their options, in deciding what their strategy needs to address, and in determining how different mechanisms could be employed to achieve their ultimate political goals. Selecting a technique of total nonviolent civilian resistance and nonviolent mechanisms of struggle may be unpopular and distrusted, especially in view of the passivity associated with these methods. However, the PLO's renunciation of violence, in return for securing Israeli recognition, may have given added legitimacy to this method. What would be required is not only a statement of what the PLO would not do, but an effort to establish what it could do. The question remains whether the PLO, reconstituted as a political entity in the proposed autonomous areas, can be a viable and democratic leadership that organizes the civilian population for the political and civilian struggles that lie ahead. Given the asymmetry of the situation and the forces aligned against them, Palestinians have to turn their own weaknesses into strengths and channel Israel's power to their own advantage. This was the promise of the *intifada*.

Conclusion

Palestinians have generally come around to accepting a two-state solution, as demanded by international legitimacy. Yet a two-state solution may always be perceived as a "compromise," with all of its attendant negative connotations and with a sense of having given up something valuable. Most obvious is that it may fall short of what each of the parties truly desires, whether a Greater Israel or a reconstituted Palestine. Still, many people view this solution positively. These include large sectors of Palestinians in the Occupied Territories, a number of PLO factions, and Israelis who support a state of Palestine coexisting alongside Israel. Contrary to the negative connotations of the word "compromise," "accommodation" in this instance would be an act of conscious choice that is based on the awareness that both sides can win.

By their explicit acceptance of a two-state solution, Palestinians have in effect liberated Jewish Israelis from their existential dilemmas concerning nationhood. Palestinians have "secularized" the conflict, away from historical claims, religious claims, and absolute and inalienable claims, into the realm of the secular, the possible, and the feasible. A two-state solution affords both parties legitimacy and a national identity. It removes political Zionism from the discourse, to focus instead on the colonial occupation of the lands taken in 1967. It leaves to the Israelis themselves the task of facing up to the implications of political Zionism and its implementation in Palestine. But it does require a reciprocal Israeli gesture—an indication that Israel too is willing to draw the line of its national existence at the doors of the Occupied Territories. Many Israelis remain fearful, since the very idea of Palestine is in a sense the negation of the idea of Israel.

Eventually the forces of history may yet merge the national identities of these two peoples destined to live together in this area. If Memmi's predictions are accurate, then there can be no compromise with colonialism and the ideologies that perpetrate it. If so, then even if Palestinians do not intend it, nor struggle for it, the racist and colonial aspects of political Zionism could yet be rendered obsolete and replaced by other ideals. While Memmi concentrates on the resistance of the colonized that works to split, erode, and finally destroy the colonizer from within, the Jewish theologian Marc Ellis looks at the process of transformation from another angle. Upon closer examination, his views appear to be the other side of the same coin. Ellis focuses on the internal contradictions of Judaism and Israeli "state power" and how the latter has corrupted Judaism.[1] He urges a return to Jewish values—to tolerance, human dignity, and reconciliation. In his view, the negation of Palestine and the Palestinians challenges everything Judaism has stood for. His solution is neither to seek nor to await a Palestinian resistance to make the contradictions no longer containable. Instead, he appeals to Jews to save themselves. Either Judaism or political Zionism must perish, or else the latter must be reconstituted in different moral terms.

For both Memmi and Ellis, the very existence of the other—the colonized, the occupied—exerts a constant pressure on the occupier, the oppressor. The colonized population forms a concrete reminder of its occupation and thus irrefutable proof of its corruption. Faced with this pressure, ever-increasing repression has to be used against a population that refuses to be dominated. So too must ever-increasing repression be employed to ward off the evils of the occupation from one's own eyes and to justify force and violence. It is a vicious circle that cannot be sustained indefinitely. Memmi talks of the inevitability of bringing down the whole structure by violent means. Ellis talks about reconstitution and reconciliation by choice.

Whether or not Judaism and political Zionism can be pried apart, as Ellis seems to suggest, is debatable.[2] Perhaps Israelis who advocate a two-state solution and Palestinians who struggle for this same goal can provide mutual reassurance and widen the circles of those who believe that conscious choices can save both peoples. Perhaps in the end, the most "radical" solution of all is for Jews and Arabs to share the land (two states, a single state, or whatever they decide), so that each nation's existence is essentially dependent on, rather than existentially exclusive of, the other.

For the time being, it appears that Zionism has made a tactical concession in return for a strategic victory. The Declaration of Principles signed in Washington in September 1993, as well as the letters of "mutual recognition" that preceded it, seemed to signal a strategic defeat for Palestinian nationalism.[3] Whether this situation is temporary or permanent depends on many factors, not least of which are the Palestinians.

The deliberate and conscious choice of Palestinians in the Occupied Territories to engage in a largely nonviolent civilian resistance, especially during the early years of the *intifada,* has clearly not been one of simple expediency. Both the selection of the technique and the strategy of resistance are commensurate with the articulated political goal, that of an independent Palestinian state alongside Israel. There could be no mistaking, however, the degree of Palestinian determination to reject the occupation and to refuse to remain subjugated.

Palestinians essentially have a window of two to five years to seriously prepare and implement their civilian resistance strategy against the Israeli occupation. After that date, strategic planning will become even more intricate. Different formulations would then be required. The reorganization of the Palestinian community into decentralized and diffuse loci of power, necessary to ensure the viability of a civilian resistance strategy, would require renewed mobilization, training, and support in the event of preparation for civilian-based defense.[4] The diffuse loci of power just mentioned would, in turn, need to be rooted in strong infrastructural supports—an area of economic development that should also be given priority during the interim phases. Such a degree of decentralization suggests some measure of democratic participation and independence of action, which the governing Palestinian council should be ready to permit.

Given the complexity of governance, and the major responsibilities facing the PLO in the "autonomous" Palestinian areas, it may be difficult to count on Palestinians reorganizing themselves within the limited time available. The immediate stages may be characterized by the usurpation and centralization of power by the reconstituted PLO. Primary responsibility for furthering the aims of national independence would then fall mainly upon its shoulders. The PLO would have to rely essentially on political and diplomatic techniques and ongoing negotiations with Israel to resolve issues in dispute. However, the basic asymmetry of the situation and the continued colonial context do not augur well for success based solely on these "political" methods. Arafat's pledge to renounce "violence" makes this an opportune time to launch a civilian resistance struggle as a way out of the dilemma in which the PLO may have locked the national liberation movement.

These difficulties should not be construed as a permanent deterrent to Palestinian action. A reinvigoration of Palestinian civilian resistance would erode Israel's political will in the occupied areas. Avenues for Palestinian action remain, and both Palestinians and the PLO could use the momentum generated by the agreements to establish the idea of Palestinian statehood within recognized borders as an objective that is both conceivable and inevitable. Palestinians would underscore their respect for international law and call attention to the responsibility of the world community to implement relevant UN resolutions. Meantime, their assumption of some kind of control over their own lives within the "autonomous" entities would help allay some Israeli fears concerning an independent Palestinian state at their doorstep. Using both political moves and civilian resistance, Palestinians would also need to keep the issue of East Jerusalem on the map[5] and address other outstanding concerns, such as the right of return and the status of Jewish settlements.

Palestinian efforts must rely on political means when needed, noncooperation when feasible, and the establishment of their alternative structures with a view to independence. Together, these efforts will push the limits of the interim agreements and challenge Israel to reach a different kind of accommodation, one that is based on acceptance of Palestinian national independence, not simply the imposition of autonomy.

Whatever unfolds in the future, Palestinians and Israelis recognize the more immediate need for separation. Perhaps both would consciously choose to achieve this "separation" peacefully. After their long and bitter history, both sides need time to heal, each within its own distinct sovereign entity. The stage would then be set for real mutuality and justice for both peoples.

Abbreviations

AAUG
Association of Arab-American University Graduates

ADC
American-Arab Anti-Discrimination Committee

ADL
Anti-Defamation League of B'nai B'rith

AIPAC
American Israel Public Affairs Committee

AMEU
Americans for Middle East Understanding

ANC
African National Congress

BBC
British Broadcasting Corporation

CBD
Civilian-based defense

CBS
Central Bureau of Statistics, Israel

DFLP
Democratic Front for the Liberation of Palestine

IDF
Israeli Defense Forces

IPS
Institute for Palestine Studies

JA
Jewish Agency

JCSS
Jaffee Center for Strategic Studies, Tel Aviv University

JNF
Jewish National Fund

JPS
Journal of Palestine Studies

MEI
Middle East International

MEJN
Middle East Justice Network

MERIP
Middle East Research and Information Project, now *Middle East Report*

NGC
National Guidance Committee

NLG
National Lawyers Guild

PASSIA
Palestinian Academic Society for the Study of International Affairs

PCSN
Palestine Center for the Study of Nonviolence

PFLP
Popular Front for the Liberation of Palestine

PHRIC
Palestine Human Rights Information Center, formerly the DataBase Project on
Palestinian Human Rights

PLO
Palestine Liberation Organization

PNC
Palestine National Council

PNF
Palestine National Front

PNS
Program on Nonviolent Sanctions in Conflict and Defense, Harvard University

UNLU
Unified Nationalist Leadership of the Uprising

UPMRC
Union of Palestinian Medical Relief Committees

WRMEA
Washington Report on Middle East Affairs, publication of the American Educational Trust

WZO
World Zionist Organization

Notes

Introduction

1. Mahmoud Darwish, "Investigation," quoted in Fawaz Turki, *The Disinherited: Journal of a Palestinian Exile* (New York: Monthly Review Press, 1972), p. 27.

2. The two general schools of thought in the study of nonviolent struggle include, on the one hand, people such as Gene Sharp and Adam Roberts, who evaluate nonviolent action in purely practical and strategic terms. On the other hand, those influenced by Gandhi insist that nonviolent struggle cannot be effective without an ideological commitment to pacifism and nonviolence. More is said about these two perspectives in a later chapter.

Chapter One

1. Benvenisti cites official Central Bureau of Statistics (CBS) figures as 860,000 for the West Bank and 560,000 for the Gaza Strip; *Jerusalem Post International Edition,* March 26, 1988. Estimated figures for early 1992 (based on different projections) set the minimum West Bank population total at 1,423,000, and that of the Gaza Strip at 767,000. See Ziad Abdeen and Hasan Abu-Libdeh, *Palestinian Population Handbook, Part I, The West Bank and Gaza Strip* (Jerusalem: Planning and Research Center, 1993), p. 26.

2. Sara Roy estimates the urban-based Gaza Strip population at 85 percent. See Sara Roy, *The Gaza Strip Survey, West Bank Data Base Project* (Boulder, CO: Westview Press, 1986), p. 10.

3. Two waves of Jewish immigration to Palestine between the late 1890s and the imposition of the British Mandate over Palestine in 1922 raised the Jewish population of Palestine to some 12 percent of the total population. At the time of the Balfour Declaration of 1917, when Jews were promised a "national home" in Palestine, Arabs comprised over 90 percent of the population. Jews owned about 2 percent of the land. By November 1947, the date of United Nations General Assembly Resolution 181, which called for the partition of Palestine into two states, Jews in

Palestine were less than one-third of the total population and owned some 7 percent of the land. The UN Partition Plan allocated 5,700 square miles of the most fertile coastal areas for Jews to establish their state (over 55 percent of the total land area). Meanwhile, Arabs would receive the remaining 4,300 square miles. John Quigley cites various sources to the effect that even in the proposed Jewish State, Jews themselves would have remained a demographic minority—499,020 Jews compared to 509,780 Arabs, compared to the Arab state, where 9,520 Jews would live among 749,101 Arabs; John Quigley, *Palestine and Israel: A Challenge to Justice* (Durham, NC: Duke University Press, 1990), p. 36. For more detailed statistics on the population composition, Jewish immigration and land distribution throughout the Mandate, see *A Survey of Palestine*. Prepared in December 1945 and January 1946 for the Information of the Anglo-American Committee of Inquiry, 1. Reprinted in full with permission from Her Majesty's Stationery Office by the Institute of Palestine Studies (Washington, DC: Institute for Palestine Studies, 1991). Also, *Supplement to Survey of Palestine*. Notes Compiled for the Information of the United Nations Special Committee on Palestine, June 1947 (Washington, DC: IPS, 1991); David Hirst, *The Gun and the Olive Branch* (London: Faber and Faber, 1977), pp. 20, 132; Appendix 1, "Population, Immigration and Land Statistics, 1919–1946," in Walid Khalidi (ed.), *From Haven to Conquest* (Washington, DC: Institute for Palestine Studies, 1987), pp. 841–844; and John Chapple, "Jewish Land Settlement in Palestine" (unpublished paper, 1964).

4. David Waines, "The Failure of the Nationalist Resistance," in Ibrahim Abu-Lughod (ed.), *The Transformation of Palestine* (Evanston, IL: Northwestern University Press, 1971), p. 219; and Doreen Warriner, *Land and Poverty in the Middle East* (London: Royal Institute of International Affairs, 1948), p. 63.

5. Theodore Herzl, *The Complete Diaries of Theodore Herzl*, 1 (New York: Herzl Press and Thomas Yoseloff, 1960), p. 88.

6. Benjamin Beit-Hallahmi analyzes how the State of Israel has exercised virtual monopoly over the definition and the terms of discourse associated with Zionism. Prior Jewish history and the experience of life in the "diaspora" are dismissed except as they substantiate the threat of anti-Semitism. In this way, Zionism and Zionist ideology have been redefined to serve Israeli state ideology. See Benjamin Beit-Hallahmi, *Original Sins* (London: Pluto Press, 1992). This said, the horrors of the Holocaust, in which some six million Jews perished under Nazism in Europe, has remained embedded in the Jewish psyche. Such an experience of absolute genocide has colored both Jewish attitudes and their perceptions toward Zionism and the State of Israel. See Tom Segev, *The Seventh Million: The Israelis and the Holocaust* (New York: Hill and Wang, 1993). There is no monolithic view; be they survivors of the Holocaust themselves or the children of survivors, many Jews—in Israel and abroad—have challenged the dominant Israeli state ideology and have struggled for a just peace for both Jews and Palestinians in the Middle East.

7. See Hans Kohn, "Zion and the Jewish National Idea," in Khalidi, *From Haven to Conquest*, pp. 807–840. There were also others who opposed political Zionism on religious grounds, believing that the creation of Israel as a state would only be fulfilled with the coming of the Messiah. Still others were anti-Zionists, who detected a chauvinism and racism in a movement that would deliberately displace Arabs in order to set up its own exclusively Jewish entity. It is noteworthy that many of the

original Jewish inhabitants of Palestine also resisted the intrusion of political Zionism from abroad. For more on these issues and other voices of dissent, see Khalidi, *From Haven to Conquest,* selected articles; and Quigley, *Palestine and Israel.*

8. Elmer Berger, "Zionist Ideology—Obstacle to Peace" (London: International Organization for the Elimination of All Forms of Racial Discrimination [EAFORD]), no. 16 (January 1981): 23, 27.

9. Attempts at a balanced and frank discussion of the impact of political Zionism on Palestinians in the United States have tended to equate the individual's criticism of Israel with anti-Semitism and with "terrorist PLO" leanings. Although political Zionism's achievements for Jews cannot be casually dismissed, the fulfillment of this Zionist enterprise culminated in the establishment of a "Jewish state," one whose existence is predicated on the necessary absence of Palestinians on its land. Early Zionist figures did not try to cloak the fact. Nowadays, criticism is muted and deflected by focusing on the "other side" and blaming the Arabs for their supposed intransigence. Or else, "liberal" Zionists have defined and channeled avenues for "legitimate" discourse into a discussion of the Occupied Territories, where the Zionist occupation has somehow overreached itself, without acknowledging the historical injustice committed against the Palestinian people on their original lands in Palestine. Examples of factual and balanced works on the subject include Simha Flapan, *The Birth of Israel* (New York: Pantheon Books, 1987); Michael Palumbo, *The Palestinian Catastrophe* (New York: Quartet Books, 1987); Paul Findley, *They Dare to Speak Out* (Westport, CT: Lawrence Hill, 1985); Maxime Rodinson, *Israel: A Colonial-Settler State ?* (New York: Monad Press, 1973); Berger, "Zionist Ideology"; and Alfred M. Lilienthal, *The Zionist Connection II: What Price Peace?* (Brunswick, NJ: North American, 1978).

10. See "The Basle Programme, 30 August 1897," translated and reprinted in Khalidi, *From Haven to Conquest,* pp. 89–91.

11. No comparable Arab bodies in Palestine were recognized by Britain.

12. Hans Kohn, an American Jewish historian and writer, states that the Zionist Organization wanted the Balfour Declaration to include the phrase "the reconstitution of Palestine as the national home" instead of "the establishment in Palestine of a national home," but that the British rejected this wording; in Khalidi, *From Haven to Conquest,* p. 827.

13. In Seeds of Conflict Series, 7, *Palestine the Twice-Promised Land* (Nendeln, Liechtenstein: KTO Press, 1978), 2, no.2, *The Jewish Cause,* p. 11. British interests in the area revolved around the need for war allies, capital and investment, and securing the trade routes to India. The settlement of Jews in Palestine would secure the support of Jews on the side of the Allies. There is extensive documentation on the collusion of British and Zionist interests in Palestine, and on the British role in facilitating the establishment of a Zionist settler colony. See for example, the Report by the Palestine Royal Commission (Peel) of 1937, in Seeds of Conflict Series, 7 (*ibid.*), 1, *The British Viewpoint* (1978), p. 12. Also see the statement by Lord Balfour to the British Government in 1919 on the calculated British refusal to consult the indigenous population about its future or its support for the Zionist enterprise. He states, "And Zionism, be it right or wrong, good or bad, is rooted in age-long traditions, in present needs, in future hopes, of far profounder import than the

desires and prejudices of the 700,000 Arabs who now inhabit the Ancient Land." "Memorandum by Mr. Balfour Respecting Syria, Palestine and Mesopotamia, 1919," quoted in Khalidi, *From Haven to Conquest*, p. 208.

14. Article 3(e) continues with a clause concerning the employment of "Jewish labor" only. See Sir John Hope Simpson, "On the Employment of Arab Labor," in Khalidi, *From Haven to Conquest*, p. 303. For an authoritative and carefully researched work on the genesis and operation of the JNF during the Mandate in Palestine, after the creation of the State of Israel in 1948, and in the West Bank and Gaza Strip after 1967, see Walter Lehn (in association with Uri Davis), *The Jewish National Fund* (New York: Kegan Paul International, 1988). Lehn notes that the idea for such a fund came as early as 1840 (p. 14). The JNF was legally registered in England in 1907, ten years before the Balfour Declaration. Lehn points out that once the British Mandate was imposed, "the JNF found itself in a congenial setting, with no legal or administrative impediments to the pursuit of its immediate or ultimate objectives—land acquisition with a view to the establishment of a Jewish state" (p. 48).

15. In Khalidi, *From Haven to Conquest*, p. 305. For more on this issue, see Lehn, *The Jewish National Fund*, pp. 164 ff.; and Meron Benvenisti, *The West Bank Handbook: A Political Lexicon* (Boulder, CO: Westview Press, 1986), p. 134. In the West Bank and Gaza Strip, millions of dollars have been invested in lands acquired by the JNF for the building of Jewish settlements, roads, and other "infrastructure." The Zionist Organization retains overall responsible for settlement policy in the Occupied Territories.

16. This provision is based on the law specifying that lands would remain in Jewish hands in perpetuity. These lands would cover 92 percent of the pre-1967 borders of Israel. See Lehn, *The Jewish National Fund*, pp. 50, 115, 118. Thus land owned by the JNF can only be used for Zionist goals, that is, for the benefit of the Jewish people. Quigley, *Palestine and Israel*, pp. 121–122, quotes sources to the effect that within the State of Israel, the government owns some 76 percent of the land, and the JNF, 16 percent. More important than actual ownership is that by virtue of the "covenant" between the JNF and the Israeli government, all state and publicly owned land would be administered under the JNF under the same procedures that apply to lands registered with the JNF.

17. The official declaration upon the establishment of the State of Israel specifies the signers as "representatives of the Jewish community of Eretz Israel and of the Zionist Movement." See Quigley, *Palestine and Israel*, p. 116. As Lehn (*The Jewish National Fund*, p. 96) explains, the creation of the State of Israel in 1948 was formalized as "the establishment of a Jewish State in the land of Israel" and not, as one would expect, a straightforward declaration of independence. He maintains that this distinction is important and was adopted deliberately. Eretz Israel depicts an entity, as yet unspecified, that could extend well beyond Israel's currently recognized borders. Berger quotes the first three paragraphs of another pertinent Basic Law, the 1952 Status Law (see note 19), where paragraph 1 reads, "The State of Israel regards itself as the creation of the entire Jewish people, and its gates are open, in accordance with its laws, to every Jew wishing to immigrate to it," "Zionist Ideology," p. 10.

18. In Quigley, *Palestine and Israel*, p. 118; and see Lehn, *The Jewish National Fund*, p. 97.

19. This law was formally passed in 1954. Most information on these laws come

from Lehn, *The Jewish National Fund,* pp. 98 ff.; Berger, "Zionist Ideology"; and Quigley, *Palestine and Israel.* Israel does not possess a constitution. Instead, a number of "Basic Laws" have assumed constitutional status. One such law concerns a "unified" Jerusalem as the capital of Israel. Another is the Law of Return (see references in note 23).

20. See Berger, "Zionist Ideology," p. 9; Sally V. Mallison and W. Thomas Mallison, "Zionism, Freedom of Information and the Law," *American Arab Affairs,* no. 24 (Spring 1988): 54; and Lehn, *The Jewish National Fund,* pp. 98, 115 ff. In 1971, the WZO/JA were split so that the WZO assumed responsibility for immigration and political activities abroad, and the JA focused on settlement and other activities in Israel. The "Status Law" was amended in 1975 to coordinate activities between both these organizations and the government of Israel; see Quigley, *Palestine and Israel,* pp. 119–120. Mallison and Mallison, "Zionism, Freedom of Information," p. 57, maintain that nothing changed as far as immigration was concerned, rather that these amendments were made to define the status of these organizations, so as to be more in tune with U.S. law and regulations pertaining to the functioning of agents of other countries.

21. Adopted by the Palestine National Council in 1968, this document is not a "covenant." Rather, as a "charter," it is a secular document, strictly delimited in time and space, and one that the Palestinians have insisted has been superseded by the Palestine National Council's Declaration of a "Palestinian State" in November 1988, and by Arafat's "mutual recognition" with Israel in September 1993.

22. See Lehn, *The Jewish National Fund,* p. 170, for information on how this covenant operates in practice in the Occupied Territories.

23. Quigley, *Palestine and Israel,* p. 126; Berger, "Zionist Ideology," pp. 9 ff. For implications of these laws for Palestinians, see Alfred Moleah, "Zionism and Apartheid: An Unlikely Alliance?" in International Organization for the Elimination of all Forms of Racial Discrimination (EAFORD) and American Jewish Alternatives to Zionism (AJAZ) (eds.), *Judaism or Zionism? What Difference for the Middle East?* (London: Zed Books, 1986), pp. 148–169.

24. See Paragraph 5 of Status Law, quoted in Berger, "Zionist Ideology," p. 16.

25. See for example, Sabri Jiryis, *The Arabs in Israel* (New York: Monthly Review Press, 1976) for a documented account of how these laws operate vis-à-vis the Palestinian citizens of Israel; also, Elia Zureik, Fouad Moughrabi, and Vincent F. Sacco, "Perception of Legal Inequality in Deeply Divided Societies: The Case of Israel," *International Journal of Middle East Studies,* 25, no.3 (August 1993): 423–442. Laws discriminate against Arabs, not only as citizens, but in the form of unequal rights to housing, education benefits, and the like. Also, Quigley, *Palestine and Israel,* pp. 131–151; and Lehn, *The Jewish National Fund.* Berger, "Zionist Ideology" (p. 17) states, "The official policy of the state is discriminatory."

26. Kahane maintained that it was impossible for Israel to be both Jewish and democratic. His solution was to call for the expulsion of all Arabs—those in the Occupied Territories, as well as the Arab citizens of the state.

27. See Palumbo, *The Palestinian Catastrophe,* pp. 4, 5, and a quote from Weitz's diary in Rodinson, *Israel: A Colonial-Settler State?* p. 16. For other documentation of Zionist policies in this regard, see Khalidi, *From Haven to Conquest.* For more on the policy of "transfer" both preceding and following the

establishment of the state, see Israel Shahak, "A History of the Concept of 'Transfer' in Zionism," *Journal of Palestine Studies, (JPS),* 28, no.3 (Spring 1989): 22–38. Also, Nur Masalha, *Expulsion of the Palestinians* (Washington, DC: Institute for Palestine Studies, 1992).

28. The Drobles plan was first formulated in 1978 and was later amended. It envisioned increasing the number of settlements and the Jewish population in the West Bank and Gaza Strip to one million within 30 years. See Lehn, *The Jewish National Fund,* p. 185; and Quigley, *Palestine and Israel,* p. 174. Lehn quotes Drobles as to the effects of this plan on Palestinians: "The Plan is a plan for Jews; I don't care if the Arabs accept it or not"; *The Jewish National Fund,* p. 185. JNF operations in the Occupied Territories often take place through subsidiaries. Lehn explains that this fact makes it very difficult to determine how much of the expropriated land in the West Bank and Gaza Strip is in the hands of the JNF and how much is in the hands of the Israeli government (pp. 140, 170, 172). He mentions the secrecy surrounding this issue, but says that by 1979, Israel had already "acquired" 66.8 percent of the land of the West Bank, pp. 172–185.

29. The Jewish author J. Klatzkin observes, "It is not by chance that Zionist policy has never tried to come to an understanding with the Arabs. It is a (designed) policy"; in T. Canaan, in Seeds of Conflict Series, 7, 3, *The Arabs—and Some Neutrals.* For similar statements by Jewish officials, see Palumbo, *The Palestinian Catastrophe;* Rodinson, *Israel: A Colonial-Settler State?;* and Khalidi, *From Haven to Conquest.*

30. Berger, "Zionist Ideology," pp. 7, 24.

31. Rodinson, *Israel: A Colonial-Settler State?* p. 69.

32. There are exceptions, notably South Africa, of which we will have more to say later.

33. The inherent existential dilemma needs to be acknowledged. Just as the PLO was required to "revise" its charter to acknowledge an Israeli legitimacy, Israel could adopt a formal constitution whose laws replace and supersede the "Basic Laws" described previously. This constitution would circumscribe Israel as the land of its citizens, both Arabs and Jews, and so define its borders officially and permanently as such. Adequate precautions could be taken to ensure the "right of return" and the fulfillment of relevant UN resolutions. The plans for self-rule for Palestinians, negotiated between the PLO and Israel in 1993, did not contain any such provisions. Essentially, the PLO exchanged recognition of Israel's "right to exist" in return for its recognition as a representative of the Palestinian "people."

34. The West Bank was officially merged into Jordan in 1950 and Jordanian law extended there. The Gaza Strip remained as an Egyptian "administered territory," where British Mandate law continued to apply.

35. Detailed and comprehensive information is readily available on the social structures of the West Bank and Gaza Strip prior to the Israeli occupation, as well as on the transformations that have occurred since then. For example, Naseer Aruri (ed.), *Occupation: Israel over Palestine* (Belmont, MA: Association of Arab-American University Graduates Press, 1983); Ibrahim Abu-Lughod and Baha Abu Laban (eds.), *Settler Regimes in Africa and the Arab World: The Illusion of Endurance* (Wilmette, IL: Medina University Press International, 1974); Quigley,

Palestine and Israel; selected issues of the *Journal of Palestine Studies;* and sources cited in subsequent notes.

36. See Sarah Graham-Brown, "Impact on the Social Structure of Palestinian Society," in Aruri, *Occupation,* pp. 223–255; and Salim Tamari, "Building Other People's Homes: The Palestinian Peasant's Household and Work in Israel," *JPS,* 11, no.1 (Autumn 1981): 31–67.

37. See Hussein Abu Al-Namel, *Gaza Strip, 1948–1967: Economic, Political, Sociological and Military Development* (Beirut: PLO Research Center, 1979, Arabic). Abu Al-Namel estimates that some 80 percent of the original inhabitants of the Strip lost their sources of income after 1948.

38. See Janet Abu-Lughod, "Israeli Settlements in Occupied Arab Lands: Conquest to Colony," *JPS,* 11, no. 2 (Winter 1982): 32.

39. Mordechai Nahumi, "Israel as an Occupying Power," *New Outlook,* 15, no. 5 (June 1972): 18; and Sheila Ryan, "Israeli Economic Policy in the Occupied Territories: Foundations of a New Imperialism," *Middle East Research and Information Project (MERIP) Reports* no. 24 (January 1974): 3–24.

40. Quoted from the *Jerusalem Post,* July 15, 1976, in Report of the National Lawyers Guild (NLG) 1977 Middle East Delegation, *Treatment of Palestinians in Israeli-Occupied West Bank and Gaza Strip* (New York: NLG, 1978), p. 12.

41. "Report of the Secretary-General U Thant on Mr. Gussing's Mission in the Occupied Territories," September 15, 1967, in Ann Lesch, "Israeli Deportation of Palestinians from the West Bank and the Gaza Strip, 1967–1978," *JPS,* 8, no. 2 (Winter 1979); Ann Lesch, "Israeli Deportation of Palestinians from the West Bank and Gaza Strip, 1967–1978 (Part II)," *JPS,* 8, no.3 (Spring 1979); and Michael Adams, *Publish It Not . . .* (London: Longman Group, 1975), p. 76.

42. Janet Abu-Lughod, "The Demographic Consequences of Occupation," in Aruri, *Occupation,* p. 255.

43. Report for 1970, in *The Arabs Under Israeli Occupation* (Beirut: Institute for Palestine Studies, 1977), p. 14. Israel Shahak cites an identical figure, in "Memorandum to the Special Committee to Investigate Israeli Practices Affecting Human Rights in the Occupied Territories," June 8, 1970, *Palestine International Documents on Human Rights, 1948–1972* (Beirut: Institute for Palestine Studies, 1972), p. 282. Also see Felicia Langer, "Four Years of Occupation," *New Perspective,* 1, no. 2 (August 1971): 32.

44. Ann Lesch, "Israeli Deportation," Winter 1979, p. 102.

45. In the few cases where Israel does permit "family reunification," permission is not necessarily granted to all the members of the same family. See A. C. Forrest, *The Unholy Land* (Toronto: McClelland and Stewart, 1972), p. 46. Close to 100,000 of the 300,000 Palestinians who fled applied to return. By the early 1970s, only about 15,000 had been allowed to do so. See Nahumi, "Israel as an Occupying Power."

46. Abu-Lughod, "Israeli Settlements," p. 33; and Raja Shehadeh and Jonathan Kuttab, *The West Bank and the Rule of Law* (Geneva: International Commission of Jurists, 1980), pp. 102–103.

47. As discussed later, settlement policy varied according to which party, Labor or Likud was in power in Israel.

48. Comprehensive documentation of these and other measures are readily

available; see Jonathan Kuttab and Raja Shehadeh, *Civilian Administration in the Occupied West Bank* (Ramallah, West Bank: Law in the Service of Man, 1982); and Raja Shehadeh, *Occupier's Law* (Washington, DC: IPS, 1985). The following section simply summarizes the relevant information and its implications for Palestinians.

49. Reprinted in *Palestine: International Documents on Human Rights*, p. 103.

50. Meron Benvenisti, *West Bank Data Base Project, 1987 Report, Demographic, Economic, Legal, Social and Political Developments in the West Bank* (Boulder, CO: Westview Press, 1987), p. 52; and Roy, *The Gaza Strip Survey*, Table 7.2, p. 140. In an article reprinted from the Israeli daily *Haaretz*, June 22, 1990, the Palestine Human Rights Information Center, *Human Rights Update, June 1990*, reports that the number of settlers was then estimated at 84,000 for the West Bank and 5,400 for the Gaza Strip (excluding East Jerusalem).

51. Estimates vary according to the sources. A report by Peace Now, "A Summary of Government Activities in the Settlements in 1991," January 22, 1992, provides this estimate of 157 settlements. The same report states that the Israeli government puts the official figure at 144. However, the number of Jewish settlers estimated by Peace Now is less than that provided by the government and other agencies. The Peace Now Report is summarized in *News From Within*, 8, no. 2 (February 5, 1992).

52. See Jan Metzger, Martin Orth, and Christian Sterzing, *This Land Is Our Land: The West Bank Under Israeli Occupation* (London: Zed Press, 1983), pp. 19–20.

53. See, for example, statements by Ariel Sharon, who occupied various posts, including minister of agriculture, defense, and housing; NLG, *Treatment of Palestinians*, p. 16. See also Ibrahim Matar, "Israeli Settlements in the West Bank and Gaza Strip," *JPS*, 11, no. 1 (Autumn 1981): 93–111.

54. This policy excluded East Jerusalem, which was officially annexed in 1967. Professor Ra'anan Weitz, head of the Jewish Agency's settlement department, interviewed on Jerusalem Radio in June 1977, spoke of settlements as having "established the facts of the map of Israel," see NLG, *Treatment of Palestinians*, p. 13. The confiscation and settlement of Palestinian lands must be viewed in the context of both Israeli colonial interests—for resources and raw materials—and the ideological elements peculiar to Zionism.

55. More is said on the Camp David Accords and their corollaries in the peace process later. For a comprehensive analysis and documentation of Israeli settlement policies, see Abu-Lughod, "Israeli Settlements," pp. 16–55. The World Zionist Organization's Five Year Master Settlement Plan formed the underpinnings of then Agriculture Minister Ariel Sharon's settlement policy. See also *Al-Hamishmar*, March 23, 1979, cited in *MERIP Reports*, no. 78 (1979): 19–20; and Matar, "Israeli Settlements," p. 99.

56. Kuttab and Shehadeh, *Civilian Administration*, p. 32. Much of the following documentation on laws and regulations pertaining to land acquisition is from Shehadeh, *Occupier's Law*, pp. 17–50.

57. Traditional Islamic, Ottoman, and Jordanian laws granted rights of land use to those who cultivated it. Private property deeds in the hands of single individuals were uncommon, unless owned by big landlords or registered after the Ottomans revised the land code in the mid-nineteenth century. During the period of Jordanian

rule, title deeds in the West Bank were in the process of being settled. However, in 1968, after occupying the area, Israel issued a military order suspending all land registration procedures.

58. Danny Rubinstein, "West Bank, New Method of Land Seizure," *JPS*, 10, no. 4 (Summer 1981): 137. Reprinted from *Davar*.

59. Shehadeh, *Occupier's Law*, p. 38.

60. Abu-Lughod, "Israeli Settlements," p. 46; and Shehadeh and Kuttab, *The West Bank and the Rule of Law*, p. 109.

61. Kuttab and Shehadeh, *Civilian Administration*, p. 32; and Shehadeh, *Occupier's Law*, p. 35. This is applicable even when people had simply been on a visit outside the area at the time. The corresponding law in Israel defines an absentee as anyone who was outside the "area" (including one's area of residence in Palestine) between November 29, 1947 and May 19, 1948.

62. Shehadeh, *Occupier's Law*, p. 35. Through use of the same "absentee" laws, the Israeli authorities have, since the early 1990s, stepped up their claims to Palestinian lands and homes in East Jerusalem.

63. Shehadeh, *Occupier's Law*, p. 54. On a visit to the Occupied Territories in July 1993, I traveled extensively in the West Bank and saw road construction in progress. Arab orchards, farms, and other cultivated areas that lay in the path of these "developments" were simply destroyed.

64. Shehadeh, *Occupier's Law*, p. 55.

65. See Jamil Hilal, *The West Bank: Economic and Social Structures* (Beirut, Lebanon: PLO Research Center, 1975), p. 284 (Arabic).

66. This terminology derives from the field of development and underdevelopment studies. Characteristic of such works is the perspective that analyzes the articulation of two unequal modes of production. In the event of the penetration of a capitalist economy into a precapitalist one, it tends to transform or destroy existing indigenous formations, or subsume them into its own. For an example of the application of this perspective in the Palestinian case, see Abdullah Abu Ayyash, "Israeli Regional Planning Policy in the Occupied Arab Territories," *JPS*, 5, nos. 3–4 (Spring/Summer 1976): 83–109.

67. R. Muslih, "Palestinian Workers in the Occupied Territories," *Shu'un Filastiniya*, part 1, no. 115 (June 1981): 14–29 (Arabic).

68. Ryan, "Israeli Economic Policy," p. 12; NLG, *Treatment of Palestinians*, p. 40; Hilal, *The West Bank*; also various authors in George T. Abed (ed.), *The Palestinian Economy: Studies in Development Under Prolonged Occupation* (London: Routledge, 1988).

69. Documentation for the years before the *intifada* show, for example, that in 1970, 39.3 percent (down from 45 percent in 1969) of West Bank laborers worked in agriculture in the West Bank, but by 1984, this figure had dropped to 22.4 percent (19 percent in 1985) of the labor force. The same period witnessed an increase in the percentage of West Bank employees in the Israeli agricultural sector. See Israeli Central Bureau of Statistics (CBS), *Statistical Abstract of Israel, 1985,* Tables XXVII/23 and XXVII/25, p. 730. See also Hisham Awartani, "Agricultural Development and Policies in the West Bank and Gaza," in Abed, *The Palestinian Economy*, pp. 143–145. Awartani quotes similar figures from the Israeli CBS for the years 1969 through 1985.

70. State of Israel, Ministry of Defense, Coordinator of Government Operations in Judaea-Samaria, Gaza District, Sinai and Golan Heights, *A Thirteen Year Survey (1967–1980)*, January 1, 1981, p. 13.

71. Roy, *The Gaza Strip Survey*, p. 38; and Ziad Abu-Amr, "The Gaza Economy, 1948–1984," in Abed, *The Palestinian Economy*, pp. 103, 105. Prior to 1967 citrus fruits accounted for 70 percent of all agricultural exports; see Roy, *The Gaza Strip Survey*, p. 44.

72. In contrast, although in 1970 only 10 percent of the Strip's labor force worked in Israel, by 1984 this figure rose to over 46 percent. During the same period, work within the Gaza Strip declined from 90 percent of the Strip's laborers to only 54 percent.

73. Israel, Ministry of Defense, *A Thirteen Year Survey*, p. 15.

74. Quoted in Abu-Lughod, "Israeli Settlements," p. 50.

75. Regulations cover wells in operation before 1967. Up to 25 percent of Israel's own annual water consumption comes from the West Bank; Benvenisti, *The West Bank Handbook*, p. 223. In 1982 the Israeli water company, Mekorot, was given control over the West Bank water supply by the military government. West Bank water resources total 600 million cubic meters. Of these, Israel uses 475 million cubic meters, while only 115 million cubic meters are allowed for Palestinian use. Abu-Amr, "The Gaza Economy," p. 108, presents a similar picture for the Gaza Strip, where scarce water resources are disproportionately exploited by Israeli settlers in the area.

76. Even in the period preceding 1967, only 7 percent of the total labor force of the West Bank was engaged in industrial work; Nahumi, "Israel as an Occupying Power," p. 19. Most of the industries were small, workshop-type ventures specializing in olive oil processing, textiles, stone quarrying, food processing, and metallurgy that employed less than 15 people; Bakir Abu Kishk, "Industrial Development and Policies in the West Bank and Gaza," in Abed, *The Palestinian Economy*, p. 166. Abu Kishk notes that there was some expansion of industry in the 1950s, but that Jordanian policy tended to favor industrial development and investment in the East Bank. Industry in the Gaza Strip also remained undeveloped, with minor investment and limited employment in this sector. Small workshops continued to dominate the industrial sector, and in 1984 they accounted for 17.6 percent of the Gaza Strip labor force; Roy, *The Gaza Strip Survey*, p. 54.

77. Benvenisti, *The West Bank Handbook*, p. 113.

78. Roy, *The Gaza Strip Survey*, p. 65, quotes Benvenisti's characterization of this situation as one of "integration and exclusion." She writes, "Integration into the dominant economy when it benefits that economy and exclusion when it does not, has created an industrial base inside the Gaza Strip of limited production, absorption and marketing capabilities. Consequently, the Strip has been unable to develop the infrastructure needed to support and promote industrial growth and remains highly dependent upon Israel to generate activity within that sector."

79. Ryan, "Israeli Economic Policy," pp. 10, 14; *Al-Fajr*, August 9, 1987; and NLG, *Treatment of Palestinians*, p. 35.

80. Sheila Ryan, "The Political Consequences of Occupation," *MERIP Reports*, no. 74 (January 1979): 6; and Sarah Graham-Brown, "The Structural Impact of Israeli Colonization," *MERIP Reports*, no. 74 (January 1979): 15.

81. Yusuf Sayigh, "Dispossession and Pauperization: The Palestinian Economy Under Occupation," in Abed, *The Palestinian Economy,* p. 262.

82. After the closure, only some 21,000 Gaza Strip workers and 30,000 West Bank workers received permits to work in Israel; see Tzvi Gilat, "Four Months Since the Closure: The Balance Sheet," *Yediot Ahronot,* August 6, 1993, *From the Hebrew Press,* October 1993. In October 1993, the Israeli authorities announced that they would be lifting restrictions against certain Palestinians entering Jerusalem and traveling to Israel.

83. Ryan, "Israeli Economic Policy," p. 12.

84. Figures for 1984, Israeli CBS, *Statistical Abstract of Israel, 1985.*

85. Roy, *The Gaza Strip Survey,* p. 33.

86. Ryan, "The Political Consequences of Occupation," p. 7; Jamil Hilal, "Class Transformation in the West Bank and Gaza Strip," *MERIP Reports,* no. 53 (October 1976): 10; and Roy, *The Gaza Strip Survey,* p. 33.

87. The peculiarity of Israel's colonial occupation of the West Bank and Gaza Strip has juxtaposed Palestinian wage labor in a direct class relationship to the capitalist classes in the Israeli economy, rather than to an indigenous Palestinian bourgeoisie class. This relationship is revealing in terms of class awareness in the Occupied Territories, but the implications are not elaborated here.

88. Reportedly said to former U.S. President Jimmy Carter; see the *Toronto Star,* October 4, 1982.

89. The latter was attributed to Israeli Chief of Staff Raphael Eitan in 1982.

90. For example, Sidney J. Boxendale, "Taxation of Income in Israel and the West Bank: A Comparative Study," *JPS,* 28, no. 3 (Spring 1989): 134–142. Boxendale demonstrates how Palestinians have been taxed at a higher rate than Israelis, including the Jewish settlers of the Occupied Territories. Moreover, to encourage Israeli settlement in these areas, Jewish settlers in the Occupied Territories received a 7 percent reduction in their income tax, compared to Israelis living within the 1948 borders. See "Young Israeli Couples 'Forced' to Live in Occupied Territories," translated from *Haaretz* of July 13, 1990, in *Al-Fajr,* July 30, 1990, p. 10.

91. The amounts of money generated in the Occupied Territories, through taxation and other means, cannot but challenge the view held in some Israeli circles that the Occupied Territories constituted an economic burden on Israel, and that Israeli allocations for the development of these areas have been low because of low revenues. Benvenisti claims that throughout the first 19 years of occupation, until 1985, US$600 million to US$700 million was "contributed" by West Bank Palestinian residents to the Israeli economy. He maintains that this amounts to a virtual "occupation tax"; *The West Bank Handbook,* p. 92. Apart from regular taxes, others include income tax and property tax. Moreover, exorbitant taxes have been imposed on businesses and industries in the Occupied Territories. Equipment imported for medical and educational purposes is subjected to high taxes. Taxes are paid upon leaving the Occupied Territories, duties are imposed for the marketing of West Bank and Gaza Strip produce in Israel, taxes are levied for the issuance of various licenses and permits, and payments are required for a multitude of other reasons.

92. These developments may explain occasional overtures from Israeli officials

indicating they may accept some form of limited autonomy for Palestinians. Israel would retain control over the lands and resources of the Occupied Territories, while at the same time relieving itself of the responsibility to ensure a basic level of Palestinian subsistence. Palestinians are well aware that both their economic and political costs to Israel have begun to outweigh the benefits. A comparative example from South Africa may be instructive. There, the South African government faced similar dilemmas emanating from its policy of apartheid. Black South Africans were able to use their presence as an indispensable labor force to organize trade unions and engage in massive labor struggles. These activities proved quite effective in putting pressure on "white" South Africa to eventually reform its system.

93. The Occupied Territories were envisioned as becoming the equivalent of Mexico in the North American Free Trade Agreement (NAFTA); see, for example, Asher Davidi, "Israel's Economic Strategy for Palestinian Independence," *Middle East Report,* no. 184 (September-October 1993): 24–27. Also see Mary Jenin, "Is Land of Milk and Honey for Israel Only?" *Breaking the Siege,* (October–November 1993): 9; *New York Times,* September 18, 1993; and Chapter Five.

94. A similar pattern has existed in the service sector, where Israel issued numerous military orders to restrict the autonomy and self-sufficiency of indigenous Palestinian institutions. A study of this sector, including health and education, is omitted here.

95. In Benvenisti, *The West Bank Handbook,* p. 143. Section 2 of the proclamation reads, "All laws which were in force in the Area on June 7, 1967, shall continue to be in force as long as they do not contradict this or any other proclamation or order made by [the West Bank area commander] or conflict with the changes arising by virtue of the occupation by the Israeli IDF of the Area"; in Kuttab and Shehadeh, *Civilian Administration,* p. 10.

96. Benvenisti, *The West Bank Handbook,* p. 196.

97. Under the Jordanian Law of Municipalities of 1955, municipal governments in the East and West Banks were public institutions that enjoyed political authority and financial independence. A municipality had the legal responsibility to perform its official functions, such as providing services to the population, financing and approving development projects, issuing building permits, levying taxes, and the like, free from external interference. Mayors were elected, although some were dismissed and replaced by appointees of the government. Under the Israeli occupation, all powers concerning municipalities were usurped by the military government. Military Order 194—"Order Concerning the Municipalities Law—1967," reads as follows: "Granting the 'Person Responsible' all the powers vested in the Jordanian King, Government, Ministers or Direct Commissioner by virtue of the Municipalities Law of 1955 and making several amendments to that law"; Kuttab and Shehadeh, *Civilian Administration,* p. 39.

98. Shehadeh and Kuttab, *The West Bank,* p. 115.

99. These earlier elections were supported by Jordan but opposed by the PLO, as the latter feared the extensive influence of pro-Jordanian authorities; see Emile Sahiliyeh, *In Search of Leadership: West Bank Politics Since 1967* (Washington, DC: Brookings Institution, 1988), pp. 36 ff.

100. See Abdul Jawad Saleh, *Israel's Policy of De-Institutionalization: A Case*

Study of Palestinian Local Governments (London: Jerusalem Center for Development Studies, 1987); and Shehadeh and Kuttab, *The West Bank,* p. 115.

101. See NLG, *Treatment of Palestinians,* p. 45. In 1978, Israel tried another tactic to marginalize and bypass the popularly elected councils. It created the collaborationist Village Leagues, an alternative leadership that it anticipated would be more supportive of the Camp David agreements. Though they received money, arms, and support from Israel, the Village Leagues were discredited and boycotted by Palestinians. By 1984 they had lost much of their significance, and by the end of the first few weeks of the *intifada,* the last vestiges of the leagues disappeared.

102. See Emile Nakhleh, *The West Bank and Gaza* (Washington, DC: American Enterprise Institute for Public Policy Research, 1979), p. 15.

103. Benvenisti, *The West Bank Handbook,* p. 67.

104. The ban was lifted sometime later. *Sumud,* roughly translated as "steadfastness," refers to the staying power of the people on the land and the preservation of their identity and society in the face of continued occupation and dispossession.

105. After 1984 more flexibility was allowed in the receipt of funds from abroad. This was to reduce the costs to Israel of maintaining Palestinian municipal services. Development projects were the most likely to be rejected. Benvenisti notes that most public investment "goes towards improving services with only a small part going to economic development"; *The West Bank Handbook,* p. 180. Israel insisted on controlling even those funds originating in the United States, which in 1986 amounted to $14.9 million; (up to about $25 million by the early 1990s); see Eugene Bird, "At the Grass Roots, Westerners Say, 'Rein in Israel,' " *Washington Report on Middle East Affairs,* September/October 1993, p. 17. Similar problems confront nongovernment private voluntary organizations (PVOs) in the Occupied Territories, particularly Israel's "selective approval" of development projects. Benvenisti writes, "Whereas PVO intention had been to invest 45.8 percent of their total budget in economic development and 30 percent in public works, the Israeli authorities reversed the proportions—30% for economic development and 44% for public works"; Meron Benvenisti, U.S. *Government Funded Projects in the West Bank and Gaza (1977–1983) (Palestinian Sector)* (Jerusalem: West Bank Data Base Project, 1984), p. 10.

106. In Kuttab and Shehadeh, *Civilian Administration,* p. 47.

107. Benvenisti, *The West Bank Handbook,* p. 167.

108. See *Breaking the Siege,* 5, no. 3 (August-September 1993): 7. Keep in mind that UN Security Council Resolution 242 of November 1967 called upon Israel to withdraw from "territories" it occupied during the 1967 War (ostensibly UN Resolutions 242 and 338 were to form the basis for the negotiations) and that the Occupied West Bank and Gaza Strip themselves (including East Jerusalem) comprise some 21 percent of the original Mandate Palestine.

109. In a single year, by the end of 1980, more than 33 Palestinian mayors and officials in the Occupied Territories were reported to be under house arrest; *The Middle East,* February 1981, p. 32. Other officials have been imprisoned or deported, such as mayors Mohammed Milhem of Halhoul, Fahd Qawasmeh of Hebron, and Abdul Jawad Saleh of Al-Bireh.

110. Benvenisti, *The West Bank Handbook,* p. 10; also see Fayez Sayegh, "The Camp David Framework for Peace," Association of Arab American University

Graduates, *Special Report,* no. 3 (Belmont: MA: AAUG, February 1979), p. 14. The full text of the accords can be found in AAUG *(ibid.),* p. 82. Also see "Israeli Cabinet Communiqué," September 2, 1982, in *JPS,* 12, no. 6 (Winter 1983): 212.

111. Benvenisti explains, "The autonomous region will not have geographic borders, for it will be personal-communal autonomy, not territorial"; *The West Bank Handbook,* p. 11.

112. In 1985 there were renewed efforts to assign Palestinian figures to replace the Israeli municipal officials. In Nablus, in 1986, the person chosen as mayor was assassinated by Palestinians, and as a consequence many candidates in other West Bank towns withdrew their candidacy.

113. Kuttab and Shehadeh explain this distinction, and how this conforms to Israel's interpretation of the Camp David Accords, which requires it to "withdraw" but not necessarily "abolish" the military government; Kuttab and Shehadeh, *Civilian Administration,* p. 14. Another order, Military Order 950, "amends" the original Order 947 to read, "In order to remove any doubt, nothing in the provisions of this Order restricts or abrogates any privilege or power vested in the Commander of the Israeli Defense Forces in the area or in whoever was appointed by him or his agents"; Article 6(b) of Military Order 947 *(ibid.,* p. 26).

114. See Kuttab and Shehadeh, *Civilian Administration,* pp. 8, 14, 181; Benvenisti, *The West Bank Handbook,* p. 24; and Shehadeh, *Occupier's Law,* p. 70.

115. There is continued debate over Israel's use of the British Emergency Regulations (which were widely criticized by Jews themselves in early Palestine as "Nazi"). These were officially repealed by the British in 1948, before the creation of the Israeli state. Moreover, legislation enacted by Jordan during the years of its rule over the West Bank effectively and legally superseded these earlier laws. Israel, however, insists that neither the British nor the Jordanians had officially repealed these laws, and on this basis claims that it is legal to enforce them in the Occupied Territories.

116. See NLG, *Treatment of Palestinians,* p. 65.

117. NLG, *Treatment of Palestinians,* p. 65, quotes a 1968 radio interview with Israeli General Shlomo Gazit, then military administrator of the Occupied Territories, to this effect.

118. For example, *Boston Globe,* February 7, 1990; and *Al-Fajr,* July 16, 1990, p. 13, and June 25, 1990, p. 13.

119. See Andrea Lorenz, "Malnutrition in West Bank and Gaza," *Washington Report on Middle East Affairs,* September/October 1993, p. 64. She states that this number includes only those demolitions carried out in 1993. Other reports state that house demolitions by means of antitank missiles began in 1992; see "Israel Uses War Policy of Pursuit and Punishment: Israeli Anti-Tank Missiles Destroy Palestinian Homes," in *"From the Field," A Monthly Report on Selected Human Rights Issues,* Palestine Human Rights Information Center (PHRIC), February 1993. The report notes 19 homes were demolished and 83 were seriously damaged, leaving about 1,000 people homeless.

120. In its April 1991 *Human Rights Update,* the PHRIC lists a total of 5,529 curfew days for the West Bank since the beginning of the *intifada,* and 4,416 for the Gaza Strip. By the end of March 1993, these figures had almost doubled, with a total of 14,852 curfew days for both the West Bank and Gaza Strip; see PHRIC, *Human Rights Violations Summary Data Through 31 March 1993.*

121. They must, however, return within three years, or else risk losing their residency rights in the Occupied Territories. In 1993, there was news about the lifting of some of these restrictions.

122. See Al-Haq, *Punishing A Nation: Human Rights Violations During the Palestinian Uprising, December 1987–December 1988* (Jerusalem: Al-Haq, 1989), p. 229.

123. This initial period of detention was extended to one year during the *intifada.*

124. By the sixth year of the *intifada,* more than 18,000 Palestinians had been placed under administrative detention; see PHRIC, *Human Rights Update,* March 1993. These do not include the tens of thousands of Palestinians who had been detained and then released, or else imprisoned for varying periods. By the end of 1988, the first year of the *intifada,* these were estimated at between 30,000 and 40,000; see PHRIC, *The Cost of Freedom: Palestinian Human Rights Under Israeli Occupation, 1988, A Special Report* (Chicago: DataBase Project on Palestinian Human Rights, 1989), p. 16.

125. Shehadeh, *Occupier's Law,* p. 146. During the *intifada,* there were reports of Palestinians placed in detention or imprisoned for expressing their desire for peace and a two-state solution. One example concerns the case of a journalist, Yusuf Jubeh, who was issued a ten-and-a-half-month detention order in 1990. He reportedly expressed this position during an appearance before an appeal judge in June 1990. Amnesty International then adopted his case; see *Al-Fajr,* July 16, 1990. See also Amnesty International Report, 1993, "Israel and the Occupied Territories," New York, July 1993, in *JPS,* 23, no. 1 (Autumn 1993): 138–141, concerning Palestinian prisoners, deaths in detention, and other concerns.

126. Benvenisti, *The West Bank Handbook,* p. 54.

127. *Jerusalem Post International Edition,* November 17, 1987. For a summary of international concerns about charges of torture in Israeli prisons, see also George Katsiaficas, "Behind Bars in Israel," AAUG, *Mideast Monitor,* 5, no. 1 (1988). The Israeli civil rights group B'Tselem has also been investigating this issue. Its 1991 report, for example, documents dozens of such reported cases; see Ran Kislev, "We Have Already Accepted Torture," *Haaretz,* April 30, 1993, *From the Hebrew Press,* July 1993. Also, B'Tselem, "Rise in the Number of Deaths of Palestinians at the Hands of the Security Forces in the Territories, from August 1992 Through January 1993."

128. See also *Jerusalem Post International Edition,* November 14, 1987. The article notes, "To obtain the convictions they wanted, the interrogators resorted, when necessary, to perjury."

129. *Jerusalem Post International Edition,* November 21, 1988, p. 11, voices some of these concerns.

130. See Karen White, "Torture, Perjury, and Palestinian Children," *WRMEA,* February 1988, pp. 8–10; and Reverend Canon Riah Abu El-Assal et al., "Children in Israeli Military Prisons," mimeographed report.

131. The first to publicize this Form in Israel was a journalist for *Davar;* Michal Sela, "The Silence of the Physicians," *Davar,* April 30, 1993, *From the Hebrew Press,* May–June 1993. The actual Form was published in *Al-Fajr,* June 28, 1993, p. 10. Also see *New York Times,* August 14, 1993.

132. For more on the subject, see various issues of *Al-Fajr* as well as the *Human Rights Updates* issued by the PHRIC. The *Human Rights Update* of May 1990, for example, puts the total number of Palestinians who died in prison since the beginning of the *intifada* at 18. Of these, four were shot, 11 were beaten or tortured, and three were denied access to adequate medical treatment. Also see Al-Haq, *Punishing A Nation,* pp. 245 ff. In 1992, three cases of deaths resulting from torture were documented by the Mandela Institute for Political Prisoners in the Occupied Territories; see its newsletter, *Samed,* August 1993. The Israeli human rights group B'Tselem has also been involved in tracing and documenting such cases.

133. Benvenisti, *The West Bank Handbook,* p. 86.

134. Abdul Jawad Saleh, *Deportation* (Beirut: PLO Unified Information, 1977). He was allowed back along with 29 other long-term deportees. Some Palestinian observers interpret this as a trade-off: in return for maintaining the exile of the 413 alleged *Hamas* activists expelled in December 1992 (whose number by then had decreased to about 397). During my trip to the Occupied Territories in July 1993, I talked to many Palestinians who were bitter about the decision to repatriate deportees, especially since UN Security Council Resolution 799 (of December 1992) specifically demanded the immediate return of the exiled Palestinians, and since only a handful of the 30 allowed back decided to remain in the Occupied Territories.

135. Saleh, *Israel's Policy of De-Institutionalization,* pp. 131–132. To highlight the injustice of deportation, in January 1988 the Palestine Liberation Organization was to charter a boat to sail to Haifa. On board the Boat of Return, as it was called, were to be hundreds of international figures, journalists, some Israeli supporters, and about 100 Palestinian deportees. It was widely reported that Israel was responsible for the subsequent sabotage of the mission, by planting a bomb that exploded and left a huge hole in the boat. This incident highlighted two important concerns. First, it exposed Israel's deportation policy and proved that most of the deportees were indeed nationalist, responsible, and respected community figures, and not terrorists. Second, it indicated that the PLO was capable of nonviolent means of struggle, even if, as in this case, it was limited to a symbolic form of protest that finally had to be aborted.

136. Some came from the village of Beita, where two Palestinians were killed by Jewish settlers, and where a Jewish settler girl was accidentally shot by a Jewish bodyguard in April 1988. These figures do not include the 250 or so women and children—families of legal West Bank residents—who were forcibly deported to Jordan during 1989–1990, on the grounds that they were living in the Occupied Territories without valid permits. Israel subsequently announced that some of these deportees could return, though I could find no documentation to verify whether that return indeed occurred. A number of Palestinians seeking medical treatment abroad or those needing to travel for other reasons were reportedly given permission to leave the Occupied Territories on condition that they did not return for three years—in effect, deportation. (Personal interview with a young Palestinian journalist who left in this manner, Amman, Jordan, April 1990.)

137. Shehadeh and Kuttab, *The West Bank,* p. 87.

138. See Al-Haq, *Punishing A Nation,* p. 199.

139. Shehadeh, *Occupier's Law,* p. 157.

140. For full text of Military Order 101, see Shehadeh and Kuttab, *The West Bank*, appendix, pp. 126–128.

141. *Palestine Perspectives*, September/October 1986, p. 7.

142. Between 1977 and 1984 more than 10,800 relatively nonviolent incidents were recorded in the Occupied Territories (about 3,000 per year since 1983 alone). These acts included demonstrations and rock throwing. See *Palestine Perspectives* (September/October 1986): 7; Michal Schwartz, "Israeli Untouchables: Criminals Are Those Who Talk to the Palestinians," *Jordan Times*, November 10, 1986, reprinted from *Middle East International;* and White, "Torture, Perjury, and Palestinian Children," p. 9. As Benvenisti explains, "terrorist activities" may include writing slogans on walls, singing nationalist songs, making a "V" (victory) sign, displaying the colors of the Palestinian flag in any form, burning tires, throwing stones, demonstrating, and making nationalist statements to gatherings of over ten people; Benvenisti, *West Bank Data Base Project, 1987 Report*, p. 40. An estimated 20,000 Palestinians were detained annually on "security charges" over the first 20 years of occupation, that is, a total of about one half million people.

143. Geoffrey Aronson, "Israel's Policy of Military Occupation," *JPS*, 7, no. 4 (Summer 1978): 79–80.

Chapter Two

1. One example of Palestinian resistance before 1948 is the 1936 Revolt, which was directed against both the British Mandate and Zionist colonization in Palestine. It began as a prolonged general strike, but later gave way to armed resistance by some sectors within the Palestinian community. It continued on and off for three years before being crushed.

2. The initial period after the "catastrophe" of 1948, as Palestinians describe their dispersion, was one of relative disorganization and inactivity. Palestinian society was shattered by the creation of the State of Israel, and its leadership fragmented and destroyed. In the mid-1950s, armed strikes against Israel were launched from the West Bank and Gaza Strip, and fighting cells were established in the Gaza Strip. Meantime, the administrative and organizational apparatus of the movement was being formed in Kuwait, in Egypt, and later in Algeria, where, following its revolution and independence in 1961–1962, the first *Fatah* office was opened.

3. Frantz Fanon, *The Wretched of the Earth* (New York: Grove Press, 1963); and Albert Memmi, *The Colonizer and the Colonized* (Boston: Beacon Press, 1965).

4. For further explanation of these dynamics, see Fanon, *The Wretched of the Earth*, pp. 41, 59 ff.; and Memmi, *The Colonizer and the Colonized*, pp. xvii, 20, 53–54.

5. Fanon, *The Wretched of the Earth*, p. 94.

6. Fanon does not have much to say about nonviolence, which he dismisses as "passivity"; *The Wretched of the Earth*, p. 61, and Preface by Jean-Paul Sartre, p. 25.

7. Fanon, *The Wretched of the Earth*, p. 35.

8. Amilcar Cabral, "National Liberation and the Social Structure," in William J. Pomeroy (ed.), *Guerrilla Warfare and Marxism* (New York: International Publishers, 1968), p. 267.

9. For more on the centrality of armed struggle for the PLO, see the recollections of Abu Jihad (Khalil Al-Wazir) about the early days of the *Fatah* movement. Abu Jihad was one of the founding members of *Fatah* (the Movement for the Liberation of Palestine); see memoirs published in *Al-Majjalla,* nos. 430–438, May–July 1988 (Arabic). Armed struggle was enshrined in the Palestinian National Charter of 1968, where it was defined as the "only" means to liberate Palestine. This charter contains 33 articles that constitute the bylaws of the PLO. Although it was never formally revoked (though steps to that effect were taken in the summer of 1993), the PLO and many Palestinians insisted that the charter was superseded by the Declaration of Palestinian Independence at the November 1988 session of the Palestine National Council (PNC), when Palestinian statehood was declared in the lands occupied by Israel in 1967. Moreover, in the intervening years between 1968 and 1988, and in successive PNC meetings, various "programs" were drawn up to define the PLO agenda and strategy, some of which differed quite markedly from the principles that were formalized earlier in the charter. One example was the decision to acknowledge the legitimacy of diplomatic and political means of struggle in lieu of total reliance on armed struggle. Another was the gradual acceptance of the principle of a two-state solution.

10. The early thinking of what was to become the core leadership of the PLO reveals striking parallels with other national liberation movements. Abu Jihad recalls that since *Fatah*'s inception around 1954, it always consciously sought to emulate other struggles, such as the Algerian and Vietnamese; see memoirs of Abu Jihad in *Al-Majjalla.*

11. See for example, Pamela Ann Smith, *Palestine and the Palestinians, 1876–1983* (London: Croom Helm, 1984), pp. 190–192.

12. Jordan was the only Arab state that granted citizenship to Palestinians, thus creating an integral link between the two peoples that could not easily be broken.

13. For more on this debate, see, for example, Helena Cobban, *The Palestine Liberation Organization* (Cambridge: Cambridge University Press, 1984). On the debates and dilemmas confronting PLO relations with the Arab world and the Occupied Territories, see selected articles in William B. Quandt, Fuad Jabber, and Ann M. Lesch, *The Politics of Palestinian Nationalism* (Los Angeles: University of California Press, 1973), for example, Fuad Jabber, "The Resistance and Inter-Arab Politics," pp. 155–217.

14. Cobban observes that the PLO has always viewed the United States as the key "to unlocking the chronic dilemma of their statelessness," *The Palestine Liberation Organization,* p. 235.

15. Quoted in Cobban, *The Palestine Liberation Organization,* p. 215.

16. In their places of exile, such as Lebanon, the PLO constituted a veritable state structure for the huge dispossessed Palestinian population. For a comprehensive analysis of the evolving strategy of the PLO, see Yezid Sayegh, "Palestinian Armed Struggle: Means and Ends," *Journal of Palestine Studies (JPS),* 16, no. 1 (Autumn 1986): 95–113. He argues that the PLO used military means to try to weaken Israel's "political will" but that there was a lack of clarity on political objectives. This sometimes "detracted" from the effectiveness of its efforts. His conclusion suggests that the PLO is at fault for not making the force it used "credible" (p. 106) and thus costly to Israel. But since the PLO cannot match Israel's military might, "armed

struggle" was doomed to failure. A strategy is, therefore, needed to exploit the very asymmetry of the conflict to the advantage of the Palestinians, whereby widening the splits in the opponent's camp will affect Israel's political will.

17. In the West Bank, much of this lack of armed resistance has to do with the geography of the area, as well as the strict control imposed first by Jordan then by Israel. Also significant were the social structures and patterns of leadership and authority that were rooted in tradition and custom, and resistant to change. In the Gaza Strip, some armed resistance did occur until this was crushed by Israel in 1972.

18. Ian Lustick, "Changing Rationales for Palestinian Violence in the Arab-Israeli Conflict," *JPS*, 20, no. 1 (Autumn 1990): 54–80; and Cobban, *The Palestine Liberation Organization*, p. 253.

19. See, for example, Gerald Chaliand, "The Palestinian Resistance," *New Outlook*, 13, no. 5 (June 1970): 19–24. Chaliand evaluates the possibilities of "guerrilla" struggle and concludes that, given Israel's military superiority, the Palestinians cannot hope to succeed by such means. Also, Emile Nakhleh, "The Anatomy of Violence: Theoretical Reflections on Palestinian Resistance," *Middle East Journal*, 25, no. 2 (Spring 1971): 180–201. Nakhleh raises questions about the ultimate objectives of the resistance and its vision of the future Palestinian entity.

20. There are other leftist factions closely affiliated with either Iraq or Syria; the DFLP and PFLP are noted here because of their attempts to remain independent of excessive reliance on any given Arab regime, and their—like *Fatah*'s—special appeal in the Occupied Territories.

21. Another important faction was the Palestine Communist Party (now People's Party), which was very active among Israeli Palestinians and significant within the Occupied Territories until the demise of the Soviet Union during 1991–1992. It was only during the April 1987 PNC meeting that the PCP became an official part of the PLO. Its influence on the PLO is important to register, partly because of its large following in the Occupied Territories, and because its members had long advocated coexistence with Israel and political and diplomatic means of resistance over armed struggle.

22. PLO strategy initially supported dialogue with "progressive Jewish groups" only. This position was later expanded to include relations with other Israeli sectors.

23. The establishment of the Palestine National Front, the municipal elections of 1976, and the establishment of the National Guidance Committee were all part of such efforts.

24. We do not address events in the region that caused the PLO to periodically reevaluate its strategy. These include its expulsion from Jordan after the 1970–1971 Civil War, the 1973 October War between Israel and the Arab states, the evolving relationship between the PLO and Jordan, and the ouster of the PLO from Lebanon following the 1982 Israeli invasion.

25. Jamil Hilal, "Class Transformation in the West Bank and Gaza Strip," *MERIP Reports* no. 53 (October 1976): pp. 9–16; and *The West Bank: Economic and Social Structures* (Beirut, Lebanon: PLO Research Center, 1975, Arabic).

26. The huge refugee population in the Gaza Strip had no allegiance to the traditional leadership, whose economic and social bases had been seriously eroded after 1948 anyway. Palestinians were always highly politicized, and the harsh conditions of life in the Gaza Strip turned it into a pot ready to explode.

27. "Patronage" is a term used by the Palestinian sociologist Salim Tamari to describe traditional feudal social relationships of authority, dependence, and allegiance. Tamari traces the decline in these social formations before 1948 as a result of Zionist colonization. He explains, however, that these formations never approached the level of complete systems in Palestine, even during the Ottoman period. He explains factionalism and factional politics in the Palestinian community by examining changes in social structures and relations. Salim Tamari, "Factionalism and Class Formation in Recent Palestinian History," in Roger Owen (ed.), *The Economic and Social History of Palestine* (London: Macmillan, 1982), pp. 177–203. The patronage system in Palestinian society did not derive solely from landownership, but was also located in traditionally established merchant families or other prominent "notables" holding public office.

28. For a discussion of these trends, the impact of the PLO, and its relationship to the traditional elites, see Ziad Abu-Amr and Ali Jarbawi, "The Struggle for West Bank Leadership," *Middle East International (MEI), no.* 304 (July 11, 1987): 16–18.

29. Israel allegedly armed organizations of the Islamic movement and generally turned a blind eye to their demonstrations and mobilization activities. The rationale was, perhaps, that Palestinian extremism, especially with Muslim fundamentalist overtones, would vindicate Israel in its refusal to relinquish any of these territories. See Haim Baram, "The Expulsion of the Palestinians: Rabin Shows His True Colors," *MEI,* no. 441 (January 8, 1993): 3–4; and Graham Usher, "The Rise of Political Islam in the Occupied Territories," *MEI,* no. 453 (June 25, 1993): 19–20. Countries said to have extended financial support to Islamic groups, especially *Hamas,* include Saudi Arabia, Kuwait, Jordan, and Iran, as well as other non-Arab Islamic states; see Michal Sela, "The Islamic Factor," *Jerusalem Post,* October 25, 1989; Miriam Shahin, "Arafat's PR Success," *MEI,* no. 441 (January 8, 1993): 7–8; and Danny Rubinstein, "The International Balloon of *Hamas,*" *Haaretz,* February 5, 1993, *From the Hebrew Press,* March 1993.

30. For more on these two movements, their emergence and ideologies, see Lisa Taraki, "The Islamic Resistance Movement in the Palestinian Uprising," *Middle East Report,* no. 156 (January–February 1989): 30–37; Emile Sahiliyeh, *In Search of Leadership: West Bank Politics Since 1967* (Washington, DC: Brookings Institution, 1988), pp. 137–163; "Status of the Islamic Trends in the Palestinian Revolt," *Sourakia,* no. 358 (June 25, 1990): 10 (Arabic); Iyad Barghouti, *The Palestinian Islamic Movement in Palestine and the New World Order* (East Jerusalem: Palestinian Academic Society for the Study of International Affairs (PASSIA), 1992, Arabic); Ziad Abu-Amr, "*Hamas:* A historical and Political Background," *JPS,* 22, no. 4 (Summer 1993): 5–20; and later in this chapter. In a lecture at the Shoman Foundation in Amman, Jordan, on September 18, 1989, Ziad Abu-Amr pointed out that the position of the Islamic fundamentalist movement has vacillated between advocacy of a Palestinian state in all of Israel/Palestine and an acceptance of a two-state solution.

31. For more on this issue, see Ali Jarbawi, "Palestinian Elites in the Occupied Territories: Stability and Change Through the *Intifada,*" in Jamal R. Nassar and Roger Heacock (eds.), *Intifada: Palestine at the Crossroads* (New York: Praeger, 1990), pp. 287–306.

32. In the aftermath of the Gulf War when the PLO was largely discredited for its

"support" of Saddam Hussein, the Islamic forces, particularly *Hamas,* allegedly received funds from Saudi Arabia and Kuwait, the same countries that had earlier provided significant financial support to the PLO itself.

33. See, for example, Raymonda Tawil, *My Home, My Prison* (London: Zed Press, 1983), pp. 122, 187, on debates surrounding education and elections; and Raja Shehadeh, *The Third Way* (New York: Quartet Books, 1982), p. 118, on the role of lawyers.

34. Jan Metzger, Martin Orth, and Christian Sterzing, *This Land Is Our Land: The West Bank Under Israeli Occupation* (London: Zed Press, 1983), p. 148. This somewhat simplified account of the early years is elaborated, for example, in Sahiliyeh, *In Search of Leadership;* and Shaul Mishal, *The PLO Under Arafat: Between Gun and Olive Branch* (New Haven, CT, and London: Yale University Press, 1986).

35. The composition of the Palestine National Front reflected emerging political forces under occupation, mainly those that opposed the power of the traditional elites. Among its ranks were Communist figures, professionals, students, trade unionists, and others; see Sahiliyeh, *In Search of Leadership,* pp. 48 ff. The PNF emphasized such goals as the "self-determination" of Palestinians and the right to repatriate the refugees; see Metzger et al., *This Land Is Our Land,* p. 161. It engaged in largely nonviolent methods of resistance, including protests, demonstrations, resolutions, petitions, and statements. Some claim that these activities had an impact on Israel—for example, paralyzing a number of Israeli businesses through the withdrawal of Palestinian labor. Israel responded with harsh repression and concerted attempts to bolster the failing power of the traditional leaders, some of whom—whether out of expediency or genuine support—sided with the new leaders.

36. Lisa Taraki, "The Development of Political Consciousness Among Palestinians in the Occupied Territories, 1967–1987," in Nassar and Heacock, *Intifada,* pp. 53–73.

37. Mishal, *The PLO Under Arafat,* especially Chapters 5 and 6, pp. 97–149.

38. A resolution was passed at the 12th PNC meeting in 1974 that clearly stipulated that a national authority would be established on "any part" of Palestine that was liberated. This decision reflected priorities that had developed among nationalist forces within the Occupied Territories themselves and consolidated support for the PLO in these areas.

39. Much of the conflict between factional groups was fueled from the outside—for example, in the competition between *Fatah* and both the PFLP and DFLP, and attempts by the former (at times with the support of Jordan) to control the population and their indigenous institutions through the selective allocation of "steadfastness" funds. The joint Jordanian/Palestinian committee was to distribute *sumud* (steadfastness) funds, a total of $150 million that was to be collected annually from the Arab states and channeled through this fund to the occupied areas. Official institutions, primarily municipalities, educational institutions, and trade unions, were to be the major recipients. In practice, however, Palestinians noticed that certain trade unions received funding while others did not. Likewise, some mayors were regarded more favorably than others and received funding accordingly. While the administrators of *sumud* funding for the Occupied Territories in Amman insisted that there was no such discrimination, it remained a concern so long as Palestinians

themselves perceived it to be the case and resented Joint Committee policies in this regard. (Personal interview with Joint Committee officials, Amman, Jordan, June 8, 1985.) Over the years most of the *sumud* funding to the Occupied Territories was reduced to a trickle owing to the failure of Arab governments to pay their share.

40. The new city councils took the lead in publicizing complaints against the occupation and called for strikes and demonstrations. These actions had not occurred under previous councils. During this same period, the idea of organized civilian resistance against the occupation emerged as a viable option. One study points out, "The strategy of the Military Government was to discredit the new city councils and to take the popular support away from them"; Metzger et al., *This Land Is Our Land,* p. 180.

41. See Sahiliyeh, *In Search of Leadership,* p. 73.

42. Abdul Jawad Saleh, *Israel's Policy of De-Institutionalization: A Case Study of Palestinian Local Governments* (London: Jerusalem Center for Development Studies, 1987), p. 23. Sahiliyeh, however, maintains that both the PNF and NGC were used by the emerging political forces in the Occupied Territories to increase support for and cooperation with the PLO; *In Search of Leadership,* p. 49.

43. Mishal, *The PLO Under Arafat,* p. 134.

44. For an Israeli army official's view of the danger of civil disobedience, see Raphael Vardi, "The Administered Territories and the Internal Security of Israel," in Daniel J. Elazar (ed.), *Judaea, Samaria, and Gaza: Views on the Present and Future* (Washington, DC: American Enterprise Institute for Public Policy Research, 1982), p. 172.

45. Geoffrey Aronson, "Israel's Policy of Military Occupation," *JPS,* 7, no. 4 (Summer 1978): 81.

46. By the late 1970s, student unions, trade unions, and the prominent nationalist forces in the Occupied Territories had all become NGC supporters. Mobilization and resistance activities helped preserve the prominence of the NGC. For example, when the popular mayor of Nablus, Bassam Shakaa, was threatened with deportation in 1979, 13 West Bank mayors submitted their resignations in protest, and the West Bank erupted in widespread demonstrations. The Israeli authorities later backed down from this decision, and Shakaa, who was in prison at the time, was released and allowed to continue as mayor. Conversation with Shakaa, Nablus, February 1988; and see Mishal, *The PLO Under Arafat,* p. 136.

47. A similar argument is made by Mohammad Muslih, "Palestinian Civil Society," *Middle East Journal,* 47, no. 2 (Spring 1993): 258–275.

48. Projecting into a future independent Palestinian national entity is beyond the scope of the present study. Our concern here is how diffuse loci of power play a role in checking the control of a colonial state. Clearly, however, the internal strength and unity of the Palestinians are crucial to the effort of resisting occupation and to the formulating of a civilian resistance strategy. The "civilian" component in turn relies on the viability of "civil" structures in that community, which do, in this case, include popular religiously based associations.

49. Gene Sharp, *Social Power and Political Freedom* (Boston: Porter Sargent, 1980), pp. 27–44; and Anders Boserup and Andrew Mack, *War Without Weapons* (London: Frances Pinter, 1974).

50. Several Palestinian sectors that survived the dissolution of the municipalities

remained functioning throughout the occupation. The role of these institutions, in health, education, and other areas, should be noted within the context of resistance but are not dealt with in this study. For more on indigenous institutions and their roles in development and resistance, see, for example, George T. Abed (ed.), *The Palestinian Economy: Studies in Development Under Prolonged Occupation* (London: Routledge, 1988), on economic development; Sarah Graham-Brown, *Education, Repression, and Liberation: Palestinians* (London, U.K.: World University Service, 1984), p. 97, on educational institutions and restrictions to their functioning; Ibrahim Dakkak, "Development for Steadfastness," *Al-Fikr* (Spring 1984): 195, 197 (Arabic); and Arab Thought Forum, Conference Proceedings, "Conference on Development in the Service of Steadfastness," 1981–1982 (Jerusalem), which includes a number of specific recommendations for development. Also not included in the discussion are established voluntary organizations, such as charitable organizations, that played a prominent role in providing services and support to the Palestinian population under occupation. These have sometimes been criticized for their overemphasis on welfare compared to self-help ventures, and for their location in major cities, which has made access difficult for the majority of the needy population. One charitable society that did respond to changing needs is the In'ash El-Usra Society (Family Rejuvenation Society) in El-Bireh. In June 1988 the Israeli authorities raided the society, confiscated documents and other materials, and ordered the closure of sections of In'ash for two years, on charges of incitement. Only the home for the orphans and the day-care center were allowed to remain open; *New York Times,* June 21, 1988; *Al-Fajr,* June 26, 1988; and *Jerusalem Post International Edition,* July 2, 1988. Charitable societies fall under the supervision of the Israeli Deputy of Social Affairs in the Occupied Territories and face many restrictions in their activities.

51. For more on this early period, see Nahla Abdo Zubi, *Family, Women, and Social Change in the Middle East: The Palestinian Case* (Toronto: Canadian Scholar's Press, 1987), pp. 19–23; Laila Jammal, *Contributions by Palestinian Women to the National Struggle for Liberation* (Washington, DC: Middle East Public Relations, 1985); and Souad Dajani, "Palestinian Women Under Israeli Occupation: Implications for Development," in Judith Tucker (ed.), *Women and Arab Society: Old Boundaries, New Frontiers* (Bloomington: Indiana University Press and the Center for Contemporary Arab Studies, 1993), pp. 102–129.

52. In July 1993, I met with several Palestinian women activists and visited a number of their research centers. Many developments were still unfolding, and Palestinian women were caught between the pressing daily conditions on the ground and the demands of the "peace process" outside and its implications for women.

53. These comprised the Union of Women's Work Committees, 1978 (affiliated with the DFLP); the Union of Working Women's Committees, 1978 (affiliated with the Communist Party); the Union of Women's Committees for Social Work, 1981 (affiliated with the PFLP); and the Union of Palestinian Women's Committees, 1981 (affiliated with *Fatah*). See Union of Women's Work Committees, "The Development of the Palestinian Women's Movement" (West Bank, n.d.) (Arabic), and conversations with women activists in the West Bank, February 1988. Also see Eileen Kuttab, "Palestinian Women in the *Intifada:* Fighting on Two Fronts," *Arab Studies Quarterly,* 15, no. 2 (Spring 1993): 69–87; Philippa Strum, *The Women Are*

Marching: The Second Sex and the Palestinian Revolution (New York: Lawrence Hill, 1992); Kitty Warnock, *Land Before Honor* (New York: Monthly Review Press, 1990); Orayb Aref Najjar, *Portraits of Palestinian Women* (Salt Lake City: University of Utah Press, 1992); Maria Holt, *Half the People* (East Jerusalem: PASSIA, December 1992); and Penny Rosenwasser, *Voices from a Promised Land* (Willimantic, CT: Curbstone Press, 1992).

54. In early 1989, to facilitate coordination of their work, the four women's committees unified under the Higher Women's Council.

55. It was not clear how Palestinian women would respond to the political agreements between the PLO and Israel, nor how they perceived their role in the forthcoming autonomy. For some ideas on the subject, particularly the role of women in an increasingly polarized class society, see Souad Dajani, "The Struggle of Palestinian Women in the Occupied Territories: Between National and Social Liberation," *Arab Studies Quarterly*, 16, no. 2, (Spring 1994); also see Chapter Three.

56. Professionals, such as lawyers, doctors, pharmacists, engineers, and dentists, all have their own professional unions and are not discussed here.

57. Although parts of their wages were withheld for Histadrut (Israeli labor union) dues, these workers received no protection from this agency. Though in theory the Histadrut is responsible for protecting the rights of workers from the Occupied Territories, in practice, "its obligations towards the workers have remained unfulfilled"; Michal Schwartz, "The Exploitation of Palestinian Workers Under Israeli Occupation," translated from Hebrew by Israel Shahak, in *Palestine Perspectives*, September/October 1986, p. 3.

58. See for example, Communiqué No. 15 of the Unified Nationalist Leadership of the Uprising (UNLU), calling for the creation of more workers" committees and neighborhood watch committees. Also Joost Hiltermann, "The Emerging Trade Union Movement in the West Bank," *MERIP Reports*, no. 136/137 (October–December 1985): 27.

59. *Al-Fajr*, July 24, 1988, p. 8.

60. Benvenisti points out that by 1985, 140 branches of Palestinian trade unions had not received approval by the Israeli authorities; Meron Benvenisti, *The West Bank Handbook: A Political Lexicon* (Boulder, CO: Westview Press, 1986), p. 164.

61. Hiltermann, "The Emerging Trade Union Movement in the West Bank," 1985, p. 26. By July 1988, eight months into the *intifada*, a reported 21 out of the 38 members of the General Council of the General Federation of West Bank Labor Unions had been arrested, and four of the largest unions in the West Bank had been closed for two years. At least one union activist was served with deportation orders, and several administrative members were detained. *Al-Fajr*, July 24, 1988, p. 8.

62. Hiltermann, "The Emerging Trade Union Movement in the West Bank," 1985, p. 31.

63. On the role of trade unions and workers' movements during the *intifada*, see Joost Hiltermann, "Work and Action: The Role of the Working Class in the Uprising," in Nassar and Heacock, *Intifada*, pp. 143–159.

64. Abdul Jawad Saleh, "Planting Stars on the Land of Palestine," *Shu'un Filastiniya*, no. 63/64 (February/March 1977): 98 (Arabic).

65. Local residents formed voluntary committees that were responsible for

collecting funds, buying farm machinery and other implements, and working with farmers, peasants, and others. They would cultivate lands, build houses or farms, or engage in any other venture that would contribute to the self-reliance of that particular villager, farmer, or community. Men and women from all social sectors and age groups participated in these activities.

66. In just a few years the number of Voluntary Work Committees jumped from 38 to over 100, and their membership reached into the thousands. In 1983, these had approximately 7,000 members; see Issam Al-Zawawa, "Voluntary Work in the Occupied Land," paper presented at the Arab Union of Social Specialists, "Social Development Between Democratic Participation and Decision-making Policies," Tunis, November 1983, Appendix (mimeo, Arabic).

67. Such a team was formed, for example, in Qalqilya and other places; see Al-Zawawa, "Voluntary Work," p. 5.

68. By 1983 the achievements of the voluntary work committees included the planting of 34,000 olive trees, banana plants, grapevines, and fig trees and the reclamation and protection over 9,000 dunums of land from expropriation (1 dunum equals 1,000 square meters); Al-Zawawa, "Voluntary Work," p. 7, and Appendix, p. 2; for complete listing of these activities, see Table, pp. 9–11.

69. Saleh states that local residents of El-Bireh and other communities were warned against cooperating with him, and that, in some cases, participants in voluntary work committees were harassed and detained for their activities. Personal interview, Amman, Jordan, 1989. Also, Al-Zawawa, "Voluntary Work," p. 18.

70. See the *Jordan Times,* January 16, 1988.

71. Between 1982 and 1985, the number of mobile clinics rose from 30 to 235, and the number of patients treated jumped from 2,000 to 40,000. Union of Palestinian Medical Relief Committees (UPMRC), *Annual Report,* April 1986, p. 7. These clinics offer medical examinations, lab services, and basic treatments.

72. This figure includes 330 doctors, that is, approximately one-third of all doctors in the Occupied Territories; UPMRC, *Annual Report,* p. 13, and conversation with Dr. Mustafa Barghouti, a founder of the Medical Relief Committees, West Bank, February 1988.

73. Voluntary health services are offered through other groups such as the Union of Health Work Committees (with 42 health centers by the end of 1990); the Union of Health Care Committees; and the Union of Palestinian Health Care Committees; see Palestine Medical Relief Association, *Wounds of Occupation: Health Care in the West Bank and Gaza Strip* (Chicago: Palestine Medical Relief Association, n.d.).

74. *Palestine Perspectives,* (September/October 1986,) p. 7; and *Jordan Times,* January 16, 1988.

75. Conversation with Dr. Barghouti, West Bank, February 1988.

76. In July 1988 the Israeli authorities detained a group of Medical Relief Committee personnel in the West Bank. According to a newspaper account, they were held for causing "disturbances" but were later released. The same article notes that the Israeli authorities were "growing uneasy" at the work of the voluntary and popular groups, particularly those that helped Palestinians break free of their dependence on the Israeli system; see the *Boston Globe,* July 2, 1988. For more on the health situation in the Occupied Territories and the role of the Medical Relief Committees during the *intifada,* see Mustafa Barghouti and Rita Giacaman, "The

Emergence of an Infrastructure of Resistance," in Nassar and Heacock, *Intifada,* pp. 73–91; and Mustafa Barghouti, *Palestinian Health: Toward a Health Development Strategy in the West Bank and Gaza Strip* (Jerusalem: Union of Palestinian Medical Relief Committees, 1993).

77. During my visit to the offices of the Union of Palestinian Medical Relief Committees in July 1993, I learned that the dominant problem seemed to be stemming from the peace process and its impact on Palestinian institutions in the Occupied Territories. Barghouti was concerned that U.S.-Israeli plans to "empower" Palestinians (for example, in health care and education, as part of the "autonomy" plan) was simply another means of normalizing the occupation and bypassing and marginalizing the traditionally active grassroots groups; see Mustafa Barghouti, "Like Quicksand Beneath Our Feet: Palestinian Health and the 'Normalization Projects,'" *Al-Quds* newspaper, March 3, 1992; and Mustafa Barghouti, "The Administrative Approach vs. the Need for Democratic Coordination: The Case of the High Health Council," *Al-Nahar* and *Al-Fajr* newspapers, October 17, 1992.

78. As one Agricultural Relief Committee member put it, the goal is "to achieve maximum development with minimum costs"; Ismail De'ik, "Agricultural Relief Committees Protect the Land," *Volunteer Work,* September 24, 1985 (Arabic). A 1987 report of the Agricultural Relief Committees outlines the advances that have been made in recent years in crop yield, fertilization, irrigation, pesticides, and other areas. The report also refers to the problem of locating markets for Palestinian produce. It cites efforts by the European Economic Community to exert pressure on Israel to allow produce from the Occupied Territories to be marketed directly to the EEC, and not through Israel's own agricultural marketing agency, Agrexco. Israeli officials finally agreed to this request, and the first shipment of citrus fruits from Gaza took place in December 1988. Report in *Al-Fajr,* December 6, 1987, p. 6. Also see the *Jordan Times,* December 29–30, 1988, and February 1, 1989.

79. *Al-Fajr,* December 6, 1987, p. 13. Palestinian cooperatives in the Occupied Territories existed before 1967. Since then they have been active in ventures that would enhance Palestinian steadfastness on the land. Cooperatives were formed in the critical sectors of agriculture, industry, housing, and other service areas that were particular targets of repressive Israeli measures. By the mid-1980s more than 220 cooperatives were operating in the West Bank: 37 percent in agriculture, 27 percent in housing, and 36 percent in services (such as water and electricity), with a total membership of about 26,000. See David Lewis, "The Importance of Palestine's Cooperatives," *MEI* (June 14, 1985), pp. 15–16; and Palestine Cooperatives on the West Bank and Gaza, *Findings from a Study Tour by U.S. Cooperatives Representatives* (n.d.), pp. 29, 32. The Gaza Strip has about 70 registered cooperatives, of which only five are said to be active. The most important cooperative there is that of the citrus growers. Membership in cooperatives has enabled families with low incomes to buy land, build houses, and secure such services as roads, water, and electricity for their communities. Other cooperatives organized the building of clinics, schools, and other facilities. Cooperatives in the Occupied Territories were subject to Israeli restrictions on funding, licensing, and operation, and they lacked sufficient resources and planning to undertake development programs. Agricultural cooperatives were a special target, and the least likely to receive permits from the Israeli authorities,

particularly if their work centered on land reclamation and productivity; see the *New York Times,* May 15, 1988. The report of U.S. Cooperatives Representatives sums up the situation by noting that Israeli approval of cooperative projects is generally positive for "pacification" projects—projects that will contribute to some improvement in the "quality of life" of Palestinians. But the authorities "strenuously object to activities that advance the Palestinians economically," *Findings from a Study Tour,* pp. 26, 27.

80. *New York Times,* May 15, 1988.

81. Yasser Arafat, Abu Jihad, and other early founders of *Fatah* were active in the student movement in Cairo in the mid-1950s. The term *shabiba* is derived from the word *shebab,* which denotes young people (or rather, young men); it is used here to depict the youth movement in general. However, in the Occupied Territories, *Shabiba* has become the label of one branch of the youth movement affiliated with *Fatah,* while other terms have been used to identify followers of other factions.

82. In the Occupied Territories this was renamed the Palestinian Students Union. Much of the information for the following analysis is derived from Sahiliyeh, *In Search of Leadership,* pp. 116–137.

83. A comparable role is often performed by workers or peasants in other struggles.

84. Sarah Graham-Brown, "Impact on the Social Structure of Palestinian Society," in Naseer Aruri (ed.), *Occupation: Israel over Palestine* (Belmont, MA: Association of Arab-American University Graduates Press, 1983), p. 252; and Sahiliyeh, *In Search of Leadership,* p. 124.

85. Specific Israeli measures against students, schools, and universities are too extensive to be listed here. Israel's policy aimed at deliberate and frequent targeting of educational institutions. Closures, arrests, and detentions of both teachers and students, setting up of roadblocks, confiscation of identity cards, poor facilities, restrictions on books and journals, imposing curfews, interfering with students' movements, and arresting them, particularly during exam times, were all common. Many students have been killed and injured or exposed to settler violence.

86. Glen Frankel, "Ansar II: The School for Gaza Resistance Fighters," from the *Washington Post,* reprinted in the *Jordan Times,* January 12, 1988. While in prison, a boy as young as 12 years old would learn about hunger strikes, making explosives, and support networks, as well as about Israeli brutality. Also see "A School for Hatred," *Jerusalem Post International Edition,* April 2, 1988. This article maintains that in the Ansar II prison, "right under the noses of the Shin Bet and the IDF Southern Command—is nothing less than the future army of Palestine." Before the *intifada* such experiences were usually restricted to known activists. Some observers even made it a habit to contrast the special social cohesiveness and determination of prisoners with the "relative passivity" and "apathy and cynicism" of the population as a whole; Jan Abu Shakrah, "Israel's Uprooting of Palestinians: Step 3, Futurelessness," *Jordan Times,* May 21, 1986.

87. Sahiliyeh identifies four pro-PLO blocs, three of which were affiliated with the "progressive groups"—the PFLP, DFLP, and CP—and the fourth with *Fatah,* in addition to a separate Islamic bloc that attracted an increased following and influence among youth in the Occupied Territories; *In Search of Leadership,* pp. 116–137.

88. For a critical analysis and rebuttal of this concept, see Leon Hadar, "What Green Peril?" *Foreign Affairs,* Spring 1993, pp. 27–43.

89. The three main Islamic groups in the Occupied Territories are *Hamas* (an offshoot of the Muslim Brotherhood), Islamic *Jihad,* and the Islamic Liberation Party. Despite some differences in means of struggle and ideological focus, all three posit the total liberation of Palestine and the establishment of an Islamic state as the ultimate goal; see Iyad Barghouti, *The Palestinian Islamic Movement;* and Ziad Abu-Amr, "Islam as a Potential Civil/Political Order," paper presented at Birzeit University and Association of Arab American University Graduates (AAUG) Joint International Conference, Birzeit, West Bank, July 5–9, 1993.

90. Iyad Barghouti, *The Palestinian Islamic Movement;* and Abu-Amr, "Islam as a Potential Civil/Political Order."

91. One can compare for example, the extreme religious ideological foundations in the Charter of the Islamic Resistance Movement (*Hamas*) issued in August 1988 with later pronouncements by this group. For the full text of this charter, see *JPS,* 22, no. 4 (Summer 1993): 122–135. By the early 1990s, *Hamas* was appealing to "human rights" and "democracy" in order attract more support; see Iyad Barghouti, *The Palestinian Islamic Movement,* pp. 94, 143.

92. See Chapter Five for a more detailed discussion of development initiatives.

93. See for example, Gerald Butt, "Opposition's Uphill Struggle," *MEI,* no. 461 (October 22, 1993): 5; and Graham Usher, "Dissension in the Opposition," *MEI* (*ibid.,* pp. 5–6). Both authors cite the failure of the "opposition," including the Islamic groups, to construct a viable strategic alternative to Arafat's agreement with Israel.

94. See Daoud Kuttab, "Freedom and Human Rights," *MEI,* no. 461, (October 22, 1993): 8–9; and Usher, "Dissension in the Opposition," p. 8.

95. Editorial, "It Must Be Made to Work," *MEI,* no. 459 (September 24, 1993): 2.

Chapter Three

1. I was told about this incident while on a first visit to the Occupied Territories during the *intifada,* January-February 1988. Driving by the site, I was able to see the newly vacated clearing across from Dheisheh and the new army camp farther down the road. In July 1993, I saw that the military had succeeded in setting up its camp, along with the obligatory observation tower that overlooked Dheisheh. This phenomenon of observation towers, some of which are quite high, has been a regular feature of the army presence in the Occupied Territories, particularly, as I discovered, in the Gaza Strip.

2. These developments included the attention focused on the Gulf War between Iran and Iraq (perceived to be at the expense of the Palestinian cause), and growing unemployment in the Occupied Territories.

3. The late Abu Jihad was acknowledged as the main architect of this plan; see Helena Cobban, "Gunless in Gaza," *World Monitor,* 3, no. 3 (March 1990): 64. I can confirm that as of 1984, PLO institutions centered in Cyprus were commissioning studies on the feasibility of nonviolent civilian resistance in the Occupied Territories. What this author learned from people closely associated with these

projects was that they were undertaken at the specific request of Abu Jihad. Early in the *intifada,* around January or February 1988, a publication circulated in the Occupied Territories that was also attributed to Abu Jihad. It clearly spelled out the elements and conditions for a successful "civil disobedience" campaign, which would then be escalated to encompass the whole of the West Bank and Gaza Strip (Arabic, n.d., pp. 1–26). Many Palestinians believe that Abu Jihad was assassinated by the Israelis in April 1988 precisely because of his role in strategic planning for the use of nonviolent civilian resistance in the Occupied Territories.

4. See Sara Roy, "Apartheid, Israeli-Style," *The Nation,* (July 26/August 2, 1993, pp. 136–139. She writes, "Virulent factional rivalries are replacing collective effort at many levels; internal fragmentation and the unmaking of civil society are the tragic result" (p. 138). My own observations stemming from my visit to the Occupied Territories in July 1993 coincide with Roy's.

5. The UNLU comprised the four main PLO factions. Islamic *Jihad* sometimes added its signature to the UNLU's communiqués, but, according to Iyad Barghouti, was not officially represented; *The Palestinian Islamic Movement in Palestine and the New World Order* (East Jerusalem: Palestinian Academic Society for the Study of International Affairs (PASSIA), 1992, Arabic, p. 25. The UNLU was formed during the early months of the uprising to coordinate strategy in the Occupied Territories. During the first few years of the *intifada,* the UNLU largely agreed on the basic course of the struggle, and a high degree of unity was achieved among various factions. Some dissension occurred, and it increased over the ensuing months. Occasionally, leaflets would be issued in the name of one or another of the major factions or in the name of Islamic *Jihad* or *Hamas,* calling for different acts of resistance at different times than those listed in the communiqués emanating from the UNLU.

6. Contrary to the popular portrayal of collaborators by propagandists in the West as "political moderates" who were killed because of their political views, these collaborators were, in the eyes of many Palestinians, traitors to the national cause. Collaborators were individuals allegedly paid and armed by Israel, whose task was to infiltrate the Palestinian community and identify activists. These activists would be placed on the "wanted list" and often became the victims of Israeli "undercover units." Until the second year of the *intifada,* most of the traditional collaborators had already been exposed. Many were publicly shamed and driven out of their areas of residence. Some publicly recanted and shifted their allegiance to the national cause. It was not long before the hardships of the *intifada* were once again exploited by Israel to recruit new collaborators. Their infiltration into the ranks of the youth, the "strike forces," Palestinians in prisons, and other sectors posed a very serious threat to the continuation of organized Palestinian resistance. Palestinian activists felt the increased need to resort to secrecy—a measure that tended to defeat both the goals and rationale of collective mass action. The severity of this problem has been readily observable from the large number of collaborators who have been killed in the Occupied Territories, exceeding 700 by 1993. Many Palestinians have been concerned with this development, and the UNLU has repeatedly issued leaflets and warnings to be cautious and thorough in the identification of collaborators, and to attempt to use other means to persuade these individuals to desist before resorting to their assassination.

7. There were indications that a few Palestinians may have been killed for other

reasons, perhaps the settling of personal scores. There have also been indications that the Israeli authorities themselves may have exaggerated the problem. One Israeli newspaper report states that the Israeli military sometimes deliberately inflated the number of collaborator killings, as a way of diminishing its own responsibility for the number of civilian casualties; see Alex Fishman, "An Equation with More Than Two Unknown Factors," *Hadashot,* February 12, 1993, excerpt in *From the Hebrew Press,* February 1993.

8. One reason for the decline in active protests was intensified Israeli repression and the arrest and imprisonment of many thousands of *shebab*. Army regulations had changed, to allow soldiers to shoot directly at any masked or covered Palestinian, even if their lives were not in direct danger. In several instances, "wanted" youth were caught and shot in cold blood, even after they had surrendered. Some youth were listed as "wanted" simply because they were active members of the popular committees. The existence of army "undercover" units has been confirmed by Israeli officials. See Palestinian Human Rights Information Center (PHRIC), *Targeting to Kill: Israel's Undercover Units* (Washington, DC: Center for Contemporary Arab Studies, Georgetown University, and PHRIC, 1992); and successive articles in the Hebrew Press, for example, Alex Fishman, "Mista'aravim," *Hadashot,* July 17, 1992, *From the Hebrew Press,* September 1992; and Guy Ehrlich, "The Price of Cherry," *Zman Tel Aviv,* February 19, 1993, *From the Hebrew Press,* March 1993. Also see *The Samson Unit,* a documentary on undercover units, shown on the ABC television program "Day One," May 2, 1993. ("Samson" and "Cherry" are the code names of these units operating in the Gaza Strip and West Bank, respectively.)

9. If an injury was serious enough, the youth would be taken for emergency care at the nearest hospital or clinic. In most cases the victim would refuse to stay for further treatment because all patients were required by the Israeli authorities to register their names at the hospital. There are many documented instances of Israeli troops storming hospitals, beating staff and patients alike, and simply dragging out the injured youth they were seeking.

10. See, for example, *Al-Fajr,* March 20, 1988, p. 8.

11. Palestinians in the Occupied Territories generally viewed Saddam Hussein as the only Arab leader who dared to confront the United States and attack Israel. Perhaps in him they saw a symbol of salvation, if not in deed, at least in the restoration of some degree of Arab pride and dignity.

12. Daoud Kuttab, "Israel's Harsh but Ineffective Measures," *Middle East International (MEI),* no. 322 (April 2, 1988): 3.

13. Some analysts put the total cost to Beit Sahour residents at around US$5 million; see various issues of *Al-Fajr* for that period.

14. Other communities considered emulating this act. For various reasons, however, they decided not to do so. I was on a visit to Ramallah at the time (October 1989) and attended some of the debates on the issue.

15. This was a rather remarkable development given the fact that alternative Palestinian products were not readily available, or else tended to be of inferior quality to Israeli products. Yet Palestinians willingly gave up Israeli cigarettes, sweets, soft drinks, medications, and the like. Only on very rare occasions was it necessary to exert pressure to enforce the boycotts. Even then, pressure would consist mainly of appeals to one's nationalist feelings. For example, in a social gathering,

anyone caught smoking Israeli cigarettes would be shamed in front of his friends and urged to throw them out in favor of an Arab brand.

16. Early in the *intifada,* East Jerusalem residents conformed to strike calls and participated in demonstrations. Israelis themselves conceded that the myth of a "unified Jerusalem" as the "eternal capital of Israel" was shattered. However, a sense of this city's distinctiveness from the rest of the West Bank persisted. Conditions were somewhat easier, a wider variety of products were available, and schools were more likely to be open. With the exception of Birzeit University, which was denied permission to begin reopening its faculties until spring 1992, the rest of the West Bank universities were gradually allowed to reopen in September 1990. The disruption of education was a source of tension and divisiveness along class lines, especially since affluent Palestinians could send their children abroad or enroll them in schools in East Jerusalem.

17. I myself experienced an incident in East Jerusalem that underscores such an interpretation. Walking close to the Dome of the Rock during a visit in October 1989, I was confronted by a Palestinian man who ordered me to wear a head scarf. He said that it was this very lack of respect for tradition and religion that weakened the Palestinian movement and contributed to its defeat by Israel. This process whereby women became scapegoats for the failure of political action is not unique to Palestinian society and has been experienced in many struggles around the world.

18. For an in-depth analysis of the attempts of the extreme Muslim religious factions to redefine and circumscribe the role of women in the Occupied Territories, see Rema Hammami, "Women, the *Hijab,* and the *Intifada,*" *Middle East Report,* no. 164–165 (May–August 1990): 24–29.

19. Palestinian women frequently cited the example of Algeria, where women participated extensively in the struggle for national liberation, only to find themselves relegated back into the home following independence.

20. In December 1990, Palestinian women in the Occupied Territories held a major conference in which some 400 delegates participated. Several important position papers were presented that stressed the need for immediate action and urged that their concerns be brought to the attention of the national movement, so as to integrate women into the struggle at all levels. This conference was sponsored by the Bisan Research Center, "The *Intifada* and Some Women's Social Issues," Jerusalem, December 14, 1990.

21. In an ironic twist of fate, the expulsion of some 400 alleged "*Hamas* activists" in December 1992 reportedly led to the radicalization of the rest of the movement. The *Jerusalem Post International Edition,* September 4, 1993, for example, reports that since these expulsions, the membership of *Hamas* became progressively more activist, and "violent" and less religious, and that their increasingly youthful cadres included many women.

22. These were teams of experts formed in various sectors who were responsible for supplying the delegates to the peace talks with specialized information on issues pertaining to their fields.

23. Much of this information was gathered from various women activists during my visit to the Occupied Territories in July 1993. Some of what I was told could have been exaggerated because of factional competition, but there was definitely a problem concerning the cohesiveness of the women's movement that was exacerbated by demands of the peace talks. It was not clear how Palestinian women would

respond to the challenges posed by the peace agreements between Israel and the PLO. They were aware that they could be marginalized from decision-making in the interim stages, even though "development" initiatives specified in these agreements would have a significant impact on their lives; for more on this issue, see Dajani, "The Struggle of Palestinian Women in the Occupied Territories," *Arab Studies Quarterly*, 16, no. 2 (Spring 1994).

24. As I explain in Chapter Four, civil disobedience more accurately denotes a single type of nonviolent action within a whole category of nonviolent noncooperation. Civil disobedience refers to the refusal to abide by what are regarded as illegitimate laws. Taken alone, this hardly comprises a "strategy" in and of itself. Yet Palestinians under occupation relied heavily on civil disobedience as the main vehicle for their overthrow of the occupation regime.

25. This leaflet, signed by the Popular Committee for Civil Disobedience, was issued within the first three months of the *intifada*; West Bank, n.d. (Arabic).

26. Gene Sharp, *The Politics of Nonviolent Action*, Three volumes. One, *Power and Struggle*; Two, *The Methods of Nonviolent Action*; Three, *The Dynamics of Nonviolent Action* (Boston: Porter Sargent, 1973).

27. The Palestine Center for the Study of Nonviolence in East Jerusalem was headed by Mubarak Awad before his expulsion in June 1988. The center continued to be operated by PCSN staff. The survey is in two parts: Part 1, "*Intifada: Palestinian Nonviolent Protest: An Affirmation of Human Dignity and Freedom*," May 31, 1988, reviews the first 17 communiqués issued by the UNLU. Part 2, "*Intifada: Palestinian Nonviolent Protest: An Affirmation of Human Dignity and Freedom*," May 1989, analyzes communiqués nos. 18–39. Categories listed more or less coincided with those of the first 17 communiqués, with some differences that reflected the changing conditions over subsequent months of the *intifada*. The results of this survey show that out of a total of 163 actions called for in the first 17 communiqués, 95.1 percent were "specifically nonviolent in nature." Specific acts are broken down into 27 categories and range from strikes and boycotts to withholding taxes, praying and fasting, raising the Palestinian flag, breaking curfews, creating alternative institutions, generating support activities, resigning from the occupation administration, and noncooperation. Only eight acts out of 163 were listed as violent. These include calls for stone throwing and the use of gasoline bombs. Of the subsequent communiqués (18–39), out of a total of 291 calls for specific acts, the majority, that is, 263 (90.4 percent) were nonviolent, while only 28 (or 9.6 percent) could be characterized as violent acts. Of the latter, 2.1 percent referred specifically to actions against collaborators, a problem that had assumed special significance by then.

28. This story was related to the author by a Palestinian who said he witnessed the incident.

29. One account reports the incident as a sit-in at a mosque and states that the villagers only carried olive branches; see PHRIC Report, March 8, 1988.

30. West Bank, n.d. (English).

31. Jerusalem, January 14, 1988, reprinted as Mubarak Awad and Jonathan Kuttab, along with Bassam Ayyub, Gabi Baramki, Ibrahim Qara'in, and Sari Nusaybah, "The Palestinians' Fourteen Demands," *Journal of Palestine Studies (JPS)*, 17, no. 3 (Spring 1988): 63–66.

32. See the *Christian Science Monitor,* March 22, 1988, on the initial employment of Israeli army reservists to replace Palestinians. A report in the *Jerusalem Post International Edition,* March 19, 1988, refers to the employment of foreign labor; also Azmy Bishara, "The Uprising's Impact on Israel," in Zachary Lockman and Joel Beinin (eds.), *Intifada: The Palestinian Uprising Against Israeli Occupation.* A MERIP Book (Boston: South End Press, 1989), pp. 217–231.

33. For a detailed examination of this case, see Ronald M. McCarthy, "Resistance Politics and the Growth of Parallel Government in America, 1765–1775," in Walter H. Conser, Jr., Ronald M. McCarthy, David Toscano, and Gene Sharp (eds.), *Resistance, Politics, and the American Struggle for Independence, 1765–1775* (Boulder, CO: Lynne Rienner, 1986), pp. 472–527.

34. McCarthy, "Resistance Politics," p. 507. For more on parallel governments, see Sharp, *The Politics of Nonviolent Action,* p. 423.

35. I had several conversations with people in the Occupied Territories who acknowledged the absence of long-term strategic planning. They expressed concern over the excessive euphoria and shared the fear that disappointment would be paralyzing, once people realized that they could not achieve independence as quickly as they had hoped. These same people, however, had few ideas for linking means and ends, or for cautioning people not to expect quick results—indeed, to expect that conditions could well get worse before they ever get better.

36. Palestinians generally distinguished between Israeli soldiers and police, toward whom they evinced less fear, and Israeli settlers, whom Palestinians tended to dread more, because of the tradition of indiscriminate settler violence against them.

37. Sharp, *The Politics of Nonviolent Action,* p. 701; and Chapter Four.

38. I was told about this incident by the woman involved. Many of the incidents that follow were recounted to me during my trip to the Occupied Territories in January-February 1988, either by people involved or by eyewitnesses to the events.

39. Palestinians in the West Bank insisted that this was a true story. Elsewhere, I came across a fictionalized version of the same event in an Arabic publication.

40. Research on the topic was being carried out by the Early Childhood Resource Center in East Jerusalem and by the Gaza Community Mental Health Program. For a moving account of the traumatization of young children, see Eyad Sarraj, "Peace and the Children of the Stone," *Breaking the Siege* (August–September 1993): 4–5. Sarraj is a psychiatrist and founder of the Gaza program.

41. Palestinians found themselves torn between their natural desire to protect their families and children, and their determination to persist in the *intifada* at almost any cost. They realized they would never enjoy freedom or security until the occupation ended. Much of the traumatization of young children occurred in their own homes—for example, when Israeli soldiers barged into houses, destroyed belongings, and beat family members, or when houses were deliberately demolished by explosives or missiles.

42. For example, the Neturei Karta. Among others, Shas and Agudat Israel are usually described as non-Zionist and have won votes in various elections in Israel, notably in 1988; see *Israel and Palestine,* no. 146 (November 1988): 12. Shas was also part of Rabin's Labor-led government of 1992. "Non-Zionist," however, should not be confused with sympathetic attitudes toward Arabs.

43. Three parties that were victorious in the 1988 Israeli elections—Tekhiah

(three seats), Tsomet (two seats), and Moledat (two seats)—openly advocated some form of "transfer" of Palestinians from the area, expulsions that could include Israeli Palestinians as well; see Maxim Ghilan, "Anatomy of a Disaster," *Israel and Palestine,* no. 146 (November 1988): 15.

44. See for example, *Israel and Palestine,* no. 158 (June 1990): 24–30. (It was only in early 1991 that Prime Minister Shamir formally renounced any Israeli claims to Jordan.)

45. For more about fundamentalist groups in Israel and their influence, see Ian S. Lustick, "Israel's Dangerous Fundamentalists," *Foreign Policy,* no. 68 (Fall 1987): 118–140.

46. For an overview of the history of the relationship between Western and Oriental Jews in Israel, see Moise Saltiel, "Is Israel a Democracy?" *Israel and Palestine,* no. 157 (May 1990): 11–17. Saltiel notes that together, by 1988, Oriental Jews and Arabs comprised over 70 percent of the Israeli population; see also Ella Shohat, "Sephardim in Israel: Zionism from the Standpoint of Its Jewish Victims," *Social Text,* 19/20 (Fall 1988): 1–37; and Deena Hurwitz, Asher Brauner, and Jonathan Boyarin (eds.), *The Eastern Aspect: Other News from Israel. Essays from Eton Aher* (Santa Cruz, CA: Resource Center for Nonviolence, April 1993).

47. Oriental Jews are overrepresented among the rank and file of the army, the very same soldiers sent to beat and kill Palestinians during the *intifada;* see *Israel and Palestine,* no. 156 (March 1990): 13–15. Also Adam Keller, *Terrible Days: Social Divisions and Political Paradoxes in Israel* (Amstelveen, The Netherlands: Cypres, 1987).

48. Jewish fundamentalism predated the rise of Islamic fundamentalism in these areas, and could arguably have provided the impetus for the growing strength of the latter.

49. Upon assuming power in 1992, Rabin vowed to halt "political" settlements and permit only the establishment of those needed for "security" reasons. Excluded from these provisions were areas around Jerusalem, housing units already under way (estimated at about 11,000 at the time), and those reflecting a "natural increase." In October 1993, in a move that signaled the Clinton administration's acknowledgement that settlement activity had not been halted, the U.S. government decided to deduct $437 million dollars from its $2 billion dollars of loan guarantees to Israel for 1994; see the *New York Times,* October 6, 1993; and Donald Neff, "Cutting the Loan Guarantees?"*Middle East International (MEI),* no. 461 (October 22, 1993): 9–10. For more on the ongoing settlement activities under Rabin, see PHRIC, "Settlement Freeze—What Does It Really Mean?" *From the Field: A Monthly Report on Selected Human Rights,* September/October 1992.

50. In June 1990 a narrow Likud government was formed with the support of the rightist and religious groups. For the full text of the document of the government's program, see the *Jerusalem Post International Edition,* June 23, 1990, p. 2. For more on this government's composition, see *Israel and Palestine,* no. 158 (June 1990): 26–30. In June 1992, the Labor Party won the elections and established a government with the support of a coalition of some of the leftist groups (Meretz) and Shas.

51. For more on these "costs," see, for example, *Christian Science Monitor,* March 22, 1988, and March 28, 1988; *Jerusalem Post International Edition,* March

19, 1988, April 9, 1988, and April 30, 1988; *Jordan Times,* January 23, 1988, and February 18–19, 1988; and *New York Times,* May 16, 1988.

52. This is to say nothing of the costs of "suppressing" the *intifada* itself, estimated to be in the hundreds of millions, though exact figures are difficult to come by. Some reports cited the amount needed at about US$160 million per month.

53. On August 18, 1988, for example, Israeli sources reported that they had decided to "preempt" the outbreak of Palestinian demonstrations even before they occurred. To this end, the Israeli authorities imposed curfews, declared closed areas, and took a variety of measures of collective punishment. The army received explicit orders that soldiers could shoot Palestinian stone throwers on sight. Israeli soldiers and civilians alike (the settlers, in this case), had already been given permission to shoot at anyone suspected of holding a "bottle" (a firebomb); see *Jerusalem Post International Edition,* June 25, 1988.

54. *Jerusalem Post International Edition,* June 25, 1988; and *Boston Globe,* June 18, 1988.

55. *Jerusalem Post International Edition,* May 26, 1990.

56. Report cited in the *Boston Globe,* June 10, 1988; and the *New York Times,* June 10, 1988.

57. *Al-Fajr,* July 16, 1990, reviews the Amnesty International 1990 report, citing the number of deaths among Palestinians not directly involved in demonstrations.

58. Report of a medical fact-finding mission by Physicians for Human Rights, *The Casualties of Conflict: Medical Care and Human Rights in the West Bank and Gaza Strip* (Somerville, MA: Physicians for Human Rights, March 30, 1988), p. 4. One Israeli denial was published in the *Jerusalem Post International Edition,* May 26, 1990.

59. Article from *Kol Ha'ir,* translated and printed in *Al-Fajr,* May 27, 1988, p. 10.

60. See *Al-Fajr,* June 12, 1988, p. 12, for statements by two Knesset members, Matti Peled of the Progressive List for Peace and Meir Vilner of the Democratic Front for Peace and Equality.

61. See Daoud Kuttab, "A Profile of the Stonethrowers," *Journal of Palestine Studies (JPS),* 17, no. 3 (Spring 1988): 14–23. Also, *Jerusalem Post International Edition,* February 27, 1988, p. 3. In a report from the Hebrew press, supplement to *Haaretz,* March 11, 1988, reprinted in *PHRIC Report,* March 23, 1988, pp. 18–22, one Israeli soldier states,

> We were standing there at a checkpoint. Along came a good-looking woman, well-dressed and proud, in a way that succeeded in making my commander nervous. Although he usually exhibited extraordinary self-control and sensitivity, he suddenly became very angry and got into the "taming of the shrew" syndrome. Her pride was interpreted as a personal assault against us. It is necessary to humiliate them, not because we are sadists, but to make it clear who is the adult and who is the child. It is not good that there is such confusion and the pyramid must be re-erected on its foundations. Such a woman, walking proudly, tears down the whole system.

62. See Zeev Schiff and Ehud Ya'ari, *Intifada* (New York: Simon and Schuster, 1990). Also *Jerusalem Post International Edition,* July 7, 1990; and *Al-Fajr,* July 2, 1990, p. 3, and July 9, 1990, p. 3, on the trial of Colonel Yehuda Meir on charges of ordering soldiers to break the bones of Palestinians. Beatings, in this context, were described as a "policy" rather than an aberration.

63. For more on instructions issued to the army, see the text of a letter by the chief of general staff, Lieutenant General Dan Shomron, to Israeli Defense Forces (IDF) commanders in the Occupied Territories, in *Jerusalem Post International Edition,* March 5, 1988.

64. *Jerusalem Post,* February 1988, also quoted in Amos Elon, "From the Uprising," in the *New York Times,* March 17, 1988, p. 12.

65. Schiff and Ya'ari, *Intifada,* pp. 160, 290.

66. *Ibid.,* p. 136.

67. For an example of such an initiative early in the *intifada,* see, "Two Military Legal Experts Warn of Criminal Liability in Beatings by Soldiers," in the *Jerusalem Post International Edition,* January 26, 1988, p. 4. A few news reports surfaced about soldiers who were punished for their role in the brutal beatings of Palestinians, or for shooting them in cold blood without provocation. One report cited an incident where Israeli high school students in paramilitary training were invited by Israeli soldiers to participate in the beating of Palestinian prisoners. This reportedly took place at Ofer, a detention center near Ramallah. The case was publicized by Ya'ir Tsaban, a Knesset member from Mapam, who claimed that there was a "cover-up" to the investigation. According to an article in *Hadashot,* one student claimed, "We asked if we could beat them up as much as we felt like, and we were told, why not?" The same student reportedly did beat a prisoner and maintained, "He looked like a pile of dough when I got through with him, bones and flesh"; *Hadashot,* May 16, 1988, translated and reprinted in *Al-Fajr,* May 28, 1988, p. 11. Apparent reference to the same case appears in Schiff and Ya'ari, *Intifada,* p. 154. One report maintained that a sergeant involved in the case was court-martialed, though another report denied that; *Jerusalem Post International Edition,* May 28, 1988.

68. *Jerusalem Post International Edition,* June 11, 1988, p. 13. Israelis are expected to start their military service at age 18, when they serve for three years. They then remain on "reserve" and are called upon for service until age 55.

69. *Jordan Times,* February 23, 1988, citing an Israeli army survey.

70. *Jerusalem Post International Edition,* January 9, 1988.

71. *Ibid.*

72. *Al-Fajr,* March 13, 1988, p. 4, quotes an article from *Haaretz* to the effect that 96 of these men were "high-ranking army reserve officers."

73. *Hadashot,* April 4, 1988, translated and reprinted in *Al-Fajr,* April 10, 1988, p. 10.

74. *Jerusalem Post International Edition,* June 11, 1988, p. 12. By the summer of 1990 more than 100 reservists had reportedly been jailed for refusing to serve in the Occupied Territories. Another method used by reservists to avoid serving in the Occupied Territories was to have themselves certified "psychologically unfit." For more on the increased resort to this method, see Shacher Shnitzer, "Anyone Who Wants to Get Out of Our Army Must Be Nuts," *Challenge,* 4, no. 5 (September 1993): 36–37.

75. *Jerusalem Post International Edition,* June 11, 1988, p. 3. One focus of the Council for Peace and Security was to dispel the prevailing myths and fears among Israelis concerning security. In June 1988, 210 Israeli generals and officers who were members of this council began to voice their call for negotiations directly with the PLO and for the withdrawal of Israel from the Occupied Territories; see *Al-Fajr,* June 19, 1988, p. 5. Israel's concerns about its "security" should be assuaged by American reassurances to sell Israel the most advanced military technology and assure Israel's "qualitative superiority."

76. Schiff and Ya'ari, *Intifada,* p. 168.

77. See for example, *Breaking the Siege,* June–July 1991, p. 6, for a translation of an article that appeared in the weekend supplement of *Haaretz,* May 3, 1991. In this article, "On Duty at Ansar II Prison," Israeli reservist Ari Shavit compares Ansar II prison (in the Gaza Strip) to a "concentration camp."

78. It was reported that the collapse of this "joint" Labor-Likud government was due to Prime Minister Shamir's refusal to accept the Baker Plan, U.S. Secretary of State James Baker's plan to open a dialogue between Palestinians and Israeli representatives in Egypt to discuss elections in the Occupied Territories. The Labor Party, led by Shimon Peres, was pressuring for some kind of acceptance of this plan. When this failed, after months of negotiations and stalling, Peres was fired, and the rest of the Labor Party resigned in protest.

79. The Prevention of Terror Act forbade any Israeli citizen, Israeli official, or Palestinian resident to meet a PLO member in any capacity or context, even to discuss peace. The penalty for such an offense could be up to three years in jail. Michal Schwartz, "Israeli Untouchables: Criminals Are Those Who Talk to the Palestinians," *Jordan Times,* November 10, 1986, reprinted from *Middle East International.* Many in Israel criticized this law as being unprecedented in a democratic country. It assumed criminality before the offense. Over the years, a number of Knesset members and other Israelis defied this law by meeting with PLO members. In June 1988, for example, four members of a group of 29 Israeli leftists who had met with PLO officials in Romania in November 1986 were convicted of violating the Prevention of Terror law. This was reportedly the first actual conviction under the law. The four were sentenced to six months in prison and a one-year suspended sentence, as well as to fines and expenses in the amount of US$2,500 each. The court rejected testimony of several prominent witnesses that the purpose of the meeting was to discuss peace and that the PLO had moderated its position and was not a terrorist organization. See the *New York Times,* July 1, 1988; *Jerusalem Post International Edition,* June 11, 1988; and *Al-Fajr,* June 5, 1988. In 1990, the Israeli peace activist Abie Nathan was given a six-month prison sentence for meeting with PLO officials. For meetings between right-wing Knesset members and PLO officials, see *Israel and Palestine,* no. 137 (October 1987): 11 ff.

80. In its 15th session of 1981, the Palestine National Council (PNC) resolved to allow dialogue with progressive Jewish groups, though still condemning contacts with Zionist parties. By the 18th session of the PNC, however, explicit calls for "developing relations with democratic forces in Israel" were approved; see *Al-Fajr,* May 3, 1987, and April 12, 1987.

81. Also see Schiff and Ya'ari, *Intifada,* pp. 137–138, 290; and others who expressed concern over the erosion of democratic principles in Israel. They reveal that growing numbers of Israelis agreed that freedom of speech and writing should

be curtailed in order to suppress news of the *intifada* and avoid further damage to Israel's image.

82. National Public Radio in the United States broadcast reports on some of these cases, June 4, 1988.

83. *Al-Fajr,* June 12, 1988, p. 4.

84. On September 6, 1993, Awad was allowed back for the first time in five years to participate in a conference in Jerusalem. It was not clear whether this was to be a prelude to his permanent repatriation.

85. Faisal Husseini, head of the Arab Studies Society, was placed under administrative detention for almost 14 months until June 1988, as well as for frequent shorter periods during the *intifada*. He was later allowed to join the Palestinian delegation at the peace talks in Washington, DC.

86. This incident was recounted to the author by an American-Jewish visitor to the area. Though some observers dismiss this and other such incidents as "errors," the degree of indiscriminate violence against Palestinian civilians throughout the *intifada* suggests otherwise.

87. Such observations apply essentially to the responses of Israeli Jews. The reactions of Israeli Palestinians are discussed in a later section.

88. Irene Ertugul, "Working Together for Peace," *MEI,* (January 9, 1987): 16.

89. For more on this campaign, see the *Jordan Times,* April 12, 1987; and *Al-Fajr,* February 27, 1987, and December 5, 1986. In Israel, the lobbying efforts of this committee have reportedly been supported by, among others, Knesset member Ran Cohen of the Citizens Rights Movement and Professor Edy Kaufman, director of the Truman Institute at the Hebrew University; see the *Jerusalem Post International Edition,* October 31, 1987, p. 5.

90. *Boston Globe,* May 22, 1988.

91. Israel Shahak provides a monthly service, *From the Hebrew Press,* which is available by subscription in the United States. Included in each packet are lengthy translations of selected articles on given themes—for example, settlement activity, repressive measures against Palestinians, and the like. The explicit analyses they provide have no parallel in the U.S. mainstream media.

92. Ertugul, "Working Together for Peace," p. 16; and *Al-Fajr,* February 27, 1987, and March 29, 1987.

93. Circulation of these papers was always restricted to areas within the "Green Line." These publications were distinctly critical about the activities of the Israeli authorities in the Occupied Territories, particularly during the *intifada*. For more on this case, see the *Jerusalem Post International Edition,* May 14, 1988, p. 7.

94. *Jerusalem Post International Edition,* May 14, 1988, p. 7. Another three of its Jewish editors and one Palestinian editor from Ramallah were detained and imprisoned. The editors and publisher were formally charged with links to a "terror" organization. While in prison, the same publisher accused the authorities of "forcing" a confession from him "under duress"; *ibid.,* June 4, 1988. Also while in prison, the two female Jewish editors, Roni Ben Efrat and Michal Schwartz, were reportedly both beaten by other prisoners, while prison officials did nothing to intervene. "Attacks on Roni Ben Efrat and Michal Schwartz in Prison," from press releases, May 30, 1988, and May 31, 1988, in *DataBase Project on Palestinian Human Rights,* June 1, 1988, p. 23; includes an affidavit by Roni Ben Efrat,

p. 24. In another development, Hadas Lahav, the Jewish wife of the publisher, was also detained, allegedly to put pressure on her husband. She accused her interrogators of "emotional torture, humiliation and harassments, including sexual." Translated from *Haaretz*, "The Shin Bet Tried to Make Me Crazy," May 26, 1988, *ibid.*, p. 25.

95. Yigal Ilan, in *Haaretz*, January 5, 1990, cited in *Israel and Palestine*, no. 157 (May 1990): 15.

96. *Al-Fajr*, April 19, 1987, p. 6.

97. This petition was organized by the New Jewish Agenda, text printed in *Al-Fajr*, July 26, 1987.

98. *Courage Along the Divide*, produced and directed by Victor Schonfeld with Jenifer Millstone, associate producer, SPI, London.

99. For a detailed account, see also Deena Hurwitz, "Nonviolence in the Occupied Territories," *Israel and Palestine*, July 1986, p. 22.

100. Similar cases have been documented in other areas in the Occupied Territories, for example, in Beita, where in June 1988 a group of Palestinians and about 100 Israeli Jews cooperated jointly in planting trees, as an expression of their support for the residents. This nonviolent activity was forcibly obstructed by Israeli soldiers, who ordered all the Israelis out. *Al-Fajr*, June 12, 1988, p. 14; and *Boston Globe*, June 11, 1988.

101. *Al-Fajr*, June 12, 1988, p. 4. During the conference these writers signed a six-point "Peace Treaty" in which they advocated an independent Palestinian state in the Occupied Territories. For the text of the treaty and its signatories, see *Al-Fajr*, June 19, 1988, p. 8. One of the Palestinian signatories was later deported.

102. For more on this movement, see *Al-Fajr*, April 3, 1988, p. 9, and *Israel Scene*, April/May 1990, supplement to the *Jerusalem Post International Edition*, May 1990. Some North American cities, such as Boston, formed their own groups of Women in Black, who conducted the same silent weekly protests. See also the documentary film *The Struggle for Peace: Israelis and Palestinians*, by Elizabeth Fernea, producer, and Steve Talley, director, 1991.

103. See Union of Palestinian Working Women's Committees, *Newsletter*, January 26, 1988.

104. Beth Goldring, "Searching for the Palestinian Gandhi," *Al-Fajr*, July 19, 1987, p. 6.

105. Israel Shahak, "Violence Against Nonviolence," *Jordan Times*, June 24, 1987, reprinted from *MEI*.

106. Peretz Kidron, "Revival of the Peace Movement," *MEI* (June 11, 1988): 9.

107. As of June 1988, The 21st Year had over 1,500 members; see the *Jerusalem Post International Edition*, June 11, 1988, and *Israel Scene*, April/May 1990, supplement to the *Jerusalem Post International Edition*, May 1990.

108. The 21st Year, "Covenant for the Struggle Against the Occupation" (Jerusalem, n.d.). Also reprinted in *Tikkun*, June–July 1988. An opening statement reads, "The Occupation, then, is not only a deplorable situation affecting the lives of Palestinians; it has an equally pernicious effect on the very political and spiritual substance of Israeli society."

109. One important feature of its political action campaign was to send groups into the Occupied Territories as "Witnesses of the Occupation." This tactic performs

a double function, both as a "moderating presence" in the areas and as a fact-finding mission; The 21st Year, *Political Actions* (Jerusalem, n.d.).

110. In their discussions with soldiers, they were careful to avoid any phraseology that could be construed as "incitement," for example, by telling people not to serve. Instead, they discussed various options and the rationale behind refusing to serve in the Occupied Territories.

111. *Jerusalem Post International Edition,* June 11, 1988, p. 11.

112. Michal Schwartz discussed these same concerns during my visit to her Jerusalem office in July 1993. Her view was that progressive Israeli groups would only be shaken from their lethargy when they perceived a revival of political action on the part of Palestinians. Perhaps then, she thought, more people would be convinced that, in fact, all was not well on the political front.

113. In July 1993, I talked to some prominent Palestinians who had been involved at one level or another in the peace talks. They expressed grave concern that there were no "alternatives" being developed on the ground in the Occupied Territories to provide backing and support to these talks, or as something to fall back on should the negotiations be suspended at any time. In retrospect, their concerns could be explained by the secret negotiations going on between Israel and the PLO, which overlapped with the "public" talks proceeding in Washington. The PLO's (especially Arafat's) refusal to countenance any alternative resistance (albeit civilian and nonviolent) makes "sense" in this scenario. In view of long-term strategic planning, however, Arafat's reliance on a single channel and means of change may require reconsideration.

Chapter Four

1. William Gamson, *The Strategy of Social Protest* (Homewood, IL: Dorsey Press, 1975), p. 57.

2. Paul Wehr, "Nonviolent Resistance to Occupation: Norway and Czechoslovakia," in Severyn T. Bruyn and Paula M. Raymon (eds.), *Nonviolent Action and Social Change* (New York: Irvington, 1979), p. 214.

3. Paul Wehr, "Self-Limiting Conflict: The Norwegian Resistance," in Paul Wehr, *Conflict Regulation* (Boulder, CO: Westview Press, 1979), pp. 69–100.

4. Ibid., p. 98. Also, M. Skodvin, "Norwegian Non-violent Resistance During the German Occupation," in Adam Roberts (ed.), *Civilian Resistance as National Defence* (Middlesex, England: Penguin Books, 1967); for a comparative examination of the Danish case, see J. Bennett, "The Resistance Against the German Occupation of Denmark, 1940–1945," in Roberts, *Civilian Resistance as National Defense*. Bennett discusses the role of the civilian population in "obstructing" the Germans through such means as boycotts and work slowdowns, and in making their situation "difficult" (pp. 187–188). He does concede, however, that the Danes engaged in some "violent" resistance as well, especially sabotage (p. 192).

5. Gene Sharp, "The Significance of Domestic Nonviolent Action as a Substitute for International War," in Bruyn and Raymon, *Nonviolent Action and Social Change,* p. 245. Sharp cites many cases, both historical and contemporary, where nonviolent struggle has been used effectively; see Gene Sharp, *The Politics of Nonviolent Action,* 1, *Power and Struggle* (Boston: Porter Sargent, 1973). Much of

the volume is devoted to such comparative analyzes, and includes ancient Rome and Hungarian resistance against Austria (1850–1867), pp. 75–102.

6. Sharp, *The Politics of Nonviolent Action*, p. 810; and Hakan Wiberg, "What Have We Learnt About Peace?" *Journal of Peace Research*, 28, no. 2 (1981): 135–136.

7. Gene Sharp, *Civilian-Based Defense: A Post-Military Weapons System* (Princeton, NJ: Princeton University Press, 1990), p. 7. This book is Sharp's most recent work on the topic. His earlier studies include *National Security Through Civilian-Based Defense* (Omaha, NE: Association for Transarmament Studies, 1985) *Making Europe Unconquerable: The Potential of Civilian-Based Deterrence and Defense* (Cambridge, MA: Ballinger, 1985). He cites many concrete "prototypes" of such struggles (mainly in Europe) and provides realistic assessments of their potential. See also Sharp, in Bruyn and Raymon, *Nonviolent Action and Social Change*, p. 248. Wiberg, "What Have We Learnt About Peace?" refers to civilian defense in both capacities: as a struggle against foreign aggression and as a response to domestic coups.

8. See Stephen King-Hall, *Defence in the Nuclear Age* (London: Victor Gollancz, 1958); Gustaaf Geeraerts (ed.), *Possibilities of Civilian Defence in Western Europe* (Amsterdam: Swets and Zeitlinger, 1977), which includes an essay on Swedish defense policy; Adam Roberts, "Civilian Resistance and Swedish Defence Policy," ibid., pp. 121–153; Adam Roberts, "Civilian Defence Twenty Years On," *Bulletin of Peace Proposals*, 9, no. 4 (1978): 293–300; Desmond Ball (ed.), *Strategy and Defence: Australian Essays* (London: George Allen and Unwin, 1982); and the report of the Alternative Defence Commission, *Defence Without the Bomb* (London and New York: Taylor and Francis, 1983).

9. Sharp, *Civilian-Based Defense*, p. 3.

10. Also see Gene Sharp, *Social Power and Political Freedom*, (Boston: Porter Sargent, 1980), pp. 27 ff.; and Anders Boserup and Andrew Mack, *War Without Weapons* (London: Frances Pinter, 1974).

11. Religion is a powerful symbol in Arab society, and certainly both Islam and Christianity contain elements and traditions that can be mobilized in the service of a nonviolent civilian campaign. Palestinian strategists could work on this aspect in the preparation for civilian resistance, in order to locate and legitimize this resistance within a broader framework of an accepted and trusted cultural tradition. See also Richard B. Gregg, *The Power of Nonviolence* (New York: Schocken Books, 1959).

12. The term "civilian resistance" used throughout this study is not totally synonymous with "nonviolent resistance." Instead, it emphasizes how nonviolent methods can be exercised within the framework of a civilian resistance struggle—for example, during the *intifada*. This designation allows the Palestinian struggle in the Occupied Territories to remain at once both integral to and distinct from the whole Palestinian national movement.

13. See, for example, Sharp, *Making Europe Unconquerable*. Lithuania (newly independent of the former Soviet Union) is a timely case of a nation that is seriously investigating a civilian-based defense strategy. Sharp and others at the Albert Einstein Institute in Cambridge, Massachusetts, and the Program on Nonviolent Sanctions (PNS) at Harvard University have been involved in consultancy work on this project and have hosted speakers and panels on the issue.

14. See Alex P. Schmid, "Possibilities and Limits of Social Defense" (The Netherlands: State University at Leiden, Center for the Study of Social Conflicts, 1983), p. 29. Mimeographed Report.

15. Sharp, *The Politics of Nonviolent Action,* p. 4.

16. *Ibid.,* pp. 19–24.

17. One could argue that any social movement requires that the "challengers" undergo a change in consciousness, or what Doug McAdam calls "cognitive liberation," see Doug McAdam, *Political Process and the Development of Black Insurgency, 1930–1970* (Chicago: University of Chicago Press, 1982), p. 48.

18. For more on this critique of Sharp, see Brian Martin, "Gene Sharp's Theory of Power," *Journal of Peace Research,* 26, no. 2 (1989): 213–222.

19. McAdam, *Political Process,* p. 37, explains that social movements can occur even where power is highly concentrated in existing social structures. He writes, "The insurgent potential of excluded groups comes from the "structural power" that their location in various politico-economic structures affords them."

20. References to Fanon and Memmi in previous chapters illustrate how the emergence of guerrilla struggles is analyzed within precisely such contexts. Key to this idea is that even oppressive social structures could not exist without some measure of "obedience" by the population. McAdam, *Political Processes,* p. 37, quotes Michael Schwartz to emphasize that any resistance can wield power: "On the one hand, these power relations define the functioning of any ongoing system; on the other hand, the ability to disrupt these relationships [is] precisely the sort of leverage which can be used to alter the functioning of the system"; from Michael Schwartz, *Radical Protest and Social Structure* (New York: Academic Press, 1976), pp. 172–173.

21. Ideology (of whatever strand) plays a role in legitimizing sociostructural arrangements in virtually every society. It serves the functions of masking sources of raw power and of rendering existing regimes acceptable and legitimate. This issue is central to the Palestinian-Israeli conflict as well.

22. Some of these issues are elaborated in Chapter Five.

23. Assessments of the likelihood of success of social movements, be they violent or nonviolent, vary according to the "costs" incurred by the opponents. Nonviolent action may raise "costs" by exposing the degree of violence needed to repress it; hence, this method effectively wields power largely by defeating the political will of the opponent to continue its rule. For some theories on the sociostructural origins and dynamics of social movements and revolutions, see Samir Amin, Giovanni Arrighi, Andre Gunder Frank, and Immanuel Wallerstein, *Transforming the Revolution: Social Movements and the World System* (New York: Monthly Review Press, 1990); Jack A. Goldstone (ed.), *Revolutions: Theoretical, Comparative, and Historical Studies* (New York: Harcourt Brace Jovanovich, 1986); Jack A. Goldstone, Ted Robert Gurr, and Farrokh Moshiri (eds.), *Revolutions of the Late Twentieth Century* (Boulder, CO: Westview Press, 1991); and Theda Skocpol, *States and Social Revolutions* (Cambridge: Cambridge University Press, 1979).

24. It is impossible to do justice to other struggles in this study, whether these be historical or current. Each would require the same painstaking identification and analysis of its specific sociostructural components and of the resources at hand for each opponent and each resistance, as well as an examination of various "complicating" variables, including religious, ideological, cultural, and others, and the interna-

tional and regional considerations and developments at different moments in time. Comparative examples cited here are for illustrative purposes only.

25. Many of these developments came about with the settlement of the British and the expansion of the mining industry. Harold Wolpe, for example, points out that the British profited from black South African labor because the migrant labor system allowed the British to assume responsible solely for the "productive" costs of labor, while "reproductive" costs were to be met in the reserves. Harold Wolpe, "Capitalism and Cheap Labor-Power in South Africa: From Segregation to Apartheid," *Economy and Society,* 1, no. 4 (November 1972): 425–457; and Harold Wolpe, "The Theory of Internal Colonialism," in Ivar Oxaal, Tony Barnett, and David Booth (eds.), *Beyond the Sociology of Development* (London: Routledge and Kegan Paul, 1975), pp. 229–253. A similar situation exists in the Occupied Territories, though there are differences between the abilities of the West Bank and Gaza Strip to sustain "reproductive" costs.

26. According to Pomeroy, this decision was not made until 1961, see William J. Pomeroy (ed.), *Guerrilla Warfare and Marxism* (New York: International Publishers, 1968), p. 42.

27. In Pomeroy, *Guerrilla Warfare and Marxism,* p. 269. As in the Occupied Territories, there were a variety of regulations defining illegal activities. In South Africa, strikes were illegal, as were any "unlawful acts or omissions, actual or threatened, aimed at bringing about any political, industrial, social or economic change"; Sharp, *The Politics of Nonviolent Action,* p. 542.

28. On the role of labor and trade unions in South Africa, see C.R.D. Halisi, Patrick O'Meara, and N. Brian Winchester, "South Africa: Potential for Revolutionary Change," in Goldstone et al., *Revolutions of the Late Twentieth Century,* pp. 272–298; and Tom Lodge, Bill Nasson, Steven Mufson, Khehla Shubane, and Nokwanda Sithole, *All, Here, And Now: Black Politics In South Africa In the 1980s* (New York: Ford Foundation–Foreign Policy Association, South African UPDATE Series, 1991). Many nonviolent campaigns in South Africa were directed against specific laws, such as the Pass Laws that restricted the movement of black South Africans outside their Homelands. For more on the nonviolent struggle in South Africa, see selected reports in Program on Nonviolent Sanctions, *Transforming Struggle: Strategy and Global Experience of Nonviolent Direct Action* (Cambridge, MA: PNS, Harvard University, 1992), pp. 87–96. This publication summarizes presentations at the Program on Nonviolent Sanctions in Conflict and Defense (PNS) at Harvard between 1983 and 1991. It documents cases of nonviolent struggles in Africa, Asia, Eastern Europe and the USSR, Latin America, the Middle East, North America, and Western Europe. It also summarizes papers that address research issues, strategies, and techniques of nonviolent action. See also PNS, *Nonviolent Sanctions Seminar Synopses, Fall 1991* (Cambridge, MA: PNS, Harvard University); Doug Bond, Michelle Markley, and William Vogele (eds.), *Nonviolent Sanctions Seminars, Synopses Spring 1992* (Cambridge, MA: PNS, Harvard University); and Doug Bond, Joe Bond, and Yong-Joo Kim (eds.), *Nonviolent Sanctions Seminars, Synopses Fall 1992* (Cambridge, MA: PNS, Harvard University).

29. Sharp, *The Politics of Nonviolent Action,* p. 666. For more on the Indian case see Narayan Desai, *Towards a Nonviolent Revolution* (Varanasi, India: Sarva Seva Sangh Prakeshan, 1972).

30. Sharp, *The Politics of Nonviolent Action,* p. 667.

31. For more on the strategy underlying *satyagraha,* see Desai, *Towards a Nonviolent Revolution,* p. 119; Wiberg, "What Have We Learnt About Peace?" p. 135; and Gene Sharp, *Gandhi as a Political Strategist* (Boston: Porter Sargent, 1979). Specific tactics used included marches, courting imprisonment, civil disobedience, economic boycotts, sit-ins, appeals, noncooperation, mass resignations, and others.

32. Sharp, *The Politics of Nonviolent Action,* p. 5.

33. *Ibid.,* p. 110. Both Sharp and other theorists of nonviolent action were influenced by the tradition of Gandhi and the nonviolent struggle against British colonialism in India.

34. The examples of certain phases of black South African struggles against apartheid in recent decades and the Vietnamese guerrilla struggle against U.S. forces in the 1970s both come to mind.

35. The elements and mechanisms involved in formulating a strategy to induce precisely these outcomes are explained in detail in Chapter Five. Many writers, including Sharp, agree that whether a society is "democratic" or characterized by resistance to foreign colonial rule is not the main issue here. Clearly, nonviolent action may be facilitated by a democratic setting. In contrast, because under colonial rule the opponent may be more able and willing to use violent repression to stifle any opposition, nonviolent action may be a particularly effective technique; Sharp, *The Politics of Nonviolent Action,* pp. 109–110, and Sharp, in Bruyn and Raymon, *Nonviolent Action and Social Change,* p. 243.

36. Other analysts of nonviolent struggle tend to apply terms that overlap with those of Sharp, for example, George Lakey, "The Sociological Mechanisms of Nonviolent Action," *Peace Research Review,* 2, no. 6 (1968): 1–102.

37. Sharp, *The Politics of Nonviolent Action;* and Chapter Three.

38. Sharp, *The Politics of Nonviolent Action,* p. 315.

39. Lewis Killian, *The Impossible Revolution* (New York: Random House, 1968), pp. 50, 51.

40. This technique was frequently wielded by organized labor in the black South African movement in its struggle against white apartheid rule; see Halisi et al., "South Africa"; and Lodge et al., *All, Here, And Now.*

41. For Sharp's analysis of nonviolent action during the *intifada,* see Gene Sharp, "The *Intifada* and Nonviolent Struggle," *Journal of Palestine Studies (JPS),* 19, no. 1 (Autumn 1989): 3–14; Philip Grant, "Nonviolent Political Struggle in the Occupied Territories," in Ralph E. Crow, Philip Grant, and Saad E. Ibrahim (eds.), *Arab Nonviolent Political Struggle in the Middle East* (Boulder, CO: Lynne Reinner, 1990), pp. 59–75; and Souad Dajani, *Intifada* (Amman, Jordan: Center for Hebraic Studies, University of Jordan, 1990).

42. Mubarak Awad, "Non-Violent Resistance: A Strategy for the Occupied Territories," *JPS,* 13, no. 4 (Summer 1984): 22–37.

43. R. Scott Kennedy, "The Golani Druze: A Case of Non-violent Resistance," *JPS,* 13, no. 2 (Winter 1984): 48–65.

44. Sharp, *The Politics of Nonviolent Action,* pp. 579, 601–602.

45. *Ibid.,* p. 595.

46. *Ibid.*

47. Sharp's earlier writings identify the first three basic mechanisms, those of

conversion, accommodation, and nonviolent coercion; see *The Politics of Nonviolent Action*. His study *Civilian-Based Defense* identifies a fourth mechanism, that of disintegration. Lakey, "The Sociological Mechanisms of Nonviolent Action," lists three mechanisms that basically overlap with Sharp's initial categorization; conversion, persuasion, and coercion.

48. Sharp, *The Politics of Nonviolent Action*, p. 706; and Lakey, "The Sociological Mechanisms of Nonviolent Action."

49. Both the Occupied Territories and South Africa come to mind as cases where the oppressed group has long been so dehumanized by the oppressor as to make radical "conversion" virtually impossible.

50. Sharp, *The Politics of Nonviolent Action*, p. 733; and Lakey, "The Sociological Mechanisms of Nonviolent Action."

51. Lakey, "The Sociological Mechanisms of Nonviolent Action," p. 13.

52. Sharp, *The Politics of Nonviolent Action*, p. 741; also see Lakey, "The Sociological Mechanisms of Nonviolent Action," p. 10.

53. Sharp, *Civilian-Based Defense*, p. 64.

54. Parallels to war are obvious, where military might is used to induce the total defeat and disintegration of the opponent. Examples of successful nonmilitary struggles of this sort include the fall of the shah's regime in Iran in 1979 and the sudden overthrow of the Marcos regime in the Philippines in 1986. The latter case illustrates clearly the dynamic wielding of "people power"; see Richard J. Kessler, "The Philippines: The Making of a "People Power" Revolution," in Goldstone et. al., *Revolutions of the Late Twentieth Century*, pp. 194–218.

55. Fanon, Memmi, and Rodinson, referred to earlier, all suggest that disintegration of the colonial regime is an inevitable outcome of the decolonization process. In an example from our times, it is inconceivable that the struggle of blacks in South Africa for their national and civil rights would succeed without the total dismantling of the system of apartheid that had oppressed them.

56. Boserup and Mack, *War Without Weapons*, p. 155. They cite Clausewitz' use of this term; and see Chapter Three.

57. The terms "defense" and "offense" are used here in accordance with Boserup and Mack's definition; *War Without Weapons*, p. 157. In their view, the nonviolent resisters comprise the "defense," as this depicts their actions in the early phases of a struggle. In the Occupied West Bank and Gaza Strip, as in other actual cases, it may be difficult to maintain a clear distinction between the two terms. They may be interchangeable, as the party of the "defense" goes on the offensive against the opponent. It may be helpful, therefore, to qualify the meaning of the "defense" by distinguishing between strategic and tactical levels. While the nonviolent resistance remains "defensive" in its strategic purpose—as expressed by the continued emphasis on strengthening its own center of gravity—it may go on the offensive tactically, in its use of nonviolent action to undermine the opponent.

58. Boserup and Mack, *War Without Weapons*, p. 158.

59. "Unity" here refers to unity in the strategic sense, in terms of the internal coherence of the strategy. It comprises the idea of consensus over the ultimate objective of the resistance, agreement on the loci of power to be targeted (concentrated or strengthened in the case of the resistance, and attacked in the case of the opponent), and adherence to the techniques of struggle. Unity in the tactical sense

may or may not be feasible or required, depending on the circumstances. Thus room is left for diversity and flexibility in the resistance.

60. Boserup and Mack differentiate between the "aim" of war and the "purpose" of war. While the former, in their view, remains consistent in every struggle—to defeat the enemy and achieve victory—the "purpose" of war is political in nature and varies in each conflict; see *War Without Weapons,* Chapter 10, "Nonviolent Defense in Classical Strategic Theory," pp. 148–183.

61. Our examination of Israeli society indicated that its sources of power vis-à-vis the Palestinians derive mainly from (a) its army, (b) its government and public, and (c) its international alignments. See Chapter Five for specific applications.

62. Boserup and Mack, *War Without Weapons,* p. 171.

Chapter Five

1. Extensive excerpts of the "Declaration of Principles" outlining the interim self-rule plan were published in the *New York Times,* September 1, 1993. The full text, including all annexes, can be found in *Journal of Palestine Studies (JPS),* 23, no. 1 (Autumn 1993): 115–121.

2. Salim Tamari contrasts the "steadfastness" of this period with the "populism" of the *intifada.* He describes the former as a passive strategy for staying on the land, compared to the latter, the active and dynamic mass and populist efforts to undermine—if not "dismantle"—the occupation regime. Salim Tamari, "The Palestinian Movement in Transition: Historical Reversals and the Uprising," in Rex Brynen (ed.), *Echoes of the Intifada: Regional Repercussions of the Palestinian-Israeli Conflict* (Boulder, CO: Westview Press, Westview Special Studies on the Middle East, 1991), pp. 13–29.

3. Meron Benvenisti, *U.S. Government Funded Projects in the West Bank and Gaza (1977–1983), Palestinian Sector* (Jerusalem: West Bank Data Base Project, 1984).

4. See for example, coverage in the *Jordan Times,* October 15, 1985, and February 11, 1986.

5. Sara Roy discussed these issues in a seminar organized by the Center for Middle East Studies at Harvard University, March 25, 1993.

6. See, for example, *Al-Fajr,* August 17, 1992, pp. 1, 16, which reports that these teams involved more than 300 professionals in various fields.

7. In July 1993, I was told that these teams were gradually inviting other factional groups to participate, regardless of their positions on the peace talks. While the Palestinian community clearly needed leadership and effective coordination of efforts, the overcentralization and monopolization of development affairs by these teams was deeply resented by some of the local Palestinians. What activists feared most was that the work of these teams was legitimizing the "empowerment" process favored by Israel and the United States, in a context that ultimately promised no more than the "normalization" of the occupation: Palestinian "self-rule" under permanent Israeli sovereignty. After the signing of the Declaration of Principles and the formation of newer committees, the importance of these teams declined.

8. Salim Tamari, "The Next Phase: Problems of Transitions," in Palestinian

Academic Society for the Study of International Affairs (PASSIA), *Palestinian Assessments of the Gulf War and Its Aftermath* (Jerusalem: PASSIA, April 1991), pp. 11–23. Samir Huleileh, a Palestinian economist in the Occupied Territories, praises the *intifada* for its success in linking the struggle against occupation with self-preservation of social, cultural, and political formations. However, he cautions that the economic activities of the *intifada* were dealt a "death blow" by the Gulf War and attending Israeli measures in the Occupied Territories. He urges "prevention of the imminent collapse of the Palestinian economy" as the immediate national priority. For Huleileh, new strategies should aim not at economic development as such, but at a unified movement that would link institution building to political struggle; Samir Huleileh, "The Gulf Crisis and the Palestinian Economy: New Tasks and Challenges," in PASSIA, *Palestinian Assessments of the Gulf War,* pp. 35–53.

9. Economic imperatives underlying this situation have made their way into the proposals for interim self-rule in the Occupied Territories. A major focus of these plans is the investment of millions of dollars to "develop" the infrastructure of the Occupied Territories, starting with the Gaza Strip.

10. Albert Memmi, *The Colonizer and the Colonized* (Boston: Beacon Press, 1965), writes of comparable movements among other colonized peoples, as they recreate their sense of identity and nationalism vis-à-vis their oppressor, and as they take pride in a newfound sense of empowerment and dignity.

11. It has yet to be seen how much "independent" development Palestinians will be allowed, and how closely their plans will be linked to the vested interests of both Israel and Jordan. Many questions have to be decided: priorities, allocation of funds, the currency to be used, and others; see Daoud Kuttab, "The Economic Debate," *Middle East International (MEI),* no. 462 (November 5, 1993): 4–5.

12. Several sources refer to the financial crisis within the PLO due to the cutoff in aid from various Gulf States following the Gulf War. One report maintains that PLO remittances fell from $30 million a month to $7 million by 1993, causing bankruptcy in many PLO-funded Palestinian institutions in the Occupied Territories; Mary Cook, "Arafat-Rabin Agreement Comes at Depth of PLO Financial Crisis," *Washington Report on Middle East Affairs (WRMEA),* November/December 1993, p. 48. Similarly, the *Jerusalem Post International Edition,* September 4, 1993, p. 2, quotes a Palestinian source to the effect that funding to the Occupied Territories dropped from $120 million in 1990 to $40 million in 1992.

13. One issue was how the conflicting interests of various Arab states could be bridged to mediate effectively with the United States; Helena Cobban, "The PLO and the *Intifada,*" *Middle East Journal,* 44, no. 2 (Spring 1990): 207–234. Reports alluded to separate deals being struck. Kuwait, for example, was reported to be aiding the PLO's rival, *Hamas,* in the Occupied Territories, and Saudi Arabia allegedly promised to send aid to Israel, even in the absence of a peace settlement; see Yizhar Be'er, "*Hamas:* A Challenge for Both the PLO and Israel," *Haaretz,* May 14, 1991, *From the Hebrew Press; New York Times,* June 19, 1991; and *Dayton News,* July 1, 1991, on export agreements between Israel and Saudi Arabia.

14. See James Zoghby, "New Thinking for Israeli-Palestinian Peace," a working paper (Washington, DC: Coalition for Post-War United States Policy in the Middle East, March 1991); Naseer Aruri, "The Palestinians After the Gulf War: What Options?" in Center for Policy Analysis on Palestine, *The Palestinians After the Gulf*

War: The Critical Questions (Washington, DC: Center for Policy Analysis on Palestine, Symposium Proceedings, March 27, 1991), pp. 3–13; Helga Baumgarten, "The PLO's Political Program and the Gulf Crisis," in PASSIA, *Palestinian Assessments of the Gulf War*, pp. 73–99; Sara Roy, "The Political Economy of Despair: Changing Political and Economic Realities in the Gaza Strip," *JPS*, 20, no. 3 (Spring 1991): 58–70; and conversations with professionals from the West Bank.

15. Palestinians in the Occupied Territories may work at a variety of levels: on the one hand, to cultivate independent power bases (alternative institutions and parallel organizations), and on the other, to create a parallel government that is backed by the PLO. It is interesting to note that the Islamic movement in the Occupied Territories has been positioning itself to play precisely the role envisioned in the former—setting up "alternative" structures of civil society to counterbalance the influence of *Fatah* and the PLO in the forthcoming autonomy. *Hamas,* for example, is said to be expanding its social support networks and working at the grassroots level to attract Palestinians to its activities; see the *New York Times,* November 7, 1993.

16. Anders Boserup and Andrew Mack, *War Without Weapons,* (London: Frances Pinter, 1974), p. 169.

17. George Lakey, "The Sociological Mechanisms of Nonviolent Action," *Peace Research Review,* 2, no. 6, (1968):53, refers to elements of the opponent's relationship to the resistance. Starting with the "area of toleration," the opponent's perception of a given "campaign," Lakey then examines how actions by the resistance may alternately cause "confusion," "violence," "nonviolence," or "making concessions," depending on how the opponent evaluates the situation. Several of these elements are relevant to the Palestinian case.

18. Settler violence against Palestinians is more difficult to control, and such control may only be achieved indirectly, if and when Israeli soldiers and the Israeli government are willing to intervene.

19. During my visit to the Kalandia refugee camp near Jerusalem (January–February 1988), young Palestinian male activists there were adamant about not resorting to lethal weapons. By way of explanation, they said, "They will massacre us." They insisted that they would only use stones and perhaps knives as a last resort, "to defend their families." During another visit to these areas in October 1989, I found that virtually all these young men, between 20 and 30 in all, had been imprisoned or were in hiding. They were punished, not necessarily for any violent activities, but for stone throwing and other *intifada*-related activities.

20. For more on the effect of the *intifada* on Israel, see Mark Tessler, "The Impact of the *Intifada* on Israeli Political Thinking," in Brynen, *Echoes of the Intifada,* pp. 43–97; and Azmi Bishara, "The Third Factor: Impact of the *Intifada* on Israel," in Jamal R. Nassar and Roger Heacock (eds.), *Intifada: Palestine at the Crossroads* (New York: Praeger, 1990), pp. 271–287. Only rarely did Israel experiment with less violent techniques; see the *New York Times,* September 10, 1990; and Palestine Human Rights Information Center (PHRIC) *Monthly Update* for July 1990, "Special Report: Arens' Uprising Policy," pp. 306–308.

21. See, for example, Israel Shahak, "Israel's Army and the *Intifada,*" *MEI,* no. 354 (July 7, 1989): 16–18.

22. For more information on officially sanctioned army violence in the Occupied

Territories and on expressions of dissent by army personnel, see No'omi Levitzky, "The Chief," *Hadashot,* March 22, 1991, in *From the Hebrew Press;* Israeli lawyer Avigdor Feldman, "The Bone Breaking Codex," *Haaretz,* October 10, 1990, *From the Hebrew Press.* Also Yizhar Be'er, "Why Harass Them?" *Haaretz,* March 24, 1991, *From the Hebrew Press,* cites the letter signed by "dozens" of reservists (who hold very right-wing views) calling for withdrawal from the Gaza Strip. Sara Leiboritz-Dan, in "All the Pain Came Out on the Paper," *Hotam,* October 26, 1990, *From the Hebrew Press,* examines the book *Collapse,* by a 22-year-old soldier chronicling his one and a half years of service in the Occupied Territories and the violence and racism against Arabs. In another article, this same soldier discusses how his entire generation has been "corrupted," "void of all ethical values," in Miri Poz, "I Wished They Would Not See My Tears," *Davar,* Friday Supplement, October 20, 1990, in *From the Hebrew Press.* See also Shmuel Shom-Tov, "Refusal Now," *Kol Ha'ir,* December 14, 1990, *From the Hebrew Press.* From another Shahak collection, see Gabi Nitza, "The Armed Struggle of the General Security Service," *Hadashot,* December 7, 1990, which describes the random violence perpetrated against civilians, including breaking into their homes, beating the residents, issuing threats, and intimidation. On racism toward Arabs, see Member of the Knesset Shulamit Aloni, "Monstrous Orders Which Are Conceivable," *Politika,* January 1991, *From the Hebrew Press.* Aloni discusses the "higher value" placed on Jewish life and the "legitimate" acts tolerated against Arabs that would be unthinkable had they been committed against Jews. Israelis express their pride that these incidents are exposed in the media and in the way this exposure underscores their "democracy" at work. The other side of the coin remains, however, that the perpetrators of violence are rarely sanctioned for such crimes which would clearly be intolerable in any other context.

23. See PHRIC, *Monthly Updates.* By the end of March 1993, some 54 Palestinian deaths were attributed to Israeli settlers/civilians; see PHRIC *Monthly Update,* January–March 1993.

24. For more on settlers, see various issues of the *Jerusalem Post International Edition* for July 1989. In the aftermath of the signing of the Israeli-PLO accords of September 1993, Israeli settlers in the Occupied Territories escalated their violent attacks against Palestinians, while some Palestinian factions increased their own armed attacks against settlers. For more on the significance of these events and the dangers of exploding settler violence, see Peretz Kidron, "Few Clues from the Elections," *MEI,* no. 462 (November 5, 1993): 5–7; and Haim Baram, "Undermining the Accords," *ibid.,* p. 7. The *New York Times* of November 17, 1993 also reported that the Israeli army would act "firmly and aggressively" to stop further "disturbances" by settlers. Also, the *New York Times,* December 6, 1993, reports some Israeli government officials referring to settlers as "fanatics" and "terrorists."

25. Occasional Israeli news reports have depicted some Israeli Jews distinguishing between "us and them," legitimizing their own Zionist conquest of Palestine, yet concerned, if not yet actually condemning, the actions of settlers as obstacles to peace; National Public Radio reports from Israel, between March and June 1988.

26. Schiff and Ya'ari devote an entire section to problems between Jewish settlers and Israeli soldiers during the *intifada.* They maintain that, instead of praising the soldiers, Israeli settlers often hurled abuse at the army for being too "soft" where

Palestinians are concerned; Zeev Schiff and Ehud Ya'ari, *Intifada* (New York: Simon and Schuster, 1990), pp. 164–168.

27. Past efforts to engage in greater civil disobedience—for example, in the form of total tax revolts, widespread strikes, and the burning of identity cards—have gone unheeded or have backfired as a result of harsh Israeli countermeasures. See, for example, the *Jerusalem Post International Edition,* June 25, 1988, p. 1; Ziad Abu-Amr, "The *Intifada* Is on a Stony Road," *MEI,* no. 327 (June 11, 1988): 16–17; and Salim Tamari, "The Uprising's Dilemma: Limited Rebellion and Civil Society," *Middle East Report,* no. 164–165 (May–August 1990): 4–9.

28. The emerging Palestinian authority may find it necessary to rein in the more extremist elements in their society that could give Israel the excuse to reenter. This necessity may cancel the potential impact of nonviolent civilian resistance. On the other hand, Palestinian residents may find themselves forced at some point to engage in civil disobedience against their own leadership and governing body. Whatever the context, it seems inevitable that some kind of preparation would be needed both to deter outside aggression and to defend against it if required—all elements of a civilian-based defense strategy examined earlier.

29. Tessler, "The Impact of the *Intifada* on Israeli Political Thinking," p. 63.

30. See Hanan Ashrawi, "Israel's Real Intentions," in Center for Policy Analysis Report, *The Palestinians After the Gulf War,* p. 21.

31. Israel Shahak opines that only direct action by the United States against Israel, in the form of economic sanctions, could force Israeli concessions, *WRMEA,* July 1991, p. 20.

32. Hanna Siniora is the editor of *Al-Fajr* newspaper. For more on the incident, see *Al-Fajr,* June 14, 1987, p. 8; *Jordan Times,* June 6, 1987, and June 11, 1987; and *Newsweek,* June 29, 1987, p. 30.

33. See *Al-Fajr,* June 14, 1987, p. 1.

34. *Jordan Times,* June 6, 1987.

35. *Al-Fajr,* June 14, 1987.

36. For an update on this issue and the implications for the autonomy stage, see Kidron, "Few Clues from the Elections," p. 6. Earlier sections reviewed how discrimination and racism are institutionalized even against Israeli Palestinians. See Uzi Ornan, "The Art of Obfuscatory Formulation," *Haaretz,* May 17, 1991, *From the Hebrew Press.* Ornan openly labels Israel as an apartheid state and documents laws and measures that establish it as such. Polls occasionally taken in Israel indicate more support for preserving Israel's Jewish character than preserving its democratic character; in an August 1988 poll this comparison was 75 percent to 49 percent; see Tessler, "The Impact of the *Intifada* on Israeli Political Thinking," p. 72.

37. Another case that caught Israeli attention occurred during the first year of the *intifada.* Mubarak Awad, the deported director of the Palestine Center for the Study of Nonviolence (PCSN), stated his willingness to convert to Judaism in order to qualify for "return" to Jerusalem under the Israeli Law of Return. It is likely no coincidence that Israeli newspaper reports were soon filled with debates on the issue of "who is a Jew." (The issue is whether those converted in the Reform movements are also considered Jews and what criteria are required for such conversion to be legal.) Though the event quickly blew over, Awad essentially forced Israeli society to confront its institutionalized racism against Palestinians. Racism in Israel occurs

among Jews themselves. For example, the airlifting of Ethiopian Jews to Israel, in the summer of 1991, that coincided with the immigration of Jews from the Soviet Union, caused concern in some Israeli circles. Various Israeli newspapers openly discussed stereotyping and racism against the "uncivilized" Jew from Ethiopia, and how Soviet Jews felt especially concerned that attention to the former would detract from the benefits they felt were their due. See Uzi Benziman, "Polls Recently Conducted Among Soviet Jews," *Haaretz,* May 31, 1991; Amnon Birman, "Zionism as a Butterfly Collector," *Kol Ha'ir,* May 31, 1991; and Nurit Wargoft and Daphne Bar-Shamir, "They Are Wild, They Are Primitive," *Kol Ha'ir,* May 31, 1991, all in, *From the Hebrew Press, Collection on Soviet and Ethiopian Jewish Immigrants.*

38. See "The Oslo Agreement: An Interview with Nabil Shaath," *JPS,* 23, no. 1 (Autumn 1993): 5–14.

39. Israel under Prime Minister Shamir appeared willing to do whatever was necessary to ensure permanent control over the West Bank and Gaza Strip, and his policies were not seriously opposed by the United States. Citing a *Maariv* article, Pinhas Inbari, *Al-Hamishmar,* May 22, 1991, in *From the Hebrew Press,* n.d., states that United States Secretary of State James Baker "proposed to the Defense Minister Moshe Arens, a deal by which the [pro-American] Arab states would renounce their economic boycott of Israel in exchange for some attenuation of conditions of the Palestinians in the [Occupied] Territories." Arens rejected this offer, "just as he refused, on principle, to even begin to negotiate another version of the deal, by which the termination of the [Arab] boycott would be offered in exchange for the cessation of the Israeli settlement drive." For more on Shamir's categorical refusal to give up the Occupied Territories, see Israel Shahak, "Yitzhak Shamir, Political Biography," *From the Hebrew Press,* 1990. The article outlines the principles of the Lehi "Party" to which Shamir belongs, whose position on war reflects, "an eternal war against all those who satanically stand in the way of the realization [of our] aims," and whose solution for "the fate of aliens," is that it would be "solved through population exchanges."

40. For more on the position of successive U.S. administrations on the Arab-Israeli conflict and on changes in public opinion in the United States, see Fred Khouri, "United States," in Brynen, *Echoes of the Intifada,* pp. 265–305; Fouad Moughrabi, "The *Intifada* in American Public Opinion," in Nassar and Heacock, *Intifada,* pp. 241–257; Don Peretz, *Intifada: The Palestinian Uprising,* (Boulder, CO: Westview Press, 1990), pp. 167–181; Noam Chomsky, "Israel's Role in U.S. Foreign Policy," in Zachary Lockman and Joel Beinin (eds.), *Intifada: The Palestinian Uprising Against Israeli Occupation.* A MERIP Book (Boston: South End Press, 1989), pp. 253–275; and Naseer Aruri, "The United States and Palestine: Reagan's Legacy to Bush," *JPS,* 18, no. 3 (Spring 1989): 3–22.

41. The PLO had to repeat the same pledges in order to qualify for "mutual recognition" with Israel in 1993.

42. See Khouri, "United States," p. 278.

43. The official position of the United States in recent decades was that the West Bank and Gaza Strip (including East Jerusalem) were "occupied areas" whose final status would be determined through negotiations. Though other members of the UN Security Council interpreted Resolution 242 to require Israeli withdrawal from all the areas captured in the 1967 War (this is specified, for example in the French and Chinese versions, as "the territories"), the English version was deliberately left

vague. The British Lord Caradon, one of the drafters of this resolution, insisted that regardless of the language, it was understood by all the parties concerned that Israel was required to withdraw from all these territories; see Sheldon Richman, "Israel's 1967 Attack Was Aggression; Israel's Current Occupation Is Illegal," *WRMEA,* July 1991, p. 40. Israel, as represented by earlier Likud governments, always insisted that it had fulfilled this resolution by withdrawing from the Sinai desert.

44. See Khouri, "United States"; Chomsky, "Israel's Role in U.S. Foreign Policy"; and Aruri, "The United States and Palestine."

45. For an outline of Israel's strategic alliance with the United States, see Aluf Ben, "Strategy on a Regional Basis," *Haaretz,* September 21, 1993, *From the Hebrew Press,* November 1993.

46. This analysis of the role of Palestinians and the Arab regimes appears borne out in official U.S. pronouncements and policies toward the region. There were indications that both the Bush and Clinton administrations' policies in the region were informed by (if not based on) studies prepared by pro-Israel think tanks in Washington, DC, notably a 1988 report published by the Washington Institute for Near East Policy, "Building for Peace, an American Strategy for the Middle East." A cofounder of this institute, Martin Indyk, was subsequently appointed as Clinton's National Security Council's Middle East adviser. Indyk had also worked with the American Israel Public Affairs Committee (AIPAC) and was a communications adviser to former Israeli Prime Minister Itzhak Shamir. A centerpiece of Indyk's strategy was the "dual containment" of Iran and Iraq, and of (religious) "extremism" in the area; for Indyk's remarks on these issues, see Special Assistant to the President Martin Indyk, Remarks on the Clinton Administration's Approach to the Middle East, Washington, DC, May 18, 1993, excerpts reprinted in *JPS,* 22, no. 4 (Summer 1993): 159–162. Indyk confirms, "We are committed to deepening our strategic partnership with Israel in the pursuit of peace and security." And on the Israeli-Palestinian conflict, Indyk's statement reads in part, "But to achieve their objectives there can be no substitute for engaging in negotiations without knowing the final status of the West Bank and Gaza Strip." For more on pro-Israel figures within the Clinton administration's appointees, see Richard H. Curtiss, "The Good News Is That So Far There's Not Much Bad News," *WRMEA,* February 1993, pp. 8–12; and Grace Halsell, "Clinton's Indyk Appointment One of Many from Pro-Israel Think Tank," *WRMEA,* March 1993, pp. 9–11, 89. For more on the marginalization of the Palestinians in U.S. policy concerns, see Noam Chomsky, "The Israel-Arafat Agreement," *Z Magazine,* October 1993, pp. 19–25. For a historical review of the U.S. "alliance" with Israel, see Douglas Little, "The Making of a Special Relationship: The United States and Israel, 1957–1968," *International Journal of Middle East Studies,* 25, no. 4 (November 1993): 563–585. He also refers to U.S. policy since the mid-1950s of containing "radical Arab nationalism" and links support of Israel to U.S. concerns over threats to its vital interests in the region posed by Israel's development of nuclear weapons.

47. Khouri, "United States," p. 266, traces the evolving relationship between Israel and the United States, until it "became the cornerstone of U.S. Middle East Policy." He quotes Thomas Dine, executive director of AIPAC (in 1986): "The U.S. only moves on the peace process after the closest consultations with . . . Israel" (p. 294).

48. Israel has sometimes contributed an increase in tension between the two governments and not only with regard to its intransigence over the Palestinian issue. A series of incidents over the last decade or so left some U.S. government officials rather disapproving of Israel. One concerns the Pollard spy case in 1985, which was followed by Israel's involvement in the Iran-Contra scandal during the Reagan administration. Another was Israel's alleged involvement with the former dictator of Panama, Manuel Noriega, and its connections with arms shipments to drug dealers in Latin America. Last but not least, was its persisting trade and military cooperation with the apartheid regime in South Africa, during the period of international boycotts of this regime.

49. The latter would have violated U.S. contractual agreements with the United Nations itself. In the event, after months of wrangling, a U.S. federal judge finally ruled in June 1988 that the U.S. government could not close the mission; *New York Times,* June 30, 1988.

50. In the spring of 1993, Americans were informed that the Anti-Defamation League of B'nai B'rith (ADL) had been implicated in a campaign of gathering information from police records on various groups in the country, including Arab-Americans, Jewish peace groups, antiapartheid groups, church groups, and others—some 500 organizations and 11,000–12,000 individuals in all—and was allegedly passing information (on Palestinian-American activists) to the Israeli Mossad. In November 1993, according to the *New York Times,* November 17, 1993, the ADL was cleared of charges of illegally obtaining information, but the whole case sent shock waves among activist groups in the United States, especially Arab-Americans. Many felt threatened that their rights to free speech and assembly had been violated. For more on this case, see issues of the *WRMEA,* July/August 1993, April/May 1993, March 1993; Robert W. Bermudes, "The Ramifications of the ADL Spy Scandal," *MEI,* no. 462 (November 5, 1993): 19–20; and a list of all targeted organizations in American-Arab Anti-Discrimination Committee, "ADL Update," *ADC Times,* May–June 1993. A frequent tactic used to stifle free speech is to equate any criticism of Israeli policies with anti-Semitism.

51. Two examples of works that address this issue are Edward Tivnan, *The Lobby* (New York: Simon and Schuster, 1987); and Paul Findley, *They Dare to Speak Out* (Westport, CT: Lawrence Hill, 1985).

52. *Jerusalem Post International Edition,* July 9, 1988, p. 3.

53. The same article documents some of the trade agreements that suffered, instances of boycotts of Israeli products, refusals to extend diplomatic and political relations, and the like.

54. Simha Flapan, *The Birth of Israel* (New York: Pantheon Books, 1987); Michael Palumbo, *The Palestinian Catastrophe* (New York: Quartet Books, 1987); and Benny Morris, *The Birth of the Palestinian Refugee Problem, 1947–1949* (New York: Cambridge University Press, 1987).

55. The situation was particularly tense during the Gulf War, when the Arab-American community in the United States was subjected to constant harassment and discrimination, even from official U.S. agencies, such as police and immigration authorities. This is to say nothing of the unpopularity of airing any pro-Palestinian position at various functions, even those that purportedly opposed the war. Instances of such harassment were personally experienced by this author. I also know of

several cases of educators (such as college professors) who were dismissed from their jobs or denied tenure at their institutions because of their research on Palestinian issues or pro-Palestinian activism. The pro-Israel organization AIPAC has published pamphlets that, among other things, instruct college students on how to pressure colleges to cancel appearances by pro-Palestinian speakers, or failing that, how to confront and corner these speakers on their positions; for example, American Israel Public Affairs Committee, "The AIPAC College Guide: Exposing the Anti-Israel Campaign on Campus," *AIPAC Papers on U.S.-Israel Relations,* 7 (1984).

56. An example occurred when the distinguished Palestinian-American professor Edward Said was featured. Another example concerned the airing of the documentary movie *Days of Rage,* in which PBS was forced to carry a "wraparound" sequel at the end of the film, prior to receiving permission to have it shown.

57. In countless cases, as this author can attest, taped shows would simply be "edited" to remove the more critical and thought-provoking statements of Arab speakers. This author and many Arab colleagues went through similar experiences with the U.S. media.

58. Moughrabi, "The *Intifada* in American Public Opinion," p. 244, examines various opinion polls to trace changes in American public opinion over these issues. For example, whereas a Gallup poll in 1982 showed 32 percent of those surveyed "sympathetic" to the Israeli position, in 1988 this figure dropped to 24 percent, while those more sympathetic to the Palestinian position rose from 22 percent to 39 percent over the same period.

59. In a rather ironic reversal, pronouncements about protecting the "democratic" process were noticeably lacking during the final stages of the PLO/Israeli negotiations over "mutual recognition." While it was uncritically accepted that Rabin would obtain the approval of the Knesset before making any deal with the PLO, the United States and others could hardly wait for (what many Palestinians perceive as) Arafat's capitulation to come fast enough. Arabs have always been criticized by the United States for their supposed lack of democracy. Yet here was an instance where there was hardly any criticism of Arafat, even though he subverted the democratic process in the PLO and unilaterally decided on these agreements with Israel. (The PLO is legally bound by its charter to subject major proposals for revisions to a vote by the Palestine National Council, or PNC.)

60. Editorial by Joseph Sobra in the *Burlington Times,* April 10, 1990, reprinted in *WRMEA,* June 1990, p. 43. In September 1990 another story broke concerning Israeli efforts to suppress publication in the United States of a book by a former Mossad agent, Victor Ostrovsky, *The Art of Deception* (New York: St. Martin's Press, 1990), on the grounds that it would harm Israeli state security.

61. On June 14, 1988, for example, the Foreign Press Association held a news conference to complain about Israeli mistreatment of journalists by army personnel and settlers alike. One report noted that between 100 and 150 complaints had been received, generating concern about increased Israeli violence toward the foreign media; *Al-Fajr,* June 14, 1988, p. 4.

62. Earlier in the *intifada,* former U.S. Secretary of State Henry Kissinger was reported to have advised Israelis to close off the Occupied Territories to the press (as in South Africa) and harshly suppress the uprising; see *WRMEA,* April 1988, p. 14.

63. One incident reported in July 1988 concerned Israeli security men who posed

as ABC News personnel to capture an Arab youth "suspected" of participating in demonstrations. Many identical incidents were subsequently revealed.

64. One example was the aforementioned 14-point program that was issued early in the *intifada* and ended up being ignored by the U.S. government and given hardly any attention at all in the media. In their leaflet, Palestinians were essentially demanding respect for human rights and the application of international law in these areas. Subsequent communiqués of the Unified Leadership, such as nos. 18 and 20, reiterated some of these demands. Palestinians insisted that if these were met, it would pave the way to ending the unrest in the Occupied Territories.

65. See Middle East Justice Network (MEJN) newsletter, *Breaking the Siege*, and the *Washington Report on Middle East Affairs*, which frequently document the amounts of aid given Israel. These publications regularly point out that, apart from direct economic and military aid, the total annual aid to Israel is close to $7 billion, considering the interest on regular aid, the stockpiling of arms in Israel, joint research and development ventures, allowing Israel to spend large portions of this aid in Israel itself, and other benefits.

66. This point was illustrated in the controversy between Israel and the United States during 1991–1992, over the requested $10 billion in loan guarantees ostensibly needed for the housing of Soviet Jewish immigrants in Israel. In the fall of 1991, Israel received housing guarantees amounting to $400 million, which, after months of negotiation, failed to meet the U.S. requirement for reassurances that these funds would not be spent in the Occupied Territories. The loan was granted anyway. Even without these special loans, however, Israel has always been able to use regular U.S. economic aid to free up its own resources and forge ahead with settlement building. With the approval of $10 billion in loan guarantees (to be dispersed in amounts of $2 billion per year and reduced by amounts spent on settlements), settlement building continued with U.S. blessing. For example, Edward P. Djerejian, Assistant Secretary of State for Near East Affairs, "U.S. Aid and Assistance to the Middle East," April 28, 1993, Statement on Europe and the Middle East of the House Foreign Affairs Committee in Washington, DC, originally published in the *U.S. Department of State Dispatch*, May 10, 1993, pp. 328–330, reiterates U.S. pledges to support Israel's "security" and maintains that the "government of Israel is committed to decrease government expenditure for non-security activity in the occupied territories." This could be read as an implicit agreement with Israeli policies concerning "security"-related settlements. During Prime Minister Rabin's visit to Washington in November 1993, President Clinton pledged to give Israel additional economic and military aid to offset the "costs" of making peace. This aid package included help with the $250 million needed to build the infrastructure (roads and military bases) for the "redeployment" of troops under the terms of the accords; see the *New York Times*, November 12, 1993. This itself raises concerns that Israel is in these areas to stay, given that roads to serve settlers and the army were well under way before the Israel-PLO agreements. Additional funding of such "infrastructure" suggests that the terms surrounding the $10 billion dollars in loan guarantees are being circumvented and redefined to establish the legitimacy of an Israeli presence in the Occupied Territories.

67. Between 1948 and 1985, Israel, the largest recipient of foreign aid, received a total of US$31 billion ($10 billion in economic assistance and $21 billion in

military assistance), 60 percent of which was grants rather than loans; see House of Representatives, 99th Congress, 1st Session, 1985, *Foreign Assistance Legislation for Fiscal Years 1986–1987,* Part 3, Hearings and Markup before the Subcommittee on Europe and the Middle East of the Committee on Foreign Affairs, p. 306. All economic aid since FY 1981 and all military aid since FY 1985 have been extended as grants. In other developments, some 12 U.S. states authorized state employee investment of pension funds in Israeli bonds, as a new source of aid to Israel (a potential burden on the American taxpayer should Israel be unable to pay); see Eugene Bird, "At the Grass Roots, Westerners Say, 'Rein in Israel,' " *WRMEA,* September/October 1993, p. 17. See also Frank Collins, "Israel's Untouchable Entitlement Programs," *WRMEA,* March 1993, p. 15, who argues that by FY 1992, U.S. aid to Israel had topped $44.8 billion. Collins maintains that costs to the United States continue to rise, as most of the economic aid is used to repay the U.S. Treasury for outstanding loans (prior to 1974). He calculates the total U.S. FY 1993 grants, loans guarantees, and interest on grants to Israel, to amount to $6.321 billion. For a comparison of amounts spent on domestic programs and U.S. aid to Israel, see Richard H. Curtiss, "U.S. Aid to Israel Still off Limits in Search for Budget Cuts," *WRMEA,* April/May 1993, pp. 17–18.

68. Comparing the tone of reports on Awad with those on the 413 Palestinians who were expelled in December 1992, one finds the unchallenged characterizations of the latter as "*Hamas* activists" permeating the media, even though few of these Palestinians had been charged with any offense. The Israeli media were more discerning in this regard; some sources acknowledged that many of these Palestinians were simply thrown onto the bus without a careful check into their identities. In some cases, they were rounded up simply because they wore beards—thus automatically assumed to be members of *Hamas.*

69. See for example, the *New York Times,* September 10, 1993.

70. PHRIC, *Monthly Update,* Supplement, May 1990. Marked "Urgent," this letter, dated June 14, 1990, is addressed to Nongovernment Organizations and Interested Parties, and signed by Al-Haq and the PHRIC in the Occupied Territories.

71. See Edward Said, "The Israel/PLO Accord: A Critical Assessment," interview with David Barsamian, New York, September 27, 1993 (Boulder, CO: Alternative Radio), reprinted in *Z Magazine,* December 1993, pp. 45–54, and some Israeli observers; see for example, Graham Usher, "Why Gaza Mostly Says Yes," *MEI,* no. 459 (September 24, 1993): 19–20 (quoting Israeli officials and journalists).

72. These complex events have their roots in Israeli's 1978 invasion of Lebanon and its installation of an occupied "security zone" in the aftermath of the 1982 invasion. *Hizbullah* is a largely Shiite Lebanese movement, said to be backed by Iran, whose primary goal is to end Israel's occupation of South Lebanon. For more on the background to "Operation Accountability" (code name for Israel's July 1993 war on Southern Lebanon), see Noam Chomsky, " 'Limited War' in Lebanon," *Z Magazine,* September 1993, pp. 27–35. For some critical Israeli reactions to these raids, see Uzi Mahanaimi, "As a Military Intelligence Commander, Ehud Barak Was Against Setting Up the Security Zone," *Ha'olam Ha'ze,* August 25, 1993, *From the Hebrew Press,* October 1993. This article corrects the erroneous impression given in the U.S. media that the attacks on Lebanon were first launched in response to Lebanese *Hizbullah* attacks on Northern Israel. Also see Ze'ev B. Begin, "A Clearly Illegal

Order," *Yediot Ahronot,* August 3, 1993, *From the Hebrew Press (ibid.),* which calls the order to use "250,000 people" (Lebanese civilians turned into refugees) as a means of putting pressure on the Lebanese government "plain cruelty" and "plainly illegal." About 75 villages were totally destroyed in this "venture."

73. The two dissenters in each case were the United States and Israel. For more information on the implications of this vote in the context of the Gulf crisis, see Ian Williams, "Courted, Seduced and Abandoned After the Vote for Collective Action," *WRMEA,* March 1991, p. 35. Williams points out that few in the United States are even aware that each and every member of the 28-nation alliance in the Gulf War voted contrary to the United States in these resolutions.

74. It has often been repeated that more states around the world recognize the PLO than Israel. This fact was acknowledged by Israeli Knesset member Avraham Burg in an article in *Haaretz,* November 20, 1989, quoted in *Breaking the Siege,* December 1989–January 1990, p. 1. The declaration of a Palestinian State in November 1988 received recognition from some 124 countries. For an authoritative analysis of the application of the UN Charter to the Palestine question, as well as successive UN General Assembly and Security Council resolutions on the Palestinian issue and the Arab-Israeli conflict, see John Quigley, *Palestine and Israel: A Challenge to Justice* (Durham, NC: Duke University Press, 1990); W. Thomas Mallison, "The United Nations and the National Rights of the People of Palestine," in Ibrahim Abu-Lughod (ed.), *Palestinian Rights: Affirmation and Denial* (Wilmette, IL: Medina Press, 1982), pp. 11–22; and W. Thomas Mallison and Sally V. Mallison, *The Palestine Problem in International Law and World Order* (London: Longman Group, 1986).

75. For example, a vote taken on July 29, 1980, was 112 for to 7 opposed, with 24 abstentions; see Mallison, "The United Nations and the National Rights of the People of Palestine," p. 31. The UN Charter also provides for economic, then, if necessary, military, sanctions to be taken in order to implement the law. The Gulf War is an example of how the United States could ostensibly act through the "provisions" of the UN that contrast with its actions on the Palestinian case. For more on U.S. voting records, see Donald Neff, "The U.S. Cast the First of 29 Security Council Vetoes to Shield Israel," *WRMEA,* September/October 1993, pp. 82, 111; Donald Neff, "The Passage of U.N. Resolution 242," *WRMEA,"* November/December 1993, pp. 83, 92; and Donald Neff, The Passage of Resolution 194," *WRMEA (ibid.,* pp. 84, 92). The text of UN General Assembly resolutions on the question of Palestine can be found in four volumes published by the Institute for Palestine Studies (IPS), *United Nations Resolutions on Palestine and the Arab-Israeli Conflict, 1, 1947–1974* (Washington, DC: IPS, 1975); *2, 1975–1981* (IPS, 1988); *3, 1982–1986* (IPS, 1988); *4, 1987–1991* (IPS, 1993).

76. See UN General Assembly Resolution 36/120C of December 10, 1981. It resolved to fulfill UN Security Council Resolution 338 of 1973, which called for the implementation of UN Security Council Resolution 242 of 1967. This would take place under the "appropriate" auspices. It also called for an international conference to be convened before 1984; Mallison and Mallison, *The Palestine Problem,* pp. 418, 492–496; and IPS, *United Nations Resolutions,* p. 155.

77. See Chomsky, " 'Limited War' in Lebanon,"; and Chomsky, "The Israel-Arafat Agreement." Two events, one preceding, one immediately following the

signing of the accords, are significant. The first was the exchange of letters between Arafat and Rabin on September 9, 1993. Among other things, Arafat pledged "Palestinian acceptance of Security Council Resolutions 242 and 338" (no other U.N. Resolutions were mentioned). On September 16, 1993, the *New York Times* reported a move initiated by Israel to garner the support of the United States, Russia, Egypt, the PLO and others, to rescind, revise, and rewrite some 32 General Assembly Resolutions passed over the last few decades. Of grave concern to the Palestinians, this move underscores an attempt to erase from the historical record and the collective memory of the international community, the historical origins and realities of the Palestinian experience and their inalienable rights.

78. Norman Finkelstein, "Beyond Intervention: No Peace Without Linkage in the Middle East," *A Special Report by the Middle East Justice Network* (Boston: MEJN, November 10, 1990). The report specifies 43 such resolutions that the United States generally vetoed or abstained on. See also Norman Finkelstein, "Double Standards in the Gulf," *Z Magazine,* November 1990, pp. 27–28; and Neff, "The U.S. Cast the First of 29 Security Council Vetoes."

79. Finkelstein notes that in a comparable UN General Assembly resolution on the issue, Israel was the sole state that voted against.

80. During the Gulf crisis, the United States did support two resolutions critical of Israel for its practices in the Occupied Territories, especially after the incidents at the Dome of the Rock in October 1990, in which several Palestinians were killed. But these, like their predecessors, remained unenforced. See MEJN, *Special Report,* 1990, p. 4, which notes that the first of these resolutions, of October 12, 1990, was the first since 1982 that the United States supported that was critical of Israel.

81. MEJN, *Special Report,* p. 3.

82. Many Palestinians became disillusioned with the United States and realized that, contrary to its declarations, it was not acting as an honest broker in the conflict. They could not understand how the United States could dismiss their suffering and calls for protection; or that basic human rights for themselves should be "vetoed." Shortly thereafter, the United States broke off its "dialogue" with the PLO, and the stage was set for the subsequent Palestinian support of Iraq, which, since an Arab summit meeting in May 1990, had been the only Arab state to vocally express its attention to the Palestinian issue.

83. B'Tselem, "The Killing of Palestinian Children and the Open-Fire Regulations," *B'Tselem Information Sheet,* Jerusalem, July 13, 1993, excerpts in *JPS,* 23, no. 1 (Autumn 1993): 144–148. Others report higher figures; for example, PHRIC, "Fact Sheet: Killings by Israeli Security Forces," June 1993, reports that by May 1993, 277 Palestinian children had been killed. Also see the review of the *Save the Children Report* on the situation of children in the Occupied Territories, published May 17, 1990, in *Al-Fajr,* May 21, 1990, p. 1. Among the items of concern noted was that more than 50,000 children were reportedly injured by Israeli troops during the *intifada:* 47 percent by beating, 22 percent by bullets, and 21 percent by tear gas.

84. Karen White, "Torture, Perjury, and Palestinian Children," *WRMEA,* February 1988, pp. 8–9. Also see "The Imprisonment and Treatment of Children in Israel's Military Prisons," Report to the Subcommittee on Europe and the Middle East, U.S. House of Representatives, Washington, DC, December 1987, signed by a

committee of Palestinian lawyers and other concerned Palestinian residents of the Gaza Strip.

85. See reports and accounts of this period in *Al-Fajr; WRMEA;* PASSIA's reports; and the PHRIC *Monthly Updates.*

86. See *WRMEA,* June 1990.

87. There was evidence of deliberate cover-ups, lies, and misinformation by the Israeli authorities and the army on the extent of human rights violations, injuries, and the use of violent methods against Palestinian civilians. See, for example, Shahak's *From the Hebrew Press,* various collections, 1990–1991. Joel Greenberg, writing in the *Jerusalem Post,* concedes that Israeli sources have not been accurate in their reporting of events. Greenberg comments that "serious questions have been raised about the reliability of military reports from the field." He notes that some "unpleasant incidents" are not reported, nor are the "excesses" of soldiers investigated. As a result, Greenberg states, "credibility within the army has suffered," and he maintains that reliable documentation on the number of dead and wounded often come from the Palestinians themselves, while the army sources sometimes engage in the deliberate withholding of facts; Joel Greenberg, "The IDF's Credibility Is Under Strain," *Jerusalem Post International Edition,* July 30, 1988, p. 3; also see *Jerusalem Post International Edition,* July 7, 1990.

88. For a thorough analysis of some of these issues, see the report of the Physicians for Human Rights, 1988, *Monthly Updates* from the PHRIC, reports by Amnesty International, and others. Many foreign observers have criticized Israel's use of tear gas (much of it imported directly from the United States) particularly the lethal CS type, which, contrary to the instructions on its casings, is tossed into homes, clinics, and other closed spaces. For a revealing report on the effects of various forms of tear gas, see Donald Wagner, "CS Tear Gas, a Form of Chemical Warfare?" *MEI,* no. 320 (March 5, 1990): 18. The PHRIC provides documented and updated reports on names, ages, dates, and cause of death for all the Palestinians killed by Israeli forces during the *intifada.* By the end of March 1993, the number of injured Palestinian civilians had topped 128,000. B'Tselem, "The Killing of Palestinian Children," confirms that many Palestinians were killed and injured in situations where they posed no threat to the lives of soldiers. Discrepancies between official Israeli versions of events and other reports were highlighted in May 1988 in an incident concerning a bus carrying international participants to a Birzeit conference on the occupation. I was told about it by one of the participants. It appears the group had traveled without incident into a Palestinian village. It was not much later that the Israeli media repeated the army contention that the bus had been stoned and that the army was forced to intervene to protect the travelers. It was only when some of the passengers on the bus held a news conference to challenge the army version of events that the story was withdrawn. It had already appeared in its original version in the United States.

89. Palestinians in the Occupied Territories face enormous problems in lodging complaints against excessive army brutality. One Israeli article reports rather sarcastically on the procedure. The army would not investigate "aberrations," the "routine atrocities," unless "accompanied by sworn statements signed by Arab complainants." As the article points out, this means that after being beaten, harassed, and insulted, the Palestinian would have to proceed to an army base and

write out his complaint. Then the Palestinian is "interrogated about the veracity of his story." The article asks whether a Palestinian would hesitate in such circumstances; if he does, is it a clear sign "that his conscience isn't clear"? See B. Michael, "Thank God, No More Complaints," from *Haaretz,* June 5, 1988, excerpts in *Al-Fajr,* June 19, 1988, p. 10.

90. For example, Ivan Kauffman, "Attack on West Bank Church Goes Unreported," *WRMEA,* May 1988.

91. The author attended a meeting held by the U.S. ambassador to Israel with American citizens in the Occupied Territories where this issue was raised, Tel Aviv, February 1988.

92. Incidents involving violence against Americans during the *intifada* include the case of an American woman who was jailed because her three year old daughter made a "V" sign in front of soldiers and that of an Arab-American youth who was shot and killed and whose case remained unsolved "for lack of evidence."

93. One article, for example, quotes a leader in a prominent American Jewish organization to the effect that the American Jewish community was "running faster" than either the United States or the Israeli government on the issue; see Joe Stork and Rashid Khalidi, "Washington's Game Plan in the Middle East," *Middle East Report,* no. 164–165 (May–August 1990): 11, which quotes Seymour Reich of the B'nai B'rith, from an article in the *Washington Jewish Week,* March 16, 1989. For more on Jewish American activism, see, for example, Andrea Barron, "US Support for Peace Now Doubles," *WRMEA,* May 1988, p. 7, and Andrea Barron, "Lobbying for Mideast Peace," *WRMEA,* May 1988, p. 5.

94. The American Educational Trust, which publishes the *WRMEA,* also published Richard H. Curtiss and Parker L. Payson, *Stealth PACs: How Israel's American Lobby Seeks to Control Middle East Policy* (Washington, DC: American Educational Trust, 1990), which documents these. Notable also are Tivnan, *The Lobby;* and Findley, *They Dare to Speak Out.* Findley attributes his defeat in the 1982 reelection campaign for Congress in Illinois to his position on the Middle East. A comprehensive overview of U.S.-Israeli relations and the role of the pro-Israel lobby is also found in his recent book, Paul Findley, *Deliberate Deceptions* (New York: Lawrence Hill, 1993). He is a founder of the Council of National Interest, based in Washington, DC, with chapters around the country, which seeks to inform Americans on U.S. policies toward the Middle East, and works for the realization of a just peace there. Beyond direct payments of campaign money, pro-Israel groups exert their influence by such tactics as maintaining files and documentation on prominent U.S. officials and personalities, and using "pro-Arab" statements or sentiments to discredit (sometimes smear) these people. An investigative report by Gregory D. Slabodkin, "The Secret Section in Israel's U.S. Lobby That Stifles American Debate," *WRMEA,* July 1992, pp. 7–8, 89, reveals the existence of special files kept by AIPAC on "politicians, journalists, academics, Arab-American activists, Jewish liberals, and others it labels " 'anti-Israel.' " Slabodkin claims to be an "insider" who worked in "AIPAC's stealth section," and he reveals how the "discrediting" worked. Only a few months after this article was published, the existence of special files kept by the ADL was also revealed.

95. For a detailed analysis of these issues, see Noam Chomsky, *The Fateful*

Triangle: The United States, Israel and the Palestinians (Boston: South End Press, 1983).

96. Martin Indyk, referred to earlier (note 46), is a case in point.

97. Israel Shahak, "Relations Between Israel and the Organized American Jews," *Report no. 126,* September 20, 1993. Both he and others have examined how the organized American Jewish community reacted to the victory of the Labor Party in the 1992 Israeli elections (as too "soft"), and to activities by peace groups, such as Friends of Peace Now, in the United States. Also see, Richard H. Curtiss, "Attacks on 'Americans for Peace Now' Follow Familiar Pattern," *WRMEA,* April/May 1993, pp. 35, 92.

98. There were indications that the organized Jewish community was taken by surprise by the 1993 accords and that some sectors were positively hostile to the prospects. Shahak, "Relations Between Israel and the Organized American Jews," discerns the "vulnerability" of organized Jewry to "splits in its ranks," but suggests that these splits have been along lines even more extreme (than comparable groups in Israel, including Likud). Similarly, Leon T. Hadar, "The Peace Accord's 'Hall of Shame,' " *WRMEA,* November/December 1993, pp. 20, 94, outlines reactions from the organized American Jewish community. He notes that this community has long been instrumental in trying to "prevent" such agreements, and observes that, "for the first time, Israel's government includes players that are more inclined to reach accommodation with the PLO than are the U.S. administration and its American-Jewish supporters." This rather cursory treatment of the position of American Jews does not do justice to the evolution of perspectives and positions within this community, nor does it address the root causes of their various stands. It simply outlines one of the basic "loci" of power among the opponent's international allies that deserves attention in a Palestinian strategy. For more on the reaction of American Jews during the *intifada,* see for example, Peretz, *Intifada,* pp. 173–181.

99. For the full text of this law, see, *JPS,* 17, no. 1 (Autumn 1987): 210–211.

100. At the time of the passage of this act, many Americans, including a number of prominent American Jews, expressed their concern at the erosion of civil liberties in the United States and clear violations of First Amendment rights under this law.

101. The only U.S. government official authorized to deal with the PLO was the American ambassador to Tunis. He, in turn, could only deal with his counterpart in the PLO there. The content of their talks was also circumscribed, in that the PLO continued to be rejected as a major or essential negotiating partner in the Middle East conflict.

102. This followed the attempted landing on a beach near Tel Aviv of armed guerrillas affiliated to the Palestine Liberation Front (which is part of the PLO). No one was killed or injured in this incident, and no "terrorist" act was actually committed.

103. The Jordanian move to disengage from the Occupied Territories in late July 1988 rendered debates within the PLO over unity and consensus moot and put pressure on the PLO to devise an immediate response to fill the political vacuum. Regionally, the PLO received total Arab support during the Arab summit in Algiers that year, the significance of which was largely ignored by the U.S. media. For example, the *New York Times,* June 10, 1988, filled whole columns detailing every item of Libyan leader Qaddafi's attire down to the white gloves and ridiculing his behavior toward other Arab leaders, instead of reporting on the political implica-

tions of the meeting. In contrast, National Public Radio, June 10, 1988 cited a figure of $600 million annually that was promised by the Arab states to support the *intifada,* while the *Boston Globe* and the *New York Times* both reported figures in the range of US$300–400 million.

104. In May 1987, Jewish representatives from a number of prominent organizations in the United States met with Arafat and PLO officials in Tunis, where they discussed a negotiated end to the conflict and a two-state solution. According to Jerome Segal, of the Washington Area Jews for Israeli-Palestinian Peace, Arafat appeared to appreciate the impact of clearly recognizing Israel. For the full text of the Sharif statement, see *Al-Fajr,* June 19, 1988; and excerpts in the *New York Times,* June 22, 1988.

105. *New York Times,* June 28, 1988.

106. Interview with Ehud Olmert, a Knesset member from the Likud Party, BBC, "24 Hours," June 17, 1988.

107. *Al-Fajr,* June 19, 1988, p. 1.

108. *Jerusalem Post International Edition,* July 2, 1988, p. 2.

109. *Boston Globe,* July 3, 1988.

110. That Israel was looking to benefit economically from the accords was clear from a number of sources. Meron Benvenisti cites official Israeli statements to the effect that the Palestinian economy would remain dependent on Israel and that the agreements would only "enrich" Israel and "justify the continuing status quo"; Meron Benvenisti, "Reversal of the Arguments," *Haaretz,* September 29, 1993, *From the Hebrew Press,* November 1993. Benvenisti maintains that these areas would provide cheap labor and markets for Israeli products and that Israel would be the "boss," exercising close control over allocation of funding and investment. To quote him in full:

> Two million Palestinians of the Territories, who number a little less than a third of the total population of [mandatory] Palestine, now control no more than about 8% of water resources and 13% of the land. Their income per capita amounts to about 12% of income of the Israelis. The size of their independent economy is no greater than 5–6% of the Israeli economy. Their total industrial production is commensurate with the production of a single Israeli plant of average size. Even assuming that the development planned nowadays may somewhat improve the Palestinian standard of life, its already recognizable features do not promise any radical changes in relations between Israel and the Territories. Instead of being a colonial system ruled from the outside, the latter will become a colonial system ruled from inside.

One interesting aspect of the Declaration of Principles has received scant attention. This concerns the sections that address the issue of investment in the Occupied Territories (which many Palestinians assume is to their benefit) which could in reality encompass both Israel and Israeli enterprises in these areas—for example, Annex III: 4—" encouragement of international investment in the West Bank and the Gaza Strip, and in Israel." Other paragraphs call for "regional and inter-regional trade,"

"Palestinian-Israeli joint ventures," a "Development Program for the region, including the West Bank and Gaza Strip," a "Middle East Development Fund," and the like.

111. See a comparable analysis by Aluf Ben, "Strategy on a Regional Basis." The irony of the whole situation, as many have observed, is that Islam is labeled "fundamentalist" when it challenges U.S. imperial interests (and Israel's position in this configuration) and is praised when it refers to "fundamentalist" regimes that remain pro-Western, such as Saudi Arabia.

112. Soon after the signing of the Israeli-PLO agreements, news circulated about an imminent peace treaty with Jordan. Some observers interpreted publicity on this deal as a type of "disinformation" that masked the real priority, a deal between Israel and Syria. Haim Baram, "Peres's Secret Ace," *MEI*, no. 463 (November 19, 1993): 5–6. Baram insists his information comes from "reliable sources," and he concludes, "Syria is next, and soon."

113. Eliminating a Palestinian claim would have to be accomplished with U.S. support and with Arafat's collusion. Many Palestinians viewed Arafat's letter to Rabin of September 9, 1993 (as part of the exchange of "mutual recognition") in precisely this light.

114. CBS News on September 13, 1993, stated that President Clinton was told a few days after his inauguration in January 1993; also see the *New York Times*, September 5, 1993.

115. A careful reading of the accords supports such an interpretation. Israel's occupation is given more or less "parity" with Palestinian claims; there is nothing to suggest that the occupation is illegal under international law or should be withdrawn in full. Mentioned only is that these issues will be "negotiated" over the course of the next years following the "interim" stage.

116. See earlier references to Gene Sharp, *The Politics of Nonviolent Action* (Boston: Porter Sargent, 1973); pp. 705–755; and George Lakey, "The Sociological Mechanisms of Nonviolent Action," *Peace Research Review*, 2, no. 6 (1968): 1–102.

117. See Chapter Four; Sharp, *The Politics of Nonviolent Action*, p. 733; and Lakey, "The Sociological Mechanisms of Nonviolent Action."

118. Interview with Rabin on the "MacNeil/Lehrer News Hour," PBS News, September 13, 1993.

119. The Likud Party had been divided on the extent of "autonomy" Palestinians would be permitted. For Palestinians, Labor's proposals for "self-rule," though slightly more liberal than those of the Likud, still fall far short of the independence they seek. The mechanism of "accommodation" remains quite relevant in this context.

120. The Jaffee Center for Strategic Studies Study Group, *The West Bank and Gaza: Israel's Options for Peace* (Tel Aviv: JCSS, 1989). This study argues that with certain qualifications and under many restrictions, a Palestinian state is inevitable and the only viable solution that would bring lasting peace to the area. This study appears to have been inspired by an earlier work along the same lines; see Mark Heller, *A Palestinian State: The Implications for Israel* (Cambridge, MA: Harvard University Press, 1983).

121. Lamis Andoni, "Jordan," in Brynen, *Echoes of the Intifada*, p. 169, note 17. The Labor Party governed in Israel throughout most of those years.

122. For example, on the ABC program "This Week with David Brinkley," September 12, 1993, political commentator George Will stated very matter-of-factly, "Jordan is the Palestinian State." It was said in a way that brooked no debate and was not open to question; and with a certainty that no one would consult the democratic wishes of the Palestinian people on the matter.

123. See the *New York Times,* September 12, 1993, and the *Christian Science Monitor,* September 8, 1993. The Israeli/PLO accords contain no provisions for Palestinian refugees and descendants of those who left or were expelled in 1947–1948 and in the interim years until 1967.

124. See Chapter Four; Sharp, *The Politics of Nonviolent Action,* p. 706; and Lakey, "The Sociological Mechanisms of Nonviolent Action."

125. Some have argued that the unprecedented Israeli repression against Palestinian civilians during the same months that secret talks with the PLO were under way in Norway was intended to bring these residents to the point of total collapse, and hence, "capitulation"; see Edward Said, "The Israel/PLO Accord."

126. The rate of immigration of Soviet Jews slowed in the aftermath of the Gulf War. Between 1989 and 1993 some 460,000 Soviet Jews immigrated to Israel, with hundreds of thousands more still expected; see the *New York Times,* October 5, 1993. In June 1991 some 14,000 Ethiopian Jews were airlifted to Israel; some of them were expected to be settled in the occupied areas. Belying the claim that Israel has no "policy" to settle immigrants in the occupied lands, Pinhas Inbari, "Great Immigration for the Sake of the Great Land of Israel," *Al-Hamishmar,* May 22, 1991, *From the Hebrew Press,* revealed that Prime Minister Shamir had severely "rebuked" a Likud member of the Knesset, Ya'akov Shama'i, for the latter's proposal for making improvements in government subsidized mortgages. Shama'i's plan would have offered Israeli Jews benefits equivalent to those offered to new immigrants to enable them to buy houses anywhere in the country. Shamir's reported anger was attributed to the fact that he wanted these exclusive benefits to remain as they were, that is, to go to people willing to settle in the Occupied Territories.

127. For example, George Giacaman, "What Next for Palestinians?" in PASSIA, *Palestinian Assessments of the Gulf War,* p. 31; and Tessler, "The Impact of the Intifada," p. 60.

128. Yizhar Be'er, "The Place from Which Shouts Are Not Heard," *Haaretz* April 17, 1991, *From the Hebrew Press,* reviews a study issued by the Civil Administration entitled "Judea and Samaria in the Year 2005," to the effect that the settled lands "will be populated to their highest capacity." Less than one-third of the area of the West Bank would remain to the Arabs. This study was prepared during the last National Unity government and thus is indicative of both Labor and Likud thinking.

129. For more on the prospects of cantonization, see Michael Jansen, "Israel's Plan for 'Cantonization,' " *MEI,* no. 457 (August 28, 1993): 16–17. The fate of Palestinians may come to resemble that of American Indian tribes. By virtue of tribal treaties, some do enjoy an autonomous status, but there is no question that the ultimate source of sovereignty remains vested in the U.S. federal government.

130. In the spring and summer of 1991 a number of articles laid out a scenario whereby Israel would find a pretext to attack Syria. Though this war did not materialize, it was interesting to note that some Israeli sources went so far as to admit

that Israel posed the existential threat to Syria, rather than the other way around. In 1993 the Rabin government evinced some "flexibility" over a "compromise" over the Golan Heights, particularly if Israel were to conclude a peace treaty with Syria. Israeli warnings of forthcoming war centered next on Iran. Zionist policy had all along explicitly called for the destruction of all surrounding (Arab) states, to cause them to fragment along ethnic and religious lines. See Israel Shahak (translator and editor), "The Zionist Plan for the Middle East," based on Oded Yinon, "A Strategy for Israel in the Nineteen Eighties," *Kivunim*, a publication of the World Zionist Organization (Belmont, MA: Association of Arab-American University Graduates, Special Document no. 1, 1982). Yinon, an Israeli journalist, was formerly with the Foreign Ministry. For more on the possibility of war with Syria, see Israel Shahak, *From the Hebrew Press*, "Collection: Israel Prepares to Attack Syria," including articles from *Haaretz* of May 7, 1991, May 23, 1991, and June 7, 1991.

131. Shahak maintains that it was U.S. opposition that deterred both Likud and Labor leaders from embarking on a course of "transfers"; Israel Shahak, "Israel Will Withdraw Only Under Pressure," *WRMEA*, July 1991, p. 20. Shahak maintains that only 23 out of 120 members of the Knesset would agree to the return of territory. This assessment may seem dated in the light of later developments; nevertheless, it is important to heed Shahak's warnings. In Israel Shahak, "The Real Significance of the Oslo Agreement," *Report no. 125*, September 10, 1993, he refers to several credible Israeli sources to argue that the PLO/Israeli accords were a "deception," and that Palestinians would not gain independence. See also Tessler, "The Impact of the *Intifada*," pp. 68–69.

132. For more on Netanyahu's statements, see Alon Ben-Meir, "Likud's Plan for Territories Is Built on Outdated Vision," *Christian Science Monitor*, October 26, 1993; and *New York Times*, August 30, 1993.

Conclusion

1. Marc Ellis, "Beyond the Jewish-Christian Dialogue: Solidarity with the Palestinian People," Americans for Middle East Understanding (AMEU) newsletter, *The Link*, 24, no. 2 (May-June 1991); and Marc Ellis, *Beyond Innocence and Redemption* (New York: Harper and Row, 1990).

2. Some of my Jewish contacts insisted there is no distinction, nor is it possible to separate the two. Others pointed to different "shades" of Zionism and party affiliations, and compared those who perceive Zionism as a legitimate and justified basis for the Israeli state (and so justifying the whole history of the creation of the State of Israel), but not as applicable to the Occupied Territories. Others, we noted, view these areas as Israel's by "right."

3. These accords seemed to leave Israel with most of the benefits it wanted but without the responsibilities of dealing with an increasingly restive population and the burdens of an increasingly "costly" occupation. Many concur with this analysis. Israel Shahak points out that these agreements will only mark a change in the "method" of domination, rather than its end; Israel Shahak, "Developments in the Aftermath of the Agreement Between Israel and the PLO," *Report no. 127*, October 10, 1993. While Shahak regards this as one of the predictable outcomes of the agreement, he maintains (quoting other Israeli sources) that some consequences

remain unpredictable. One of his concerns is that this deal, concluded without consultation with either the Israeli or the Palestinian public, may unleash unexpected social and political forces. Concerning Israel, he notes the popularity enjoyed by right-wing groups. He fears this could lead to the emergence of political forces or even a government that is opposed to such "peace" with the Palestinians. He also cautions about serious conflicts in Palestinian society, especially when Arafat's promises of a better life cannot be met.

4. Organizing and training for nonviolent struggle have not been discussed here. Yet these remain relevant issues and should be considered, be it for a strategy of complete nonviolent civilian resistance or one that rests on civilian-based defense. One could make an argument that just as a military struggle would be inconceivable without prior training, so should a strategy of nonviolent civilian struggle be based on prior training and preparation.

5. Prospects for maintaining awareness of East Jerusalem were not immediately encouraging. The Jerusalem municipal elections of November 2, 1993, brought in Ehud Olmert, a Likud member, as mayor. Earlier during the campaign, some Israelis tried to join forces with Palestinians to propose joint sovereignty and to make Jerusalem a capital for both peoples. Among the advocates of this proposal was Moshe Amirav, a Jerusalem councilor. Amirav helped form a group called Peace for Jerusalem that was slated to run in the November elections; see interview with Amirav in *Al-Fajr,* July 19, 1993, pp. 8–9.

Index

Abdeen, Ziad, 163n.1
Abed, George T., 171n.68, 171n.69, 172n.71, 173n.81, 185n.50
Absentee Property Law, 13
Abu Al-Namel, Hussein, 169n.37
Abu-Amr, Ziad, 54, 172n.71, 172n.75, 182n.28, 182n.30, 190n.89, 190n.90, 212n.27
Abu Ayyash, Abdullah, 171n.66
Abu El-Assal, Reverend Canon Riah, 177n.130
Abu Jihad (Al-Wazir, Khalil), 33, 57, 58, 180n.9, 180n.10, 189n.81, 190n.3, 191n.3
Abu Kishk, Bakir, 172n.76
Abu Laban, Baha, 168n.35
Abu-Libdeh, Hasan, 163n.1
Abu-Lughod, Ibrahim, 164n.4, 168n.35, 219n.74
Abu-Lughod, Janet, 169n.38, 169n.42, 169n.46, 170n.55, 171n.60, 172n.74
Abu Shakrah, Jan, 189n.86
Abu-Sharif, Bassam, 144, 224n.104
Accommodation, as nonviolent resistance mechanism, 37, 109, 148–149
Adams, Michael, 169n.41
Administrative detention/detainees, 23–25 73, 84; youth, 53, 139
African National Congress (ANC), 103
Agricultural relief committees: grassroots organizations, 51–52; during *intifada,* 62
Agriculture: citriculture, 14; economic integration, 14–15; marketing produce, 52; self-sufficiency, 52
Aid: to Israel, 134; to Occupied Territories, 91. *See also Sumud* funds
Aker, Mamduh, 85
Al-Haq, 136, 177n.122, 178n.132, 178n.138, 218n.70
al-Hassan, Hani, 35
Aloni, Shulamit, 211n.22
Al-Qassam units, 40, 54

Alternative Information Center, 86
Alternative institutions, establishment of, 71–72, 97
Al-Wazir, Khalil. *See* Abu-Jihad (Al-Wazir, Khalil)
Al-Zawawa, Issam, 187n.66, 187n.67, 187n.68, 187n.69
American citizens: freedom of speech and information, 131; in Occupied Territories, 140
American Friends of Peace Now, 142
American Israel Public Affairs Committee (AIPAC), 131
American Jewish community, 78, 142; response to Arab-Israeli conflict, 141–143
Amin, Samir, 204n.23
Amirav, Moshe, 228n.5
Amnesty International, 79
ANC (African National Congress), 103
Andoni, Lamis, 149, 225n.121
Annexation. *See also* Land expropriation
Anticolonial movements: goals of, 32. *See also* Palestine Liberation Organization (PLO); Guinea-Bissau, 32; India, 104–105; international examples, *xvii,* 8; South Africa, 102–103
Anti-Terrorism Act (1987), 143–144
Arab Women's Congress, 46
Arafat, Yasser, *xii, xvii,* 33, 36, 110, 142, 143, 157, 167n.21, 189n.81, 190n.93, 202n.113, 216n.59, 220n.77, 224n.104, 225n.113
Arens, Moshe (Israeli Defense Minister), 79, 213n.39
Armed struggle, 34, 35; debate over, 36; Islamic *Jihad* advocating, 39–40; technique evaluation, 35
Arms Export Act, Israeli violation of, 134
Aronson, Geoffrey, 43, 179n.143, 184n.45
Arrighi, Giovanni, 204n.23
Aruri, Naseer, 168n.35, 169n.36, 189n.84, 209n.14, 213n.40, 214n.44